Adobe®
Premiere® Pro CC
Digital
Classroom

Adobe® Premiere® Pro CC

Digital Classroom

Jerron Smith and the AGI Training Team

Adobe® Premiere® Pro CC Digital Classroom

Published by
John Wiley & Sons, Inc.
10475 Crosspoint Blvd.
Indianapolis, IN 46256

Copyright © 2013 by John Wiley & Sons, Inc., Indianapolis, Indiana
Published simultaneously in Canada
ISBN: 978-1-118-63960-3
Manufactured in the United States of America
10987654321

For general information on our other products and services or to obtain technical support, please
contact our Customer Care Department within the U.S. at (877) 762-2974, outside the U.S. at
(317) 572-3993 or fax (317) 572-4002.

Wiley publishes in a variety of print and electronic formats and by print-on-demand. Some
material included with standard print versions of this book may not be included in e-books
or in print-on-demand. If this book refers to media such as a CD or DVD that is not included
in the version you purchased, you may download this material after registering your book at
www.digitalclassroombooks.com/CC/PremierePro. For more information about Wiley products, visit
www.wiley.com.

Please report any errors by sending a message to errata@agitraining.com

Library of Congress Control Number: 2013951334

Credits

President, American Graphics Institute and Digital Classroom Series Publisher
Christopher Smith

Executive Editor
Jody Lefevere

Technical Editor
Sean McKnight

Editor
Karla E. Melendez

Editorial Director
Robyn Siesky

Business Manager
Amy Knies

Senior Marketing Manager
Sandy Smith

Vice President and Executive Group Publisher
Richard Swadley

Vice President and Executive Publisher
Barry Pruett

Senior Project Coordinator
Katherine Crocker

Project Manager
Cheri White

Graphics and Production Specialist
Jason Miranda, Spoke & Wheel

Media Development Project Supervisor
Chris Leavey

Proofreading
Karla E. Melendez

Indexing
Michael Ferreira

About the Authors

Jerron Smith is an Editor, Animator & Educator. A multi-faceted artist and video producer with nearly two decades of experience, Jerron works with a wide variety of media. He has experience in both digital video/television production, and post-production as well as extensive experience in the multi-media and print design industries. He teaches professional development classes at American Graphics Institute and serves as an adjunct instructor in the Communication Arts department at the New York Institute of Technology, where he instructs courses in computer graphics, animation and video editing. He holds undergraduate degrees in Art and Education and a Masters degree in Communication Arts where he specialized in Computer Graphic technology.

The **AGI Creative Team** is composed of Adobe Certified Experts and Adobe Certified Instructors from American Graphics Institute (AGI). The AGI Creative Team has authored more than 25 Digital Classroom books, and created many of Adobe's official training guides. They work with many of the world's most prominent companies, helping them use creative software to communicate more effectively and creatively. They work with design, creative, and marketing teams around the world, delivering private customized training programs, and teach regularly scheduled classes at AGI's locations. The Digital Classroom authors are available for professional development sessions at companies, schools and universities. More information at *agitraining.com.*

Acknowledgments

Thanks to my wife, Monique, and daughters Kerowyn and Lauryn for their support during the many months of writing this book as well as the New York Institute of Technology, Terry Snyder and Dr. Michael Banks for teaching me not only how to make a cut, but more importantly why to do so. Thanks also to Cheri, Chris and the whole team at AGI for keeping me focused during this project. Special Thanks to Jeff Jacobs, Kurt Zisa and Donna Betancourt for the use of their video footage. Thanks to the following for permission to use their content in this book:

Jeff Jacobs music video footage courtesy of Jeff Jacobs and Kurt Zisa

Werewolves of Central Park and Travelogue New York video footage courtesy of Donna Betancourt and Silver Cheese Productions

Travelogue Boston video footage courtesy of Chris Leavey at American Graphics Institute

Register your Digital Classroom book for exclusive benefits

Registered owners receive access to:

 The most current lesson files

 Technical resources and customer support

 Notifications of updates

 Online access to video tutorials

 Downloadable lesson files

 Samples from other Digital Classroom books

Register at *DigitalClassroomBooks.com/CC/PremierePro*

Digital Classroom

Register your book today at
DigitalClassroomBooks.com/CC/PremierePro

Contents

Starting Up

Lesson 1: Understanding Digital Video

Lesson 2: Understanding the Workspace

Lesson 3: Prepping Files in Prelude

Lesson 4: Making the Cut

Lesson 5: Adding Transitions to Video

Lesson 6: Working with Graphics

Lesson 7: Using Video Effects

Lesson 8: Video Compositing

Lesson 9: Working with Audio

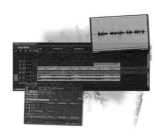

Lesson 10: Advanced Editing Techniques

Lesson 11: Outputting Your Video

Appendices

Starting up

About Adobe Premiere Pro CC Digital Classroom

Adobe® Premiere Pro lets you edit and create video for a variety of platforms. Premiere Pro provides you with the editing tools to express your creative ideas for video, film and online broadband delivery. Premiere Pro is also tightly integrated with other Adobe products such as Photoshop, Illustrator, and After Effects so that you can integrate graphics and special effects into your projects. Because Premiere Pro is a professional tool, there is a great deal you will need to understand to use it effectively for creating great video content. Fortunately the Digital Classroom provides everything you need to get up-and-running quickly.

The *Adobe Premiere Pro CC Digital Classroom* is like having your own personal instructor guiding you through each lesson while you work at your own speed to gain an understanding of essential Premiere Pro skills. This book and DVD combination includes 11 self-paced lessons that let you discover essential skills and explore the new features and capabilities of Premiere Pro on either a Mac OS or Windows computer. Each lesson includes step-by-step instructions, lesson files, and video tutorials, all of which are available on the included DVD. If you purchase an electronic book, all the resources from the DVD are available on a readers-only website. Information on how to access the files is included with the downloaded version of the book. This book has been developed by the same team of Adobe Certified Experts and Premiere Pro professionals who have created many official training titles for Adobe Systems.

Prerequisites

The *Adobe Premiere Pro CC Adobe Digital Classroom* is designed to give you the essential skills you need so you can quickly get up-and-running with video editing. Before you start the lessons in this book, you should have a working knowledge of your computer and its operating system. You should know how to use the directory system of your computer so that you can navigate through folders. You need to understand how to locate, save, and open files. You should also know how to use your mouse to access menus and commands. If you need help getting started with your operating system, the Digital Classroom series includes books covering Mac OS X and Windows. Learn more at *DigitalClassroom.com*.

Before starting the lessons in the *Adobe Premiere Pro CC Digital Classroom*, make sure that you have installed Adobe Premiere Pro CC. The software is sold separately, and not included with this book. You may use the 30-day trial version of Adobe Premiere Pro available at the *adobe.com* website, subject to the terms of its license agreement.

System requirements

Before starting the lessons in *Adobe Premiere Pro CC Digital Classroom*, make sure that your computer is equipped for running Adobe Premiere Pro, which you must purchase separately. The minimum system requirements for your computer to effectively use the software are listed on the following page.

System requirements for Adobe Premiere Pro CC

Following are system requirements for Windows and Mac OS computer systems to use Premiere Pro.

Windows

- Intel® Core™2 Duo or AMD Phenom® II processor; 64-bit support required
- Windows 7 with Service Pack 1, Windows 8, or Windows 8.1
- 4 GB of RAM (8 GB recommended)
- 4 GB of available hard-disk space for installation
- Additional disk space required for preview files (10 GB recommended)
- 1280 × 800 display
- 7200 RPM or faster hard drive (multiple fast disk drives, preferably RAID 0 configured, recommended)
- Sound card compatible with ASIO protocol or Microsoft Windows Driver Model
- QuickTime 7.6.6 software required for QuickTime features
- Optional: Adobe-certified GPU card from list below with at least 1 GB VRAM for GPU accelerated-performance
- Internet connection and registration are necessary for required software activation, membership validation, and access to online services.★

Mac OS

- Multicore Intel processor with 64-bit support
- Mac OS X v10.7, v10.8, or v10.9
- 4 GB of RAM (8 GB recommended)
- 4 GB of available hard-disk space for installation; additional free space required during installation (cannot install on a volume that uses a case-sensitive file system or on removable flash storage devices)
- Additional disk space required for preview files and other working files (10 GB recommended)
- 1280 × 800 display
- 7200 RPM hard drive (multiple fast disk drives, preferably RAID 0 configured, recommended)
- QuickTime 7.6.6 software required for QuickTime features
- Optional: Adobe-certified GPU card from list below with at least 1 GB VRAM for GPU accelerated-performance
- Internet connection and registration are necessary for required software activation, membership validation, and access to online services.★

For a list of video cards that support GPU acceleration when used with Premiere Pro you can check out the application's technical specifications at: *http://www.adobe.com/products/premiere/tech-specs.html.*

Starting Adobe Premiere Pro

As with most software, Adobe Premiere Pro is launched by locating the application in your Programs folder (Windows) or Applications folder (Mac OS). If necessary, follow these steps to start the Adobe Premiere Pro application:

Windows

1   Choose Start > All Programs > Adobe Premiere Pro. If you have the Creative Suite installed, you may have to select and start Adobe Premiere Pro from within the Creative Suite folder. (Alternatively, you can use the search field located in the Start menu to find the Premiere Pro application.)

2   From the Premiere Pro Welcome Screen you can choose to either create a new project or open an existing project. If you close the Premiere Pro Welcome Screen, it will close the application.

Mac OS

1   Open the Applications folder, and then open the Adobe Premiere Pro folder.

2   Double-click on the Adobe Premiere Pro application icon. You may also wish to drag it to the dock for easy access as you start each lesson, and use it for editing your video files.

3   From the Premiere Pro Welcome Screen you can choose to either create a new project or open an existing project. If you close the Premiere Pro Welcome Screen, it will close the application.

Menus and commands are identified throughout the book by using the greater-than symbol (>). For example, the command to save a document would be identified as File > Save.

Resetting the Adobe Premiere Pro preferences

When you start Adobe Premiere Pro, it remembers certain settings along with the configuration of the workspace from the last time you used the application. It is important that you start each lesson using the default settings so that you do not see unexpected results when working with the lessons in this book. Use the following steps to reset your Adobe Premiere Pro preferences.

Steps to reset Adobe Premiere Pro preferences

1 Quit Premiere Pro.

2 Start Premiere Pro. and immediately press the Option key (Mac OS) or Alt key (Windows). Continue to hold down the key until you see the Premiere Pro Welcome Screen.

When resetting the Premiere Pro preferences there is no confirmation message that you have been successful. Your first indication that the task has been accomplished will be the empty list of Recent Files on the Welcome Screen.

Access lesson files and videos any time

Register your book at *www.digitalclassroombooks.com/CC/PremierePro* to gain access to your lesson files on any computer you own, or watch the videos on any Internet-connected computer, tablet, or smart phone. You'll be able to continue your learning anywhere you have an Internet connection. This provides you access to lesson files and videos even if you misplaced your DVD.

Checking for updated lesson files

Make sure you have the most up-to-date lesson fi les and learn about any updates to your Premiere Pro CC Digital Classroom book by registering your book at *www.digitalclassroombooks.com/CC/PremierePro*.

Loading lesson files

The *Adobe Premiere Pro CC Digital Classroom* DVD includes files that accompany the exercises for each of the lessons. You may copy the entire lessons folder from the supplied DVD to your hard drive, or copy only the lesson folders for the individual lessons you wish to complete.

For each lesson in the book, the files are referenced by the file name of each file. The exact location of each file on your computer is not used, as you may have placed the files in a unique location on your hard drive. We suggest placing the lesson files in the My Documents folder (Windows) or at the top level of your hard drive (Mac OS).

Copying the lesson files to your hard drive

1 Insert the *Adobe Premiere Pro CC Digital Classroom* DVD supplied with this book.

2 On your computer desktop, navigate to the DVD and locate the folder named prlessons.

3 You can install all the files, or just specific lesson files. Do one of the following:

   • Install all lesson files by dragging the prlessons folder to your hard drive.

   • Install only some of the files by creating a new folder on your hard drive named prlessons. Open the prlessons folder on the supplied DVD, select the lesson you wish to complete, and drag the folder(s) to the prlessons folder you created on your hard drive.

Locating missing media

Premiere Pro creates a link between your project files and the files that you import into the Project panel. This linkage system allows you to have a very small project file, but at the same time requires that you manage the media you are using in your projects. If you move, rename, or delete files that you are using in a project you will receive a missing media warning when Premiere Pro starts up. You should always locate any missing files before attempting to proceed with your project.

The process for locating missing files is automatic and will help you find video, audio, still images, and even preview files.

1 When presented with a file browser, verify the file name at the top of the dialog box. This is the file that you are currently trying to locate.

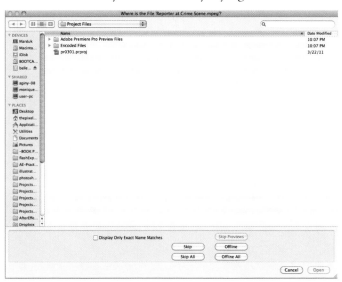

Premiere Pro requests that you locate any missing files at the time a project is opened.

2 Navigate to the missing file, highlight it, and then press the Open button to relink the file. After locating all missing files, the project will open.

If your missing files are still in the same relative folder structure as when they were first imported into your project, then Premiere Pro should locate them all once it knows the location of the first one. If it cannot automatically find other missing files, you will have to locate them manually. Once all missing files have been found or skipped, the project will open.

There are technically three options when attempting to locate missing files; you can find the file and open it, skip the specific file, or set the file as offline. Offline files can be brought online by right-clicking on them in the Project panel and choosing Link Media from the menu that appears. In addition to the ability to skip and offline individual files, you also have buttons to skip and offline all files the application is currently attempting to locate.

Unlocking Mac OS files

Mac users may need to unlock the files after they are copied from the accompanying disc. This applies only to Mac OS computers and is because the Mac OS may view files that are copied from a DVD or CD as being locked for writing.

If you are a Mac OS user, and have difficulty saving over the existing files in this book, you can use these instructions so that you can update the lesson files as you work on them and also add new files to the lessons folder

Note that you only need to follow these instructions if you are unable to save over the existing lesson files, or if you are unable to save files into the lesson folder.

1 After copying the files to your computer, click once to select the prlessons folder, then choose File > Get Info from within the Finder (not Premiere Pro).

2 In the aelessons info window, click the triangle to the left of Sharing and Permissions to reveal the details of this section.

3 In the Sharing and Permissions section, click the lock icon (🔒), if necessary, in the lower-right corner so that you can make changes to the permissions.

4 Click to select a specific user or select everyone, then change the Privileges section to Read & Write.

5 Click the lock icon to prevent further changes, and then close the window.

Working with the video tutorials

Your *Adobe Premiere Pro CC Digital Classroom* DVD comes with video tutorials developed by the authors to help you understand the concepts explored in each lesson. Each tutorial is approximately five minutes long and demonstrates and explains the concepts and features covered in the lesson.

The videos are designed to supplement your understanding of the material in the chapter. We have selected exercises and examples that we feel will be most useful to you. You may want to view the entire video for each lesson before you begin that lesson. Additionally, at certain points in a lesson, you will encounter the DVD icon. The icon, with appropriate lesson number, indicates that an overview of the exercise being described can be found in the accompanying video.

DVD video icon.

Setting up for viewing the video tutorials

The DVD included with this book includes video tutorials for each lesson. Although you can view the lessons on your computer directly from the DVD, we recommend copying the folder labeled *Videos* from the Adobe *Premiere Pro CC Digital Classroom* DVD to your hard drive.

Copying the video tutorials to your hard drive

1   Insert the *Adobe Premiere Pro CC Digital Classroom* DVD supplied with this book.

2   On your computer desktop, navigate to the DVD and locate the folder named videos.

3   Drag the videos folder to a location onto your hard drive.

Viewing the video tutorials with the Adobe Flash Player

The videos on the *Adobe Premiere Pro CC Digital Classroom* DVD are saved in the Flash projector format. A Flash projector file wraps the Digital Classroom video player and the Adobe Flash Player in an executable file (.exe for Windows or .app for Mac OS). However, please note that the extension (on both platforms) may not always be visible. Projector files allow the Flash content to be deployed on your system without the need for a browser or prior stand-alone player installation.

The accompanying video files on the DVD use the Adobe Flash Video format to make universal viewing possible for users on both Windows and Mac OS computers.

Playing the video tutorials

1   On your computer, navigate to the videos folder you copied to your hard drive from the DVD. Playing the videos directly from the DVD may result in poor-quality playback.

2   Open the videos folder and double-click the Flash file named PLAY_PRCCvideos to view the video tutorial.

3   After the Flash player launches, press the Play button to view the videos.

The Flash Player has a simple user interface that allows you to control the viewing experience, including stopping, pausing, playing, and restarting the video. You can also rewind or fast-forward, and adjust the playback volume.

A. Go to beginning. B. Play/Pause. C. Fast-forward/rewind. D. Stop. E. Volume Off/On. F. Volume control.

Playback volume is also affected by the settings in your operating system. Be certain to adjust the sound volume for your computer, in addition to the sound controls in the Player window.

Additional resources

The Digital Classroom series goes beyond the training books. You can continue your learning online, with training videos, at seminars and conferences, and in-person training events.

On-demand video training from the authors

Comprehensive video training from the authors are available at *DigitalClassroom.com*. Find complete video training along with thousands of video tutorials covering After Effects and related Creative Cloud apps along with digital versions of the Digital Classroom book series. Learn more at *DigitalClassroom.com*.

Training from the Authors

The authors are available for professional development training workshops for schools and companies. They also teach classes at American Graphics Institute, including training classes and online workshops. Visit *agitraining.com* for more information about Digital Classroom author-led training classes or workshops.

Additional Adobe Creative Cloud Books

Expand your knowledge of creative software applications with the Digital Classroom book series. Books are available for most creative software applications as well as web design and development tools and technologies. Learn more at *DigitalClassroomBooks.com*

Seminars and conferences

The authors of the Digital Classroom seminar series frequently conduct in-person seminars and speak at conferences, including the annual CRE8 Conference. Learn more at *agitraining.com* and *CRE8summit.com*.

Resources for educators

Visit *digitalclassroombooks.com* to access resources for educators, including instructors' guides for incorporating Digital Classroom into your curriculum.

What you'll learn in this lesson:

- To understand the difference between editing and delivery formats
- To understand the difference between high-definition and standard-definition video formats
- To understand the digital post-production workflow

Understanding Digital Video

Before you begin editing in Premiere Pro, it is beneficial to become familiar with some of the concepts and principles that define the art and craft of video editing.

Starting up

You will not need any files for this lesson.

See Lesson 1 in action!

Use the accompanying video to gain a better understanding of some of the concepts covered in this lesson. The video tutorial for this lesson can be found on the included DVD.

Understanding digital Non-Linear Editing

When you watch a video or film, what you are actually watching is a series of still images displayed sequentially at a high rate of speed. Each image, called a frame, is displayed on screen for a very short period of time (anywhere between 1/24th to 1/30th of a second), creating the illusion of continuous motion. In the past, the only way to edit film or video was using a linear system. That is, an editor had to advance a film reel or tape to a specific part and cut or copy from that point forward. If she or he then wanted to edit another part of the footage, they had to advance the entire reel or tape to a new location and start again. It could be a very tedious and time–comsuming process. Adobe Premiere Pro is an example of a digital NLE (Non-Linear Editor): it gives you direct and immediate access to any frame in a digital video clip at any time. In an NLE process, you use computer data instead of a physical linear medium, such as film or tape, and you can jump back and forth along your timeline at any point in the editing process. Unlike traditional graphic image processes, this is a non-destructive process because the original source footage is never lost or altered. The media links that you import or capture in Premiere Pro are only references to the original footage stored on your hard drive.

The video and audio footage that you edit in Premiere Pro can be digitized from an analog source, such as a VHS or cassette tape, or recorded directly to a digital format, as is the case with modern video cameras as well as other hard drive and compact flash-based recording devices.

Understanding video settings

In Premiere Pro, you generally work by building sequences to match the standards of the media you are going to work with instead of the intended output. There are many types of video files you can work with in Premiere Pro. The various formats, aspects ratios, codecs, and other settings used to describe video files will be explained in this book. The following terms will help you:

Dimensions: specifies the pixel dimensions of a video file; in other words, the number of pixels horizontally and vertically that compose an image or video frame. This value is usually written as a pair of numbers separated by an X, where the first number is the horizontal value and the second represents the vertical; for example, 720 × 480. Pixel is a conjunction of the words "picture" and "element" and is the smallest individual component in a digital image.

Frame rate: specifies the number of individual images that compose each second of video. Frame rate is displayed as a value of fps (frames per second).

Pixel Aspect Ratio: specifies the shape of the pixels that compose an image. Pixels are the smallest part of a digital image and different display devices (televisions, computer monitors, etc.) have pixels with different horizontal and vertical proportions.

Editing vs. delivery formats

While working through the many lessons presented in this text you are going to encounter many new concepts and terms, especially when you are dealing with video footage. When working with video in Premiere Pro you will encounter many different video formats and the codecs (compressor/decompressor) used to compress them while editing the video files throughout the lessons in this book and when working on your own. Most computer users are familiar with the term "format" used to describe files, for example, jpeg and tiff formats for images, or doc and ppt formats for Word and PowerPoint files. However, for video files, formats such as Quicktime and AVI are only containers that hold video information; much like a file folder holds paper. You can describe the relationship between formats and codecs this way: formats are the containers; codecs are the language the contents are written in.

Codec is a conjunction made from the words "compressor" and "decompressor." Codecs are mathematical algorithms used to shrink audio and video files to manageable sizes. Video files are very large; for example, 20 minutes of NTSC DV video (from a standard definition miniDV camcorder) is over 4 GB in size, which is the capacity of one single-layer DVD. Without video codecs, you could not easily save and store archived video footage; video would also never be small enough to watch online, by e-mail, or on a mobile device. To view an audio or video file, you must have a player compatible with the format and have on your computer the codec used to compress the video file, so you can decompress it.

Traditionally, the codecs used to capture and edit footage were uncompressed or offered very little compression, while the codecs used to deliver the final files to the viewers were far more compressed. With the proliferation of high-definition video equipment, this has changed: many cameras now use MPEG-2 or MPEG-4 codecs to reduce files to manageable sizes for storage and editing.

Tape-based vs. tapeless formats

Prior to the proliferation of high-definition devices, camcorders relied on physical tapes to record data. VHS, Beta-max, DigiBeta, and MiniDV are examples of tape-based formats. While the tape-based workflow served the video industry well for many years, there were drawbacks to using it. Being a physical medium, tapes would eventually degrade with reuse, so they had a limited lifespan. Additionally, since tapes are a linear format used for transferring footage stored on a digital tape to a computer—a process known as *capturing*—this could only be performed in real-time. In other words, if you had one hour of video footage to capture, it took a full hour to do so. Tapeless, also called file-based formats, use hard-disk drives or flash drives to store video footage. When using a tapeless system, a new file is created whenever the camera person presses the record/pause button on the camcorder. This offers instant access to any recorded scene without the need to cue up a specific tape location.

With the expansion of the high-definition camcorder market, consumer, prosumer, and professional-level camcorders now rely almost exclusively on tapeless, file-based storage systems. These tapeless camcorders have blurred the line between editing and delivery formats, since most of them use either an MPEG-2 or MPEG-4 codec on the recorded video.

High definition vs. standard definition

Standard definition footage adheres to the NTSC (National Television Standards Committee) or PAL (Phase Alternating Line) standards, which are the standards for video used in the United States of America and most of the rest of the world, respectively. Standard definition footage usually has an aspect ratio of 4:3; in other words, there are four horizontal units for every three vertical units of measure. Prior to the invention of high-definition television, NTSC was the only standard for broadcast video in the United States. NTSC included settings for both 4:3 and 16:9 (widescreen) aspect ratios. In the age of Digital Television broadcasts, the NTSC has been replaced by the ATSC (Advanced Television Systems Committee) standards; however, the term NTSC is still used by most video cameras, editing, and graphics applications to refer to standard definition broadcast quality video.

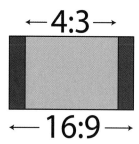

There are other aspect ratios used in video, but 4:3 and 16:9 are the most common.

NTSC & NTSC Widescreen: The NTSC presets include settings for standard (4:3) and widescreen (16:9) aspect ratios. The dimensions for both are 720x480, but the pixel aspect ratio is different, which accounts for the difference in shape. Pixel aspect ratio (PAR) is the ratio or shape of the pixels that compose each individual part of a single video frame. Both versions of the NTSC standard use a frame rate of 30 fps.

PAL & PAL Widescreen: PAL is the standard for broadcast television used throughout Europe and much of the rest of the world. PAL differs from NTSC in several key ways; such as dimensions and frame rate. It uses a frame rate of 25 fps, which is closer to the 24fps used in film and according to some video professional produces more realistic imagery. Similar to NTSC, PAL has standard (4:3) and widescreen (16:9) settings. A frame size of 720×576 is shared by both, and the pixel aspect ratio gives each their unique frame shape.

High Definition: High Definition (HD) television technology has existed for decades, but it was during the early 21st century that it became popular with average American television viewers. The term HD describes video with a higher resolution than traditional television systems, now called SD or standard definition. There are two main high definition standards for broadcast television: 720P and 1080i; many televisions and Blu-ray disk players support a third standard: 1080P.

720P: the 720P format has a resolution of 1280 pixels wide by 720 pixels high and supports a variety of frame rates, from the 24 fps used by film and the 30 fps that was part of the old NTSC standard, to 60 fps.

1080P & 1080I: the 1080 formats exist in Interlaced and Progressive versions; as with other modern digital standards, these formats support a variety of frame rates, such as 24 fps, 30 fps and beyond.

Progressive video vs. interlaced video

The two methods of displaying images on a video screen are Progressive display and Interlacing. When discussing video formats, the letter P or I are often stated at the end of the format. For example, 1080p or 1080i footage denote whether it is progressive or interlaced. In the United States, and before changing to a digital broadcasting system, televised images were sent as interlaced signals in which every frame of video was made by combining two half-images called fields.

Before the advent of high-definition LCD and Plasma screens, televisions were made by wrapping a plastic or wooden frame around a large, hollow glass device called a Cathode Ray Tube (CRT). These CRT television screens were composed of a series of even and odd numbered lines called scan lines, and each frame of video was displayed by illuminating these lines starting at the top of the screen. Interlacing was created to display video signals on this type of TV set and worked by illuminating one set of lines first (even or odd numbered), and then moving back to the top of the display to illuminate the other set. In this way, the display would show the second set of lines when the first set of lines began to fade; the result was a complete picture for the viewer. This process occurred 60 times a second with NTSC broadcast television. Unlike Interlacing, Progressive display illuminates the scan lines sequentially from top to bottom.

Most modern televisions can display in interlaced and progressive mode, and the ATSC includes broadcast standards for both, while all computer monitors use progressive display only. The difference between the two display methods occurs in video camera formats as well; older NTSC or PAL cameras can only shoot interlaced video, but many newer cameras let you choose between interlaced and progressive shooting modes, for example, 50i (25 fps), 60i (30 fps), 30p (30 fps), and 24p (24 fps). When working in Premiere Pro, we highly recommend that you use the sequence settings that match the settings of the footage you are working with.

Premiere Pro presets

In Premiere Pro, your projects are organized and arranged into Sequences. The video you are going to edit is added to these Sequences, where it can be trimmed, moved, arranged, and otherwise adjusted. Before you can edit video in Premiere Pro you must create a sequence inside your project. This sequence is your main editing and assembling environment. The application includes pre-built settings for sequences called presets. With the recent proliferation of high-definition video equipment and non-tape based recording media (cameras that store video on hard drives or flash drives instead of traditional tape) you can use a wide variety of formats and specifications. Tapeless camcorders, also known as file-based devices, usually record to hard-disks, optical media, or flash memory media, instead of to videotape, and save video and audio files using formats and codecs often specific to each device. Tapeless formats supported by Premiere Pro include Panasonic P2 camcorders, Sony XDCAM HD and XDCAM EX camcorders, Sony CF-based HDV camcorders, and AVCHD camcorders.

In this section, you will learn about some of the common standards as they apply to working in Premiere Pro.

DV NTSC, DV PAL, DV 24P

The DV (Digital Video) standard comes in three varieties: NTSC, PAL, and 24P, all of which should be used in conjunction with IEEE1394 (FireWire/i.LINK) DV equipment. All three varieties of video come in standard (4:3) and widescreen (16:9) aspect ratios and have variations to support two standard rates for audio sampling: 32 and 48 kHz.

AVCHD

AVCHD is an acronym for Advanced Video Coding High Definition, a video format developed for the recording and playback of high-definition digital video. This tapeless format was created primarily for use in consumer and prosumer level camcorders, but it has also been adopted for use in some professional level equipment. The AVCHD presets in Premiere Pro support 720p, 1080i, and 1080p video footage, each at a variety of frame rates.

DVCPRO & DVCPROHD

Panasonic developed DVCPRO as a variation of the standard DV format. This tape-based format was developed to improve the standard definition DV format by increasing its robustness and feature set, and is an alternative to the DVCAM format developed by Sony. DVCPROHD was created as an enhanced version of the preceding DVCPRO format. The DVCPRO50 presets in Premiere Pro can create sequences compatible with 480i (NTSC) and 576i (PAL) video formats; the DVCPROHD presets can create sequences for footage recorded at 720p, 1080i, or 1080p in a range of frame rates from 24fps to 60fps.

HDV

HDV is high-definition digital video. The format can store up to 1 hour of high-definition video on a standard mini-DV tape by compressing the video using the MPEG-2 codec, which is the same type of compression used to create DVDs. The HDV presets in Premiere Pro can create sequences for footage recorded at 720p, 1080i, or 1080p. HDV tape was one of the first consumer and prosumer levels of high-definition recording and storage available to the public.

XDCAM, XDCAM HD, XDCAM EX, XDCAM HD422

The XDCAM format was introduced by Sony as a tapeless solution for professional level video recording and storage. The XDCAM family of products differs in everything to other formats, from recording media, frame size, and codec. The presets in Premiere Pro contain support for the range of XDCAM formats: you can work with standard definition projects using the DV NTSC sequence presets, while XDCAM HD, XDCAM EX, and XDCAM HD422 have their own presets. The XDCAM EX and XDCAM HD422 presets include support for 720p, 1080i, or 1080p footage; the XDCAM HD presets support 1080i and 1080p in a range of frame rates from 24fps to 60fps.

Overview of the post production workflow

Video productions are usually divided into three distinct, though interrelated, stages: Pre-production, Production, and Post-production. The video editing, graphics integration, and compositing that you perform in Premiere Pro is part of the post-production stage. Once a video project has been recorded, the work of the post-production professionals (editors, graphic designers, composers) begins. Large studio or production companies hire different individuals or outside contractors for post-production work. Smaller post-production teams share multiple positions or have one person perform the post-production work. A general post-production workflow is shown in the following figure.

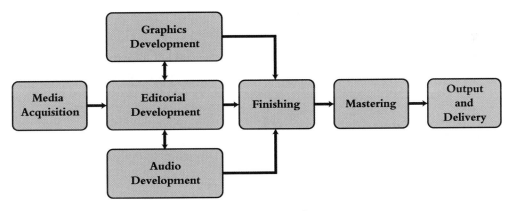

Specific post-production workflows vary depending on the production company and project.

Media acquisition

During media acquisition, you can add footage to the Premiere Pro project, which can come from a single source, or a variety of tape-based or tapeless sources. Footage that comes from an analog source, such as a VHS or Beta tape, must be digitized; digital tape-based sources, such as DV footage, are captured; tapeless formats are ingested. An important aspect of the media acquisition phase is the storage and organization of media assets. Video files use a lot of hard drive space and can be better stored on external devices, which allows you to become modular, thus easily transporting footage and project files from one computer to another. At the same time, we recommend you develop an intuitive and easy-to-navigate folder structure to store your footage and help you locate specific footage items when needed in the latter stages of post-production.

Editorial development

Editorial development is the phase when a project is assembled. The diagram above portrays this phase as a single block of time and effort, but it is a multi-stage process where you can go through the initial editing steps to develop a rough cut, submit it for client or collaborator feedback, and then refine it in a sequential process of edits and revisions that lead into the finishing phase. Often each successive revision (called a cut) refines the pacing, tone, and theme or narrative of the work leading into the next phase. During this phase, stand-in graphics and audio are added into the edit while the finished products are developed.

Graphics development

The graphics development phase is often concurrent with editorial development. Titles, effects shots, and compositing are integrated into a project in this portion of the workflow. This phase does not involve just one step, but a sequence of successive revisions that begin with initial concepts and rough art work and end with the development of the final graphics and effects added to the finished project.

Audio development

The third concurrent phase represented here is audio development. As is the case with graphics and editorial, this phase involves a sequence of successive revisions leading to the creation of finished audio tracks added into the edit. This phase can include audio refinement to clean up noise and the creation of Foley sound effects and background music beds.

Finishing

The finishing phase is where stand-in graphics and audio are replaced with the finished elements, and any final edits and transitions are added in Premiere Pro to create a final cut.

Mastering

The mastering phase involves compiling all the elements that the client needs, and assembling them into a single bundle for handoff. Depending on the required deliverables, this may be as simple as adding multiple individual sequences into a single master sequence for output to a tape or file. It could also include preparing a variety of different projects with different titles, graphics, or audio for delivery to different regions or markets.

Output and delivery

Output and Delivery is the process of creating the final, playable media for handoff to the client or audience. Depending on the scope of the project, this phase can take different forms. It may involve outputting your master sequence to a tape-based format for handoff to a broadcast television station, authoring a DVD or multimedia playback component, or compressing your source footage for streaming delivery on the Web.

Self study

1 In this lesson, you learned about some of the technical details that will affect the decisions you make when setting up and outputting your video projects. It is important to keep in mind that as new video, image, and audio formats are developed and support for them is added to Premiere Pro you will want to constantly improve your knowledge base.

2 The Adobe website (*www.adobe.com*) offers tutorials and white papers on technical and design issues that relate to your use of Premiere Pro and along with sites like Wikipedia (*www.wikipedia.com*) can be an excellent source to help further your professional development.

Review

Questions

1 What are names of the two different standards that govern video for American and European television?

2 What are the three high definition video standards?

3 What are the frames rates for American television, European television and film?

Answers

1 The ATSC (Advanced Television Systems Committee) is the name of the set of standards that govern American television and PAL (Phase Alternating Line) is the standard used in Europe. In the United States the set of standards that were in use before the age of digital television broadcasts were called the NTSC (National Television Standards Committee).

2 The three standards for high definition video are:

720p: the 720p format has a resolution of 1280 pixels wide by 720 pixels high and supports a variety of frame rates, from the 24 fps used by film and the 30 fps that was part of the old NTSC standard, to 60 fps.

1080p & 1080i: the 1080 formats exist in Interlaced and Progressive versions; as with other modern digital standards, these formats support a variety of frame rates between 24 to 30 fps.

3 American television uses a frame rate of 30 fps, while European television uses a frame rate of 25 fps and film uses a frame rate of 24 fps.

What you'll learn in this lesson:

- To navigate the Premiere Pro interface
- To customize the program interface
- To manage your media in the project panel

Understanding the Workspace

In this lesson, you will gain an understanding of the key elements of the Premiere Pro interface and how to configure them to better suit your needs.

Starting up

In this lesson, you will work with the project files from the pr02lessons folder. Make sure that you have loaded the prlessons folder onto your hard drive from the supplied DVD. The Starting up section at the start of this book provides detailed information about loading lesson files, resetting your workspace, locating missing media, and opening the files in CC. If you have not already done so, please review these instructions before starting this lesson.

When opening the Premiere Pro project files used in this lesson you may experience a missing media message. You must locate any missing media before trying to proceed through the lesson. For more information refer to "Locating missing media" in the Starting up section of this book.

See Lesson 2 in action!

Use the accompanying video to gain a better understanding of some of the concepts covered in this lesson. The video tutorial for this lesson can be found on the included DVD.

Understanding the Premiere Pro interface

Adobe Premiere Pro uses a docked, panel-based interface. The entire interface configuration is called a workspace; the application has five pre-built workspaces to accommodate different working styles and the different tasks you need to accomplish. You will perform most of your editing work in the different panels of the program's interface. These panels allow you to import and organize your media and preview your video and audio footage. The Timeline, where most of the actual video editing is performed, is also a panel.

Understanding the default Editing workspace

There are many different panels available in the Premiere Pro interface; the next figure shows the panels available in the default Editing workspace. This workspace is specifically intended to maximize the size of your viewers, while still giving you access to important features, such as the Project panel and Timeline.

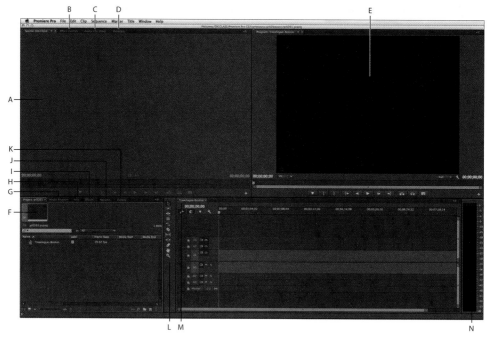

A. Source Monitor panel. B. Effect Controls panel. C. Audio Clip Mixer panel. D. Metadata panel. E. Program Monitor panel. F. Project panel. G. Media Browsers panel. H. Info Panel. I. Effects panel. J. Markers panel. K. History panel. L. Tools panel. M. Timeline panel. N. Audio Meters panel.

A. Source Monitor: The Source Monitor can be used to playback and preview individual clips. You can also use the Source Monitor to prepare clips before you add them to a sequence. In the Source Monitor, you can set In and Out points, add markers, and specify how the clip will be added to the Timeline. You can view clips in this monitor by dragging and dropping them into the Source panel or by double-clicking them.

B. Effect Controls panel: Special effects can be added to video and audio clips on the Timeline. Some effects, for example, can change color video to black-and-white, while others alter the color balance of an image or can help to simulate the look of film. The Effect Controls panel allows you to edit effects that have been applied to your clips. To access these, you must select it in the Timeline by clicking it. If you do not have a clip selected, the panel remains blank. You can also use the panel to access the inherent Motion, Opacity, and Audio properties of clips.

C. Audio Mixer: You can use the Audio Mixer to adjust settings while listening to audio tracks and viewing video tracks. Each Audio Mixer track corresponds to a track in the Timeline of the active sequence. You can also use the mixer to add effects, change the volume of relative tracks, or to record audio directly into sequence tracks.

D. Metadata panel: Metadata is a set of information that describes the content or properties of a file. Video and audio files automatically include information regarding their file size, format, creation date, and duration. Metadata can also include additional information, such as location, director, scene, shot, etc. The metadata panel allows you to edit and view these properties so you can use them to organize and sort your files, or share with other Adobe applications.

E. Program Monitor: The Program Monitor is your live monitor; it is used to playback and preview only the clips on the Timeline.

F. Project panel: Video editing is a non-destructive editing process because you do not edit the original content of your files. The Project panel contains references to all the footage files (video, audio, and images) that you have imported into Premiere Pro in addition to the sequences, titles and other supporting material you create in the application.

G. Media Browser panel: The Media Browser helps you browse and preview files on your hard drive. You can leave the Media Browser open and dock it, just as you would any other panel. The Media Browser gives you quick access to all your assets while you edit.

H. Info panel: The Info panel displays information regarding the currently selected item in the Project panel or Timeline.

I. Effects panel: The Effects panel is a repository for all the video and audio effects and transitions available in the application. You can place transitions such as Dissolves, Dip to Black, and Page Peels between clips to allow you to transition from one clip to another. You can add effects such as Black and White, Levels, and Balance, to individual clips, to change their appearance or audio qualities.

J. Marker panel: You can use the Marker panel to see all the markers in an active clip or sequence. The panel displays marker information such as In and Out points, comments and color coding tags.

K. History panel: The History panel stores a list of the actions you have performed to change the state of your project in the current working session. As an alternative to using Edit > Undo, or the keyboard commands Ctrl+Z (Windows) or Cmd+Z (Mac OS), you can use this panel to jump back to any previous state in the current work session. However, you should note that changes you make to the program that affect panels, windows, or preferences are not stored in the History panel. Also, when you close and reopen Premiere Pro, the History panel is automatically reset and you lose access to the previous states of your project.

L.Tools panel: This panel stores the various editing tools you can access in the application. The cursor changes appearance based on the tool that is active and the type of content that you are hovering over.

M. Timeline panel: You perform the majority of your editing work on the Timeline panel, including adding clips, positioning them, and changing their properties. You can also use the Timeline to add effects and transitions to the video and audio clips in your project. Each sequence in the project is a separate, independent Timeline. When multiple Timelines are visible, the panel uses a tabbed display similar to a web browser to separate each.

N. Audio Meters panel: This panel is a VU (Volume Units) meter. It shows the volume of clips that are on the Timeline. The display in this panel is active only when you preview the video and audio clips on the Timeline.

Understanding the tools

Premiere Pro has eleven different tools that were designed to perform a single specific task useful during the editing process.

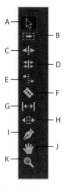

*A. Selection tool. **B.** Track Selection tool.**C.** Ripple Edit tool.*
***D.** Rolling Edit tool. **E.** Rate Stretch tool. **F.** Razor tool. **G.** Slip tool.*
***H.** Slide tool. **I.** Pen tool.**J.** Hand tool. **K.** Zoom tool.*

A. Selection Tool: Use this tool to select clips, menu items, buttons, and other objects found in the user interface. We recommend you configure the Selection tool to be selected by default after using the more specialized editing tools, since most clip and interface interaction requires using the Selection tool.

B. Track Selection Tool: Use this tool to select all clips to the right of the cursor in a sequence. Click a clip with this tool to select the clip and the ones to the right on a *single* track. Hold the Shift key and click a clip to select the clip and the ones to the right on *every* track.

C. Ripple Edit Tool: You can use the Selection tool to trim the start or end of a clip in the Timeline; however, you might create an empty space between the clips on your Timeline. Use the Ripple Edit tool to trim the In or Out point of a clip, close gaps caused by the edit, and preserve all edits to the left or right of the trimmed clip.

D. Rolling Edit Tool: Use this tool to simultaneously change the In and Out points of a pair of adjacent clips on the Timeline: the Rolling Edit Tool trims the In point of one clip and the Out point of the other clip, leaving the combined duration of the two clips unchanged.

E. Rate Stretch Tool: This tool is used to shorten or lengthen a clip in the Timeline. The Rate Stretch tool speeds up or slows down the playback of the clip without trimming the clip, thus leaving the In and Out points of the clip unchanged.

F. Razor Tool: Use this tool to split clips in the Timeline. Click any point on a clip to split it at that exact location. To split all clips across all tracks at an exact point, press and hold the Shift key while clicking a clip.

G. Slip Tool: Use the Slip tool to simultaneously change the In and Out points of a clip in a Timeline, while keeping the overall duration of the clip unchanged.

H. Slide Tool: Use this tool to move a clip to the right or left on the Timeline while trimming any adjacent clips. The combined duration of the clips, and the location of the group in the Timeline, remain unchanged.

I. Pen Tool: All clips have a set of inherent properties that you can animate using the Effect Controls panel. Select the Pen tool to set or select key frames for clips in the Timeline.

J. Hand Tool: Use this tool to move the viewing area of a Timeline to the right or left as an alternative to the scroll bar at the base of the Timeline panel.

K. Zoom Tool: Select this tool to zoom in or out in the Timeline viewing area.

Customizing the interface

There are a series of pre-installed workspaces that come with the application to be used as a starting point so you can begin working immediately. However, since it is impossible for the application's developers to predict the needs of every user, we recommend you customize and adjust the interface to fit your specific needs and style.

In this section, you will adjust the Editing workspace to fit the needs of the project you will work with in this lesson. The first procedure is to remove panels you will not be working with at this time.

1   Choose File > Open Project. In the Open Project dialog box that appears, navigate to the pr02lessons folder that you copied to your hard drive and open the file named **pr0201.prproj**. This file contains a single sequence in the Project panel named Travelogue–Boston.

An alternative way to open a project is to use a keyboard shortcut. Choose Ctrl+O (Windows) or Command+O (Mac OS) to open an existing project.

2   Choose File > Save As. In the Save As dialog box that appears, navigate to the location on your hard drive where you saved the project files folder and then to the Lesson 2 folder. Rename the file **pr0201-working** and click the Save button. This file will be your working file for the remainder of this lesson.

Opening, closing, and moving panels

To customize the application interface, you should close, open, and reposition panels that are not necessary for the type of work you will perform in this work session.

In this section, you will customize the interface to remove some of the default panels and create a new custom editing workspace where there is more space for the Timeline. We recommend you have as much space as possible for the Timeline and monitors, since most of your work is carried out in these panels.

Using drop-zones

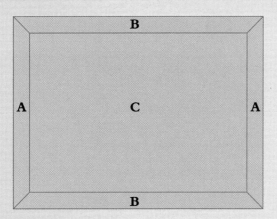

Drop-zones help you work with the docked panel layout by providing you with visual cues as you drag panels to rearrange them.

As you drag a panel, a drop-zone overlay appears above the current panel group that your cursor is hovering over. Different sections of the drop-zone become highlighted to show you what your new panel configuration will be. If either section on the sides (labeled "A" in the figure) illuminates, the panel that you are repositioning is placed to the side of the currently highlighted panel, creating a new, independent panel group vertically. The same is true for the top and bottom of the drop-zone (labeled "B" in the figure), except this creates a new panel group horizontally. The third possibility is to release your mouse while hovering over the center of the drop-zone (labeled "C" in the figure); this groups the panel that you are moving with the existing panel group, creating a new tab.

1 With the **pr0201-working.prproj** file still open, locate the Media Browser panel in the lower-left area of the interface; click the panel's name tab to make it active and to bring it to the front of the panel group. Click on the small x to the right of the panel name to close it.

Once a panel is active, you can close it by clicking the small x to the right of the panel name.

2 After closing the Media Browser panel, close the Info, Effects, Markers and History panels in the same way. When done, your interface will appear as the image below.

3 Click the Project panel's name tab and drag it to the Program Monitor panel. Place the panel onto the middle rectangular section of the drop zone so the two panels are grouped together.

Drop zones make it easier to tell the effects of your panel movement.

4 Now you will adjust the Tools panel so that you can free up even more space for the Timeline. Place your cursor at the dividing line between the Tools and Timeline panels. When the cursor becomes a double-headed arrow (◄╟►), click and drag the dividing line towards the Tools panel to shrink it.

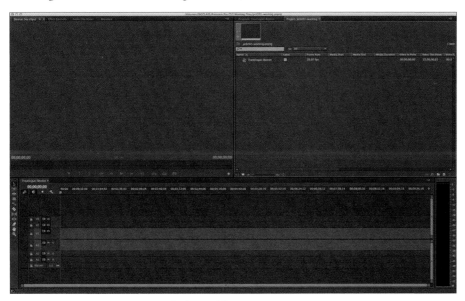

When a panel is resized, the adjacent panels adjust to fill any empty space.

5 This action creates a new group in which the Project panel and the Program monitor share space.

6 Click on the Program Monitor to make it active. Your interface should now resemble the figure below.

7 Choose File > Save or press Ctrl+S (Windows) or Command+S (Mac OS) to save the project file. The interface changes are saved with the file and will override the current workspace setting when this file is reopened.

Do not close this file, you will need it in the next section of this lesson, where you will save these interface changes as a new custom workspace.

Saving a custom workspace

As you have seen, it is very easy to customize the Premiere Pro user interface. You can also save custom workspaces so you can return to a favorite or helpful panel configuration later.

In this part of the lesson, you will save the workspace you created as a new workspace, and then reset the Editing workspace to its original configuration.

1 With the **pr0201-working.prproj** file still open, choose Window > Workspace > New Workspace to open the New Workspace dialog box.

2 Change the default name of the workspace to **Digital Classroom-Editing** and click the OK button to save the workspace. This also makes your new workspace the active one. This new workspace saves with the application and will be available to you, even if you reset the application's preferences.

You can delete Workspaces by choosing Window > Workspace > Delete Workspace. This opens the Delete Workspace dialog box, where you can choose the workspace you want to delete from a drop-down menu. You can delete any workspace except the currently active one.

3 Choose Window > Workspace > Editing to return to the Editing workspace. Notice that it still reflects the changes you made when you were customizing the workspace in the previous exercise: as you customize any workspace, you automatically append it, thus making your changes part of the current state. To return this workspace to its original configuration, you must reset it as explained in the next step.

4   Choose Window > Workspace > Reset Current Workspace. In the confirmation dialog that appears, choose Yes to reset the Editing workspace and return the Workspace to its original appearance.

5   Choose Window > Workspace > Digital Classroom-Editing to return to the custom workspace that you created. For the remainder of this lesson you will be using this custom workspace.

6   Choose File > Save or press Ctrl+S (Windows) or Command+S (Mac OS) to save the project file.

Setting application preferences

Application preferences control the overall functionality of Premiere Pro, and you can edit them at any time. The application preferences allow you to change nearly any aspect of the program, from the default length of transitions and still images, to the interface color and the frequency and number of automatic backups made for your projects.

In this section, you will configure the auto-save feature to make more copies of your project file at shorter intervals.

1   With the **pr0201-working.prproj** file still open, choose Edit > Preferences > General (Windows) or Premiere Pro > Preferences > General (Mac OS) to open the Preferences dialog box.

2   From the list of categories on the left, choose Auto Save to view the preferences for how Premiere Pro automatically backs up your files.

There are two settings for the application's Auto Save functionality: Automatically Save Every and Maximum Project Versions.

3   Change the value of the Automatically Save Every property to **10** minutes, and then change the value of Maximum Project Versions to **10** as well. Click OK.

This increases the frequency of the Auto Save function, while creating more project versions so you have a greater choice of file back-ups. While most users will admit that auto-save is a great feature, not all can agree on the best frequency for saving files. When the application runs the auto-save command, it can interrupt what you are doing and some users find this quite distracting.

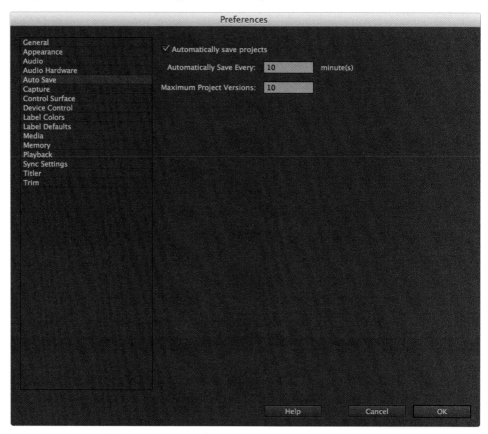

Auto Save is helpful when the application closes unexpectedly or you need to return to an earlier version of your project.

The Auto Save function does not save over your project file; instead it creates backups of your project file and saves them to the Adobe Premiere Pro Auto-Save folder. This folder is created automatically by the application and stored in the same location as your original project file.

4   Choose File > Save or press Ctrl+S (Windows) or Command+S (Mac OS) to save the project file. Do not close this file; you will need it in the next exercise.

Using the Project panel

As mentioned previously, the Project panel contains references to all the footage files (video, audio, and images) that you have imported into Premiere Pro. As such, it is the creative hub for all you will create with this application. In addition to references to your imported footage, the panel holds the Sequences and Titles that you can create within the application, and is where you locate the items you want to add to the Timeline.

Understanding media management

Media Management is the organization or management of the media you work with in a project. There are two equally important aspects to Media Management. The first is how you manage the media on your hard drives, and the second is how you organize the different media references that you import into Premiere Pro.

To ensure portability, performance, and security, many users highly recommend that you store media on an external hard disk drive. The two standard connection types for external hard drives are FireWire (400 and 800) and USB 2.0 and 3.0. Mac users also have access to a third high-speed connection format called thunderbolt. Many video editors recommend a FireWire drive because of its higher sustained bus speed, but any type of drive works for your projects, though newer technologies, such as thunderbolt and USB 3.0, also provide excellent connections for media storage drives. Depending on your system configuration, these connection types may not be available to you at this time.

The files that you will work with to complete the lessons in this book are organized into a single folder called Media Library. Within that folder, there are additional folders for each individual project. In each respective project folder, there are folders that separate the different types of media (video, audio, and still images) you will use. This type of hierarchical structure is also used to keep the project panel organized and makes it easier to locate the media you want to add to the Timeline panel.

Before you can edit any piece of footage on the Timeline, you must first add it to your Premiere Pro project. You can import a wide variety of media, including video, audio, still images, After Effects Projects, and other Premiere Pro projects.

In this section, you will import a variety of media files into your project that you can later organize and add to your Timeline.

1   With the **pr0201-working** file still open, confirm that you are using the Digital Classroom-Editing workspace that you created earlier in this lesson. If you have made any changes to the workspace, you should reset it now. If the Project panel is hidden behind the Program Monitor, click on the Project panel tab now to bring it forward and make it active.

2   Choose File > Import to open the Import dialog box, then navigate to the Media Library folder located inside the prlessons folder that you copied to your hard drive.

Select the Travelogue-Boston folder, and then select the Video subfolder to reveal the video files you will import for this lesson.

The keyboard shortcut for the import command is Ctrl+I (Windows) or Command+I (Mac OS).

3   Inside the Video folder, there is a series of video files shot in and around the city of Boston.

Click the first video file displayed in the dialog box, hold the Shift key on your keyboard, and then click the last file displayed to select every file between them.

Click the Import button to import all the selected files into your project panel.

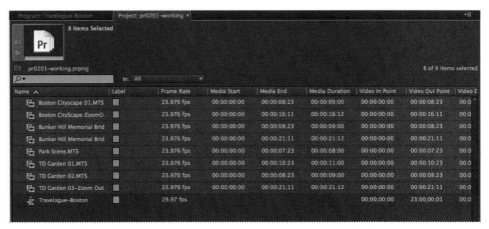

All recently imported files are automatically selected/highlighted in the project panel.

Holding the Shift key while selecting files only selects files in a sequential list. To select files non-sequentially, hold the Control (Windows) or Command (Mac OS) key and click individual files.

4   In addition to importing individual or groups of files, you can import entire folders and their content.

Choose File > Import and navigate to the Travelogue–Boston folder in the Media Library. In the Import dialog box, click once on the Audio folder to select it, and click the Import button.

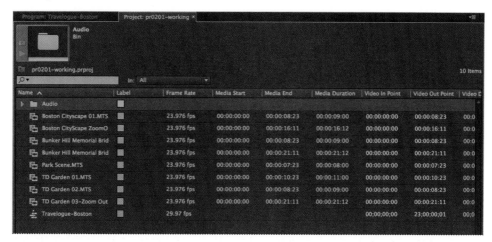

Importing entire folders is a quick way of importing multiple files, along with their content and subfolders.

When you import a folder into Premiere Pro, the application automatically creates a bin in the Project panel with the same name as the imported folder. The content of the folder on your hard drives, as well as the content of any sub-folders, is placed inside this bin.

In NLE (Non-Linear Editing) parlance, a bin is basically just the name for a file folder. The functionality of bins in the Premiere Pro Project panel is almost identical to those of the file folders on your computer.

5   Click the reveal triangle to the left of the Audio bin to show the clips that you imported. Notice that the three files that are inside of the folder on your computer's hard drive have all been imported into Premiere Pro. When importing a folder, the content of any sub-folders it may contain is also imported.

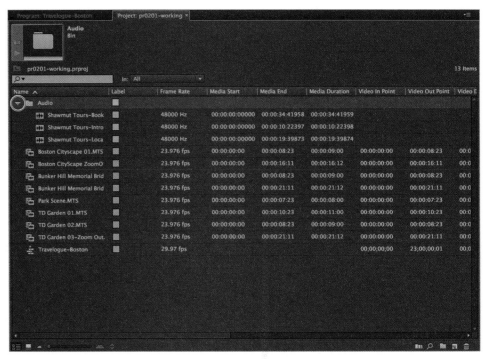

Each bin's reveal triangle can show and hide the bin's contents.

6   Choose File > Save or press Ctrl+S (Windows) or Command+S (Mac OS) to save the project file.

In the next part of the lesson, you will create a new bin to hold the video files you just imported and keep the project panel organized.

Creating and organizing bins

The term bins comes from the days of editing film when the developed film clips were stored in bins for easy organization. In the Premiere Pro project panel, bins serve as file folders to hold and organize your media assets. Bins can hold any combination of media: video, audio, still images, and even other bins. The organizational scheme you use for this exercise will create a separate bin for each different type of media used in the project.

The media management strategy that you adopt depends on the specifics of the project and the quantity of footage. For larger projects, you might break the footage into bins based on the content of the video, location, or for dramatic works, the footage needed for a specific scene (scene-based organizational system).

1   If the Audio bin is still selected, click on any empty area of the Project panel to deselect it. Then create a new bin by clicking the New Bin button located at the bottom-right of the Project panel. Rename this bin **Video** and press Enter (Windows) or Return (Mac OS) to confirm the new bin name.

When you create a new bin, it will automatically be placed inside the bin that you currently have selected. This is why it is important to remember to deselect the Audio bin in this step.

When you create a new bin, the default name is highlighted immediately so you can change it. If you click another item in the Project panel or click another pane, the name becomes deselected. To make the name editable again, right-click the bin name and choose Rename from the menu that appears. Additionally, double-clicking the name of any item in the Project panel makes the name editable.

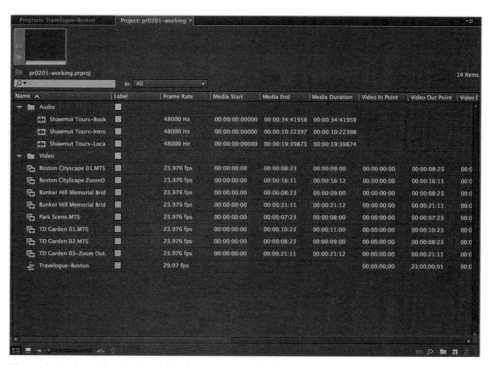

The term bin is a legacy from the days of film editing. In practice, bins function exactly like the folders on your hard drive.

2   Click the first video clip displayed in the Project panel, hold the Shift key on your keyboard, and click the last video clip to select every clip between them.

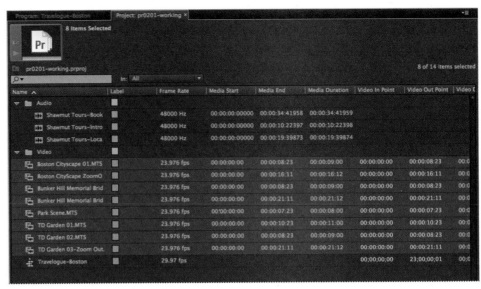

Holding the Shift key allows you to select files in sequential order.

3   Release the Shift key and then click any one of the selected files and drag it to the Video bin. When the bin's name becomes highlighted, release the mouse to move all the selected files into the bin.

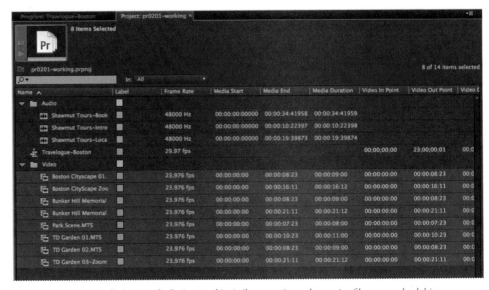

Moving and arranging media items in the Project panel is similar to moving and arranging files on your hard drive.

4 Click any empty area of the Project panel to deselect the Video bin, and then click the New Bin button again to create a third bin. Rename this bin **Boston Footage** and again press the Enter (Windows) or Return (Mac OS) to confirm the new bin name.

5 Click the Audio bin, then press and hold the Control (Windows) or Command (Mac OS), and click the Video bin to select both.

6 Release the Control (Windows) or Command (Mac OS) key and then drag either of the selected bins into the Boston Footage bin. This moves both the selected bins inside the bin named Boston Footage.

Storing bins inside one another is an efficient organizational tool and can prevent the Project panel from becoming cluttered.

7 Choose File > Save or press Ctrl+S (Windows) or Command+S (Mac OS) to save the project file.

Now that you have organized the Project panel, in the next part of the lesson you will modify the panels display so that it is easier to view the most relevant information about your media items.

Modifying the Project panel display

The Project panel displays information about each item it contains in a series of columns to the right of each item's name. This information display can be customized so that you can control which properties display and in what order. This allows you to view only the attributes that are most relevant to the type of work you are currently doing at any given time in Premiere Pro.

Adding/removing columns in the Project panel

The default column display can be changed, to add hidden panels or remove panels that you may consider extraneous.

1   Since the Project panel is very small when compared with the overall Premiere Pro interface, seeing all the columns at the same time is impossible. The first thing you will do is expand the panel to full-screen size. Note that even in full-screen mode you may not be able to view every data column in the Project panel depending on your monitor's resolution. If necessary, click on any area of the Project panel to select it. You will know it is selected when it has an orange border around it.

Click on any area of the Project panel to select it. You will know it is selected when it has an orange border around it.

With the Project panel selected press the tilde (~) key on your keyboard.

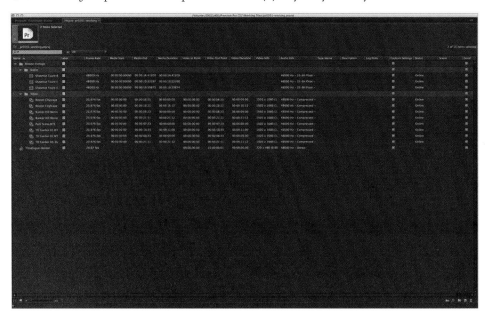

The tilde (~) key acts as a minimize/maximize toggle for whichever panel is currently active.

You can also right-click any column header in the Project panel to access a menu that allows you to edit the Metadata display.

2   The expanded Project panel makes it much easier to see each clip's properties.

Click on the menu button located at the upper-right corner of the Project panel and from the menu that appears, choose Metadata Display. Metadata is information that is attached to files that contains extra information about the file. For a video clip, metadata could include information such as the length, audio information, or frame size and rate.

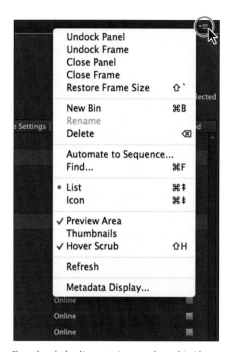

Even though the clip properties are only used inside Premiere Pro they are still listed as a part of the overall metadata properties.

3　In the Metadata Display panel click on the reveal triangle to the left of Premiere Pro Project Metadata to reveal its properties.

Click and drag the lower-right corner of the dialog box to enlarge it so that you can see all the revealed attributes. Each attribute corresponds to one of the visible columns in the Project panel.

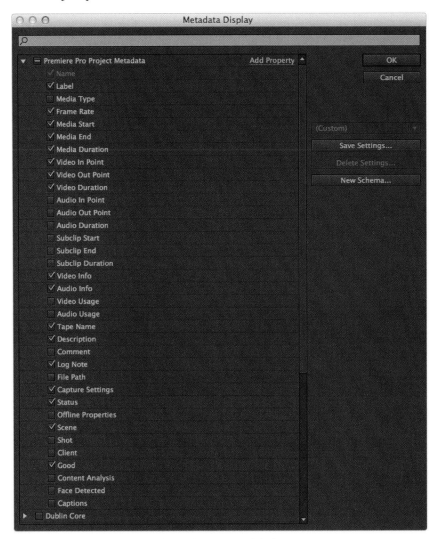

Some clip properties are turned off by default in the Project panel display.

4   In the dialog box, disable the following attributes by clicking to clear the check mark
    to the left of the attributes.

Frame Rate	Media Start	Media End	Media Duration	Video Info
Audio Info	Tape Name	Log Note	Capture Settings	Status
Scene	Good			

You do not need these attributes for the work you will do in this project. The Media
(displayed in Timecode) and Tape Name properties refer to the tape that these clips
were captured from. The Frame Rate, Video, and Audio Info and Capture settings are
the same for all the clips you will work with in this project. You will not use the other
properties, such as Scene, because they are intended for a different type of project
workflow than you will be working with here.

Understanding timecode

Timecode is used in video editing and motion graphics programs to keep track of your position
along a Timeline, tape, or any time-based medium. You can identify timecode as a series of four
numbers separated by colons or semicolons. As seen in the example above and reading from left
to right, the numbers represent: Hours;Minutes;Seconds;Frames.

You can count hours, minutes, and seconds in much the same way as you would with a standard
clock, but the counting begins at zero instead of one. The one variable with timecode is the
number of frames that make up a second, which is based on the frame rate of the media you
are dealing with. Depending on the Composition settings, you could be using the American
television standard of 30 FPS (frames per second), the European standard of 25 FPS, or the film
standard of 24 FPS. In essence, timecode provides a discrete address to each frame of video.

5   Click the OK button. The Project panel was reduced to a few columns.

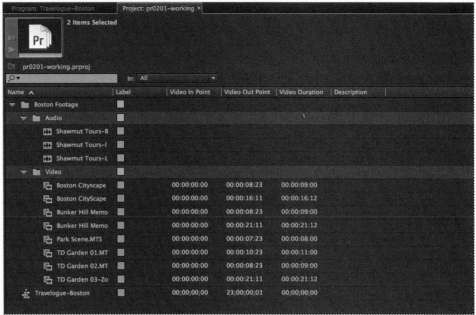

The visible columns in the Project panel can be adjusted at any time depending on the needs of your project.

6   Choose File > Save or press Ctrl+S (Windows) or Command+S (Mac OS) to save the project file.

Do not close this file; you will need it in the next exercise.

In the next section, you will edit the clip descriptions and change the order that the columns display in.

Adding a clip description

Some of the columns in the Project panel are purely descriptive; they display information about the properties of the footage you are working with. Columns such as Media Start, Media End, and Media Duration are non-editable, while others, such as Video In Point, Video Out Point, and Video Duration, can be changed as you work with your clips in Premiere Pro. Columns such as Description can be edited directly in the Project panel itself. Clip descriptions can be very helpful, especially when working on longer, more complex projects, or when working in a team environment. The Description column of the Project panel contains an editable text field that can be used to hold a wide variety of information, such as a content description, or to note intended usage.

1   With the Project panel still expanded to the full size of the screen and active, click the Description column header and drag it to the left. As you drag the column name, a dark highlight appears between each pair of names.

Drag the Description column until this highlight is between the Label and Video In Point columns, and then release it to rearrange the column order.

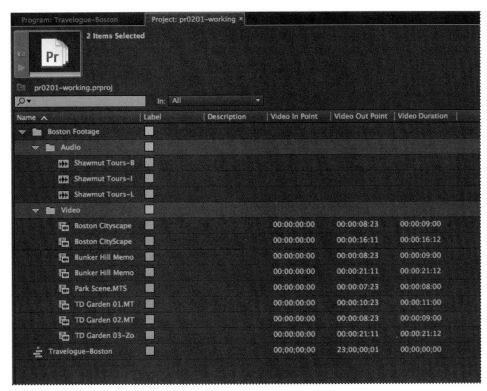

You can drag any column title to the left or right to change the arrangement of the Project panel's columns.

2   You have repositioned the Description column, but the default size of the column is very small, leaving very little room in which to add a description.

Place your cursor on the dividing line between the Description and Label column headers. When the cursor changes to a double-headed arrow, click and drag to the right to change the width of the Description column to make it approximately double its current size. Note that all the other columns move over to accommodate the size change.

After enlarging the Description column, repeat these steps for the Name column so you can see the full name of each audio and video file. Depending on the screen resolution of your monitor, enlarging the Name field may not be necessary.

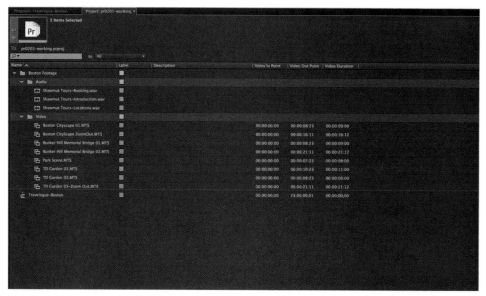

You can quickly edit visually the width of each column directly from the Project panel interface.

3 Locate the clip named **Boston Cityscape 01.mts**. You can edit a clip's Description property at any time.

Click in the clip's description field and add the following description: **Static shot of the Boston Area Skyline**.

Press the Enter (Windows) or Return (Mac OS) key on your keyboard to deselect this clip's text field and automatically select the next clip's description field.

If you do not want to select the next clip's description, you can click any empty area of the project panel with your cursor to deselect the active text field.

4 Press the tilde (~) key on your keyboard to return the Project panel to its normal screen size.

5 Choose File > Save or press Ctrl+S (Windows) or Command+S (Mac OS) to save the project file.

In your own projects, you should consider giving each clip in the project panel a unique description. This can include any information you feel is important to your editing process, such as time of day, the subject of the shot, or notes on camera position or movement.

Organizing content by columns

The columns of the project panel are used to control how the different items in the panel display. You can arrange your clips based on the content of any column.

1   In the Project panel, the default organization is alphabetically based on the name. In the case of bins, the bin name is used to arrange all the media it contains. The active panel shows either a downward or upward pointing chevron next to the column header.

2   Click the Column Name to reverse the standard ascending display order and notice how items reverse their display order in the panel and are now displayed in descending order. When working on your own projects, you can choose the order you prefer. For this project, we will place the Travelogue–Boston Sequence at the top of the display.

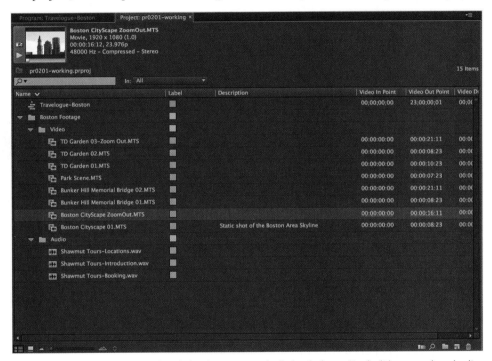

The footage display in the Project panel can be based on any currently displayed column. Simply click on any column heading to reorder the footage in the panel.

3   Choose File > Save or press Ctrl+S (Windows) or Command+S (Mac OS) to save the project file.

Choose File > Close Project to close this project and return to the Premiere Pro welcome screen.

Searching in the Project panel

If you are working on a complex project with many different footage items, it can become very difficult to find the items you are looking for in the Project panel. To make organizing and finding your footage easier, the panel has a search field that you can use to quickly find what you are looking for. Simply type the term you want to search for into the text field, and the Project panel begins to hide any item that doesn't match. For additional control, you can use the "In" drop-down menu to set the types of fields that are part of the search criteria.

As long as any text is present in the Search field, the display of the Project panel is affected. Use the X icon to the right of the text area to clear the current search.

Locating missing media

Premiere Pro creates a link between your project files and the files that you import into the Project panel. This linkage system allows you to have a very small project file, but at the same time requires that you manage the media you are using in your projects. If you move, rename, or delete files that you are using in a project you will receive a missing media warning when Premiere Pro attempts to open it. Likewise, if you edit a file name or location while a project is open in Premiere Pro, you will receive a missing media error. You should always locate any missing files before attempting to proceed with your project.

The process for locating missing files is automatic and will help you find video, audio, stills, and images. The next steps are not intended to be followed right now, but are presented here as reference for when you do encounter a missing media warning.

1 When presented with the Link Media dialog box, verify the clip and file names listed. These listed files are the ones that Premiere Pro has been unable to locate automatically while opening the project file.

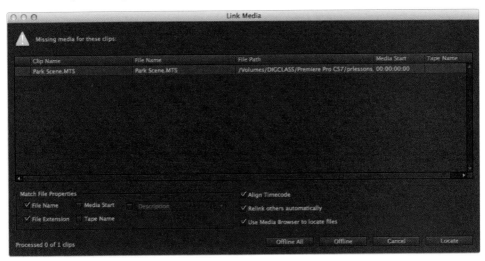

The application will automatically open the dialog box when a project with missing files is opened.

Most of the options in the Link Media dialog are pretty straight forward. However, the choices offered for dealing with missing files can use some explanation. You have three choices when dealing with the Link Media dialog box. You can have the program set the missing media as offline. In this case, the clip entry will appear in Premiere Pro without any attached media that cannot be displayed. In the Premiere Pro Project panel, offline files can be brought online by right-clicking them in the Project panel and choosing Link Media from the menu that appears. Additionally, you can cancel the search operation or attempt to locate your missing media. With the exception of some very specific workflows, you will usually choose to locate the missing media.

2   Click the Locate button. By default, Premiere Pro will open the Media Browser panel. Use the directory tree on the right to navigate to the missing file, highlight it, and then click the OK button to relink the file.

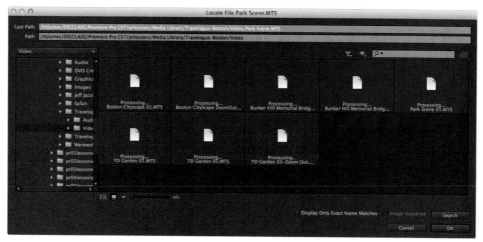

When all missing files have been recovered, the project will open.

If your missing files are still in the same relative folder structure as when they were first imported into your project, Premiere Pro will locate and automatically relink them all, once it knows the location of the first one. If it cannot automatically find other missing files you will have to locate them manually. Once all missing files have been found or skipped, the project will open.

If you prefer to use the standard file dialog box that is native to your operating system, you can uncheck the Use Media Browser to locate files check box in the Link Media dialog box.

Self study

The only way you will ever create a Project panel display that works for your specific project is by becoming familiar with the amount of variation available to you. Open the practice project again and this time work with changing the organization of the Project panel so that it is arranged based on different columns. Additionally, you can rearrange the panel display to create your own custom application interface.

Review

Questions

1   What type of content is contained in the Project panel?

2   What is the difference between the Source and Program monitors?

3   When viewing the timecode display what do the four different sets of numbers represent?

Answers

1   The Project panel contains references to all the footage files (video, audio, and images) that you have imported into Premiere Pro in addition to the sequences, titles and other supporting material you create in the application.

2   You can use the source monitor to playback and preview individual clips or to prepare clips before you add them to a sequence. The Program monitor is used only to preview the clips that have already been added to the Timeline.

3   The four different sets of numbers in a timecode display are: *Hours;Minutes;Seconds;Frames.* So the following timecode: 00;00;04;14 would represent a time mark of 4 seconds and 14 frames.

What you'll learn in this lesson:

- To understand the uses of Adobe Prelude

- To use prelude to ingest video from tapeless media

- To add metadata to video files

- To add markers to video clips

- To export media for use in Premiere Pro

Prepping Files in Prelude

Adobe Prelude is a video ingest and logging tool. It allows you to ingest footage from tapeless media, rename clips, add and edit metadata and transcode to nearly any format.

Starting up

In this lesson, you will work with the project files from the pr03lessons folder. Make sure that you have loaded the prlessons folder onto your hard drive from the supplied DVD. The Starting up section at the start of this book provides detailed information about loading lesson files, resetting your workspace, locating missing media, and opening the files in CC. If you have not already done so, please review these instructions before starting this lesson.

When opening the Premiere Pro project files used in this lesson you may experience a missing media message. You must locate any missing media before trying to proceed through the lesson. For more information refer to "Locating missing media" in the Starting up section of this book.

See Lesson 3 in action!

Use the accompanying video to gain a better understanding of some of the concepts covered in this lesson. The video tutorial for this lesson can be found on the included DVD.

What is Adobe Prelude?

To complete this section of the lesson you will need to download and install Adobe Prelude from the Adobe Application Manager.

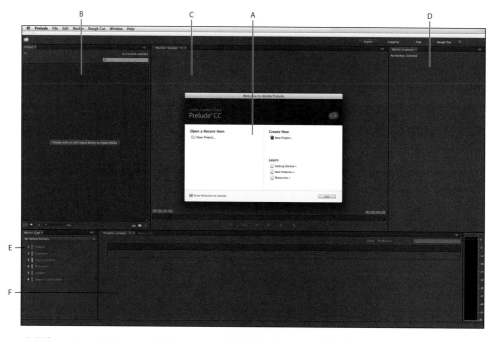

A. Welcome Screen. B. Project panel. C. Monitor panel. D. Marker Inspector panel. E. Marker Type panel. F. Timeline panel.

Adobe Prelude is a video ingest and logging tool. Ingesting is the term used to describe the process of bringing footage from your tapeless camera to your computer for editing. Logging is a term used to describe the process of annotating your video footage. While both of these two tasks can be accomplished in Premiere Pro itself, Prelude has the added ability to batch encode your source video files. You may be asking yourself why would you need Prelude if you already have Premiere Pro? Prelude can be used to improve the efficiency of your editing workflow; with it's simple streamlined interface the ingest, verification and logging of video footage is quicker and easier.

Prelude finds additional use a tool for a team-based workflow. With a simple interface designed to perform only a few specified tasks, it is a perfect tools for team members who may not be familiar with the use of Premiere Pro. Using Prelude assistant editors and even directors or producers can quickly create video sequences from ingested footage, add markers for notation and export them all to Premiere Pro for more detailed editing.

Supported formats for ingest and logging

Adobe Prelude supports a wide variety of formats for both ingest and logging.

3GP	MPE
AIFF	MPEG
ASF	MPG
AVCHD (files must remain in camera folder structure)	MXF
	P2 AVC–Intra
AVI	P2 DVCPRO HD
Canon XF	QuickTime
F4V	RED R3D
FLV	SWF
M2P	VOB
M2T	WAV
M2V	WMV
M4V	XDCAM
MP3	XDCAM EX
MP4 (some codecs from cell phones and GoPro are not currently supported)	XDCAM HD

Formats that can be ingested but not logged

Because the logging process adds or edits the metadata of your source video files not all formats are supported. This is a list of the file formats that can be ingested from tapeless media but cannot be logged. In order to log these types of footage file you must first transcode them to a more compatible format.

3G2
ARRIRAW
M1V
M2TS
MP4 (some codecs from cell phones and GoPro are not currently supported)
MTS

Ingesting video

Just like Premiere Pro the heart of Adobe Prelude is the project file. In this portion of the lesson you will create a new Prelude project file and then ingest video from the prlesson folder that you have previously copied to your hard drive.

1 From the Adobe Prelude welcome screen click on the New Project button to open the new project dialog box.

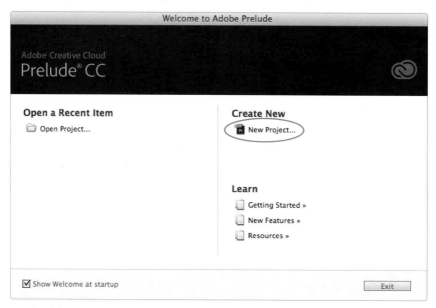

Note that clicking on the Exit button closes the application.

In the New Project dialog box you must now choose a location to save your new project. Navigate to prlessons>Lesson03. In the Save As file change untitled project to **pr0301-working**.

Click the Save button to create the new project.

2   To ingest video either double-click anywhere in the Project panel or click on the
     Ingest button at the top of the application. In the Ingest dialog box that appears choose
     Home Directory from the Recent directories drop-down menu.

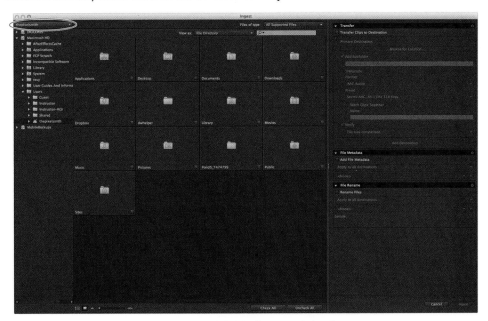

The Recent Directories menu can make it easier to quickly find the files you are looking for.

This will show you the contents of your home directory. Navigate to the Media
Library inside of the prlesson folder that you copied to your hard drive. Inside of
the Media Library navigate to Werewolves of Central Park > A Roll and locate the
Reporter at Crime Scene.mpeg file.

3 Click the checkbox field located at the lower right corner of the video clip icon to mark this file for ingest and then press the Ingest button located at the lower right of the dialog box. Ingested video clips appear in the Project panel, just as they do in Premiere Pro.

If you need to mark all files in a directory for ingest, just click the Check All button located at the bottom of the dialog box.

Understanding the Ingest dialog

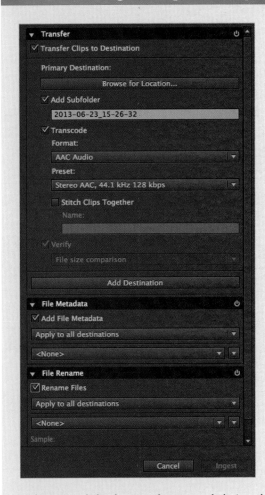

In the Ingest dialog box you have several choices that allow you to process your footage while ingesting it.

Transfer: The Transfer section is used to copy the video clips you are ingesting from your tapeless media to another location of your choosing. Additionally, when copying these files you can use the Transcode option to convert them from your camera's native file format into a wide variety of other formats.

File Metadata: The File Metadata section is used to add meta data to your video files at ingest.

File Rename: Since tapeless cameras often use generic names for vide clips the File Rename section can be used to bath rename your files at the point of ingestion.

4   In addition to individual files you can also ingest entire folders in Prelude. Again to ingest video either double-click anywhere in the Project panel or click on the Ingest button at the top of the application.

If necessary, again navigate to the Media Library located inside the prlessons folder and locate the Werewolves of Central Park folder.

Click on the checkbox for the B Roll folder, leave all setting as they were during the previous ingest operation and then click the Ingest button.

You can ingest single files, multiple files and even multiple folders using Prelude.

During Ingest you will receive a Ingest Failure Warning dialog box. Click OK to clear the message. The warning appears because of the metadata files that are also located inside the ingested folder and will not affect your work in Prelude.

Any incompatible files inside an ingested folder cause a warning dialog to appear.

5   Choose File>Save or press Control+ S (windows) or Cmd+S (Mac OS) to save your working file.

Do not close this project as you will need it in the next part of the lesson.

Organizing clips

Prelude allows you to preview, annotate and organize clips and then send them to Premiere Pro as projects.

1   With the **pr0301-working.plproj** still open, you will now organize the ingested clips in the Project panel.

2   The Project panel defaults to an icon based display. While very helpful for visually identifying your clips it can be somewhat cumbersome from an organizational standpoint. Click on the List view button at the lower left side of the panel to switch the display.

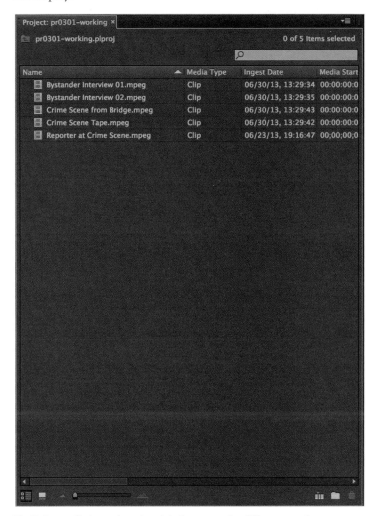

The Project panel's view mode can be switched to accommodate different user preferences.

3   Click on the Create a new bin button located at the bottom right of the panel. This creates a new bin you will use to organize the clips in this project.

Rename this bin **A Roll** and then click in any empty area of the Project panel to deselect the bin name and complete the rename operation.

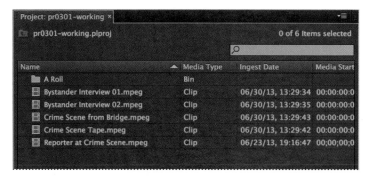

In Prelude bins are equivalent to the file folders on your hard drive

4   Click on the **Reporter at Crime Scene.mpeg** file and drag it into the A Roll bin. Note that the bin will highlight to indicate that you can place a file inside of it.

Depending on how you plan to integrate Prelude into your own workflows you could create multiple bins at this point to organize all of your footage. Since this project is being used as a gateway into Premiere Pro you will only create one folder at this time.

5   Choose File > Save or press Control+S (Windows) or Cmd+S (Mac OS) to save your working file.

Do not close this project as you will need it in the next part of the lesson.

Logging video

The process of logging video clips involves watching your video clips and then adding descriptions to them based on their content. Prior to the advent of digital video and editing technology this process involved creating written log books that listed important events in the video next to time code references for their locations. Now the process involves adding metadata to the files description and other fields

1   With the **pr0301-working.plproj** still open, double-click on the **Reporter at Crime Scene.mpeg** file to load it into the Monitor and Timeline panels.

Click the the Play-Stop toggle button at the bottom of the Monitor Panel to preview the video file. Click the toggle button again to stop the preview at any time.

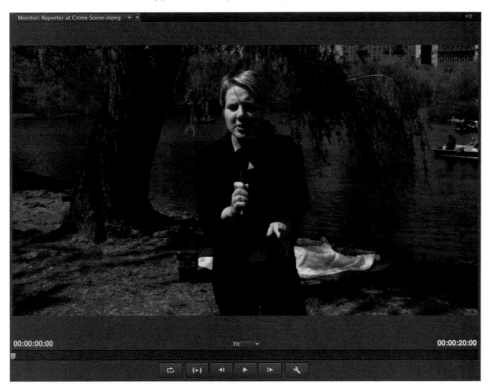

The interface and keyboard commands of Prelude are very similar to those of Premiere Pro.

You can also start/stop the playhead by pressing the Space bar on your keyboard when the Monitor or Timeline Panels are active.

2   Choose Window > Metadata to open the metadata panel then in the Project panel click on the Reporter at Crime Scene.mpeg clip to highlight it. Notice that the metadata panel fields populate once you select a file.

Now that you know the content of the video you can add a description to it.

The Metadata panel isn't included in the default Logging workspace but can easily be opened from the Window menu.

You may need to move the Metadata panel around so that you can better see the other panels of the program interface.

3   In the metadata panel click on the reveal triangle to the left of the Dublin Core metadata group. This is where you will find the file's description field.

4   Add the following text to the description text field: **News reporter opening and closing from Central Park in NYC.**

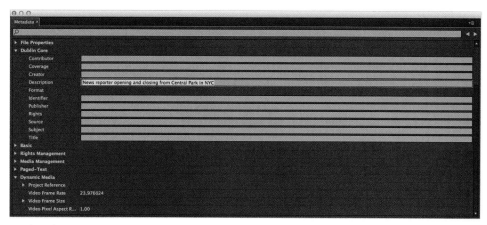

Metadata editors such as Adobe Bridge can be used to view/edit the metadata you add in Prelude.

5   In the Project panel, click on the **Bystander Interview 02.mpeg** to highlight it, and then click on the Play-Stop toggle button again to preview this file. Click the toggle button again to stop the preview at any time.

6   With the **Bystander Interview 02.mpeg** still selected, locate the Metadata panel and add the following text into the description field: Interview in park, unusable, too much background noise.

Choose Window > Workspace > Reset Current Workspace to return Prelude to the default Logging workspace. Click Yes in the dialog box that appears to ask you to confirm your decision.

The metadata that you add here in Prelude is added either to the file itself or to an XMP sidecar file that is saved to the same location as your media and will be visible when you add these files to a Premiere Pro project or when previewing them in a metadata viewer or search application.

Do not close the file, you will need it in the next section of this lesson.

In the next part of this lesson you will add comments and marks to the clips in this project in preparation of importing it into Premiere Pro.

Adding Comment markers

The metadata that you added in the previous part of this lesson can be accessed by almost any program intended to read metadata. However there are specific workflows in place for moving files between Prelude and Premiere Pro. To speed up your work you can add markers and comments to clips that are visible while editing. There are several different types of markers you can create:

Subclip: used to create In and Out points that mark subclips for editing. When the project is saved the generated subclips appear in the Project panel.

Comment: add a comment or note to a clip at a specified point in time. You use comment markers to indicate important times in a video file.

Flash Cue Point: When exporting to the Flash Video format (flv, f4v) Flash Cue Point markers can be used to trigger external scripted events or used as navigational points.

Web Link: When exported to certain video formats that support them add a URL to a point in time on a video file that can be used to provide additional information about the movie clip.

Chapter: When imported into Adobe Encore and Premiere Pro these markers are used to create chapter points for DVD and Blu-ray disk projects.

Speech Transcription: These markers are used to edit speech-to-text transcriptions created in applicatiosn such as Adobe Media Encoder or even to add such data manually.

In this part of the lesson you will create a comment and subclip markers.

1   With the **pr0301-working.plproj** still open, double-click on **Reporter at Crime Scene.mpeg** file to preview it in the Monitor and Timeline panels.

You previewed this file in an earlier step, it is video of a news anchor introducing a story and then signing off. Now you will add a marker to indicate where the intro ends. This information will help you later when you export this file to Premiere Pro.

The Prelude interface is designed to perform a few very specific tasks.

2   In the Timeline panel move the playhead to the 9 second and 10 frame (00:00:09:10) mark. The playhead's current position is displayed at the lower left of the Monitor panel.

The Prelude monitor panel is very similar to the one in Premiere Pro.

3   Choose Marker > Add > Comment Marker. This creates a new marker on the Timeline that begins at the current position of the playhead.

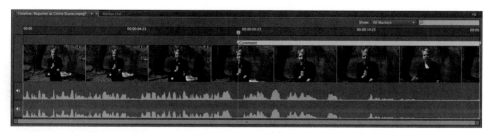

By default comment markers are assigned a duration that begins at the playhead and runs until the end of the clip.

4   In the Marker Inspector panel click the Out button to set the Out Point of the marker to the current position of the playhead. This creates a marker that only holds for a single frame.

Comment markers can be assigned any duration the user specifies.

5   Still in the Marker Inspector panel type the following into the Marker Name Field:
    Story Introduction Ends.

6   Save the changes you have made to this file by choosing File > Save or pressing Ctrl+S
    (windows) or Cmd+S (Mac OS). Since each file in Prelude is treated as an individual
    element it is necessary to save after any one of them is changed.

    Do not close the file, you will need it in the next section of this lesson.

Adding Subclip markers

Subclips allow you to digitally sub-divide a master video clip into individual segments.
This is a good way of separating long clips or multiple takes into manageable blocks of
video.

1   With the **pr0301–working.plproj** still open, double-click on the
    Bystander Interview 01.mpeg to load it into the Monitor and Timeline panels.

2   Click the the Play-Stop toggle button at the bottom of the Monitor Panel to preview
    the video file. Click the toggle button again to stop the preview at any time. This
    video contains a bystander in the park being interviewed by the reporter from the
    earlier scene.

    Only a small part of this video clip is usable, so you will now make a subclip out of
    this section.

3   Move the playhead to the 5 second and 5 frame (00:00:05:05) mark on the Timeline
    panel.

*The Monitor panel's Timecode display will show you where the playhead (also called the
Current Time Indicator) is along the Timeline. You can use the left and right arrow keys on your
keyboard to move the playhead back or forward one frame at a time.*

4   Choose Marker > Add > Subclip Marker. This places a subclip marker into the
    timeline. The In point of the subclip is set to the current position of the playhead
    while it's Out point runs until the end of the clip.

5   Move the playhead to the 18 second (00:00:18:00) mark on the Timeline and then press the Out button located in the Marker Inspector panel. This sets the Out point of this marker to the current position of the playhead.

Change the marker's name to **Bystander Interview 01–Subclip**.

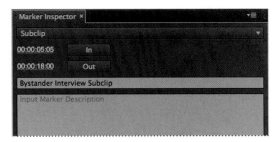

The marker's name appears in the timeline next to the start of the marker.

6   Choose File > Save or press Ctrl+S (windows) or Cmd+S (Mac OS) to save the Prelude project file. Notice that a new entry appears in the Project panel to denote the subclip you have just created.

If you want to edit the subclip or even delete it those changes will take effect the next time you save the file.

Do not close the file, you will need it in the next section of this lesson.

Creating a rough cut

Adobe Prelude is in no way a fully featured editing application. It does however have the ability to be used for simple footage assembly. This allows you to create rough cuts that can then be exported to Premiere Pro for later finishing.

1   With the **pr0301-working.plproj** still open, Choose File > Create Rough Cut. In the Create Rough Cut dialog box that appears, navigate to the Lesson03 folder on your hard drive. Change the text in the Save As text field to **Crime Scene Report** and click the Save button.

Notice that a new item with the Media Type of Rough Cut appears in the Project panel.

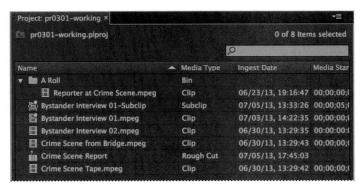

In the Project panel items can be easily recognized by their Media Type.

2   Double-click on the Crime Scene Report Rough Cut in the Project
panel to load it into the Monitor and Timeline panels and then drag the
Reporter at Crime Scene.mpeg video clip into the Timeline panel. Notice that the
Rough Cut appears in the Project panel as a new item.

Video clips can be dragged into either the Timeline or Monitor panels.

3   Choose File > Save.

When this file is exported to Premiere Pro, the Rough Cut will be converted into
a Sequence. The video that you have added here will already be present on it's
timeline. If you are using Prelude to set up all of your Premiere Pro sequences you
could continue to add additional video clips to the Rough Cut or add markers and in
general mock up a very detailed sequence. However, in this lesson we are only using
it as a part of our workflow and we will continue our work in Premiere Pro in the
next lesson.

Do not close the file, you will need it in the next section of this lesson.

Exporting to Premiere Pro

Once you have prepared your media for Premiere Pro actually exporting it is a fairly quick
and easy process. You select the content in the Prelude Project panel that you want to
send to Premiere Pro and then simply export it. Prelude bundles the content together into
a prproj file. This is a Premiere Pro project file that can be opened just using the File >
Open command once you get to Premiere Pro.

1 With the **pr0301-working.plproj** still open, click on the first item that appears in the Project panel. Hold down the shift key on your keyboard and then click on the last item that appears in the Project panel. This will select every item in between them as well.

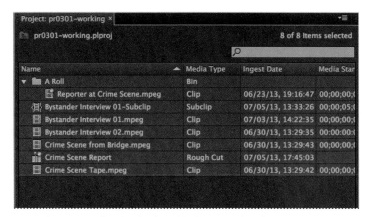

Items in the Project panel can be selected just like files on your hard drive.

2 Choose File > Export > Project. This opens the Export Project dialog box. In this dialog confirm the that the Project drop-downmenu is set to Premiere Pro and change it's name to **Werewolves of Central Park**. If necessary uncheck the Media and Use Subfolder options.

3 Click the OK button and then navigate to the pr03lessons folder and then save your exported project to this location.

In the next lesson you will use a copy of this exported file to complete the editing of this project. Once you have completed this next lesson you should have a stronger understanding of the overall editing workflow utilizing Prelude and Premiere Pro.

Congratulations you have completed this lesson.

Self Study

Now that you have learned the basics of working with Adobe Prelude you can use it to ingest video from your tapeless camcorder. When ingesting video files from your camcorder remember to check the Transfer Clips to Destination option in the Ingest dialog box, so that you can copy the files onto your hard disk drive.

Review

Questions

1   What is Adobe Prelude used for?

2   What do the terms ingesting and logging mean in relation to a video editing workflow?

3   What are subclip and comment markers used for in Adobe Prelude?

Answers

1   Adobe Prelude is a video ingest and logging tool.

2   Ingesting is the term used to describe the process of bringing footage from your tapeless camera to your computer for editing. Logging is a term used to describe the process of annotating your video footage

3   Subclip markers are used to create In and Out points that mark subclips for editing, while comment markers are used to add a comment or note to a clip at a specified point in time.

Lesson 4

What you'll learn in this lesson:

- The methodology of the continuity editing process seen in film and television
- To trim clips with the selection and razor tools
- To target and use multiple video tracks

Making the Cut

Video editing changes the arrangement and duration of video and audio clips to craft a narrative. An editor arranges footage to create a coherent story paced to appeal to the audience. Now that you have learned to organize your project, in this lesson you will discover how to edit clips on the Timeline.

Starting up

In this lesson, you will work with the project files from the pr04lessons folder. Make sure that you have loaded the prlessons folder onto your hard drive from the supplied DVD. The Starting up section at the start of this book provides detailed information about loading lesson files, resetting your workspace, locating missing media, and opening the files in CC. If you have not already done so, please review these instructions before starting this lesson.

When opening the Premiere Pro project files used in this lesson you may experience a missing media message. You must locate any missing media before trying to proceed through the lessons. Please refer to the "Locating missing media" in the Starting up section of this book.

See Lesson 4 in action!

Use the accompanying video to gain a better understanding of how to use some of the features shown in this lesson. The video tutorial for this lesson can be found on the included DVD.

The cuts-only editing methodology

In traditional film and video, continuity editing makes use of very few transitions, and the straight cut is the preferred method of getting from one scene or shot to another. When working with a cuts-only editing approach, the editor attempts to find a match cut, in which different scenes, people, or objects share a similar visual relationship. This relationship can be based on screen position, similar movement or color value, or a wide variety of other criteria. This type of cut forms the basis of the continuity editing style, the goal of which is to create a seamless and non-jarring change.

A Roll vs. B Roll

The terms A Roll and B Roll describe the primary and secondary footage shot and used in video and film productions. In an edit, B Roll is used to add or enhance the meaning of the main footage or to cover the removal of unwanted or error-ridden material. For example, in a documentary production, the A Roll would contain interview footage and the B Roll would contain exteriors, establishing shots, or footage that describes or illustrates the topics described in the documentary. In dramatic work, the B Roll might contain additional angles on the main subject or secondary subjects present in a scene.

Cut-ins and Cut-aways

Cut-ins and cut-aways are instantaneous shifts in the framing of a shot. Both techniques are related to the primary focus or action of a scene and can be used to enhance the meaning or alleviate the tedium of long scenes. Cut-ins and cut-aways are often used to show an event occurring alongside the main action of the scene. A cut-in is a cut that shifts from the main subject (A Roll) to an event occurring inside the same scene. For example, if your main scene involves two people shaking hands, a possible cut-in might be a close-up of the handshake.

A Cut-away is a cut away from the main action to other simultaneous events. For example, in the scene of the two people shaking hands, a possible cut-away might show other people entering the room. Cut-ins and cut-aways rarely add dramatic content, but usually control the pacing of longer scenes, introduce new elements to the main scene, or emphasize elements already present.

Cutting on action

Cutting on action is a standard practice of continuity editing that refers to a technique in which you cut from one shot to another that matches or anticipates the action of the first shot. In other words, a subject begins an action in one shot and seems to complete or continue it in the next, creating a visual join or bridge that prevents the viewer from noticing the cut itself. For example, a shot of someone beginning to bow can be cut to a shot of the same subject continuing the action from a different angle. A shot of a person looking up in response to a knock on a door can be cut to a shot of another person walking through a door.

In this lesson, you will use A Roll and B Roll footage to create a faux newscast. This footage is from a short film project named *Riding Hood*, about a group of folkloric creatures roaming the streets of New York City. In the scene used for this lesson, the police are investigating an attack on a pedestrian in Central Park, and a reporter from a local news network has just arrived to cover the story. You will have A Roll of the news reporter to be intercut with B Roll footage of comments from onlookers and establishing shot of the area. To complete this edit, you will trim clips in the Monitor and Timeline, add extra tracks to the Timeline to hold your clips, and learn to specify the destination track for inserted footage.

All the media used in this section of the lesson can be found in the Werewolves of Central Park folder in the Media Library. The Reporter at Crime Scene.mpeg file can be found in the A Roll sub-folder while the remainder of the footage used can be found in the B Roll sub-folder.

Trimming clips in the Source Monitor

The Source Monitor is one of the most important tools you can use to preview and trim clips in preparation for the Timeline. You can preview all footage used in Premiere Pro using the Source monitor, except for the content of Sequences, which you can preview in the Program Monitor. To preview footage, you can double-click a footage item or drag it to the Source Monitor panel.

Every clip in the project panel and on the Timeline has an In Point, an Out Point and a duration. When a clip is imported into Premiere Pro, its In and Out points are automatically set to the physical beginning and end of the clip, allowing it to run for its full duration. However, many times you might want to use a portion of a clip in your project. In such situations, you can trim the clip by setting new In and Out points using the Source monitor.

The footage used in this part of the lesson can be found in the Werewolves in Central Park folder, located inside the Media Library folder.

1 From the Premiere Pro welcome screen, click the Open Project button, or with Premiere Pro already open, chose File > Open Project. Navigate to the pr04lessons folder that you copied to your hard drive and locate the **pr0401.prproj** file. Double-click the file to open it. If necessary, you should locate any missing media files using the Link Media dialog box. You can refer to Lesson 02 for a refresher on how to do this.

In the preceding lesson, you used Adobe Prelude to create a Premiere Pro project file. This file is a copy of that file, and we have provided it as a matter of convenience. Notice that the rough cut that was created in Prelude has been converted into a sequence, and that all the folders and files have been preserved as well.

2 Choose File > Save As. In the Save Project dialog box that appears, confirm that you are still in the pr04lessons folder, rename your file to **pr0401-working**, and then click the Save button.

Before you edit your clips, it will be helpful to organize the Project panel further to make it easier to view and navigate.

3 At the bottom of the Project panel, click the List View button to switch the default icon view into a list display.

As mentioned previously, your folder hierarchy has been preserved when it was exported from Prelude.

If you cannot see the full clips names, click on the dividing line between the Name and Label column headings in the Project Panel and drag it to the right. Expand the Name field until the names of all the video clips in the B Roll folder are visible.

Expanding the Name field might place the Label or other fields outside of the visible area of the Project panel.

4 Click the clip named **Bystander Interview 01–Subclip** to highlight it, and then press and hold the Control (Windows) or Cmd (Mac OS) key on your keyboard; click the other clips visible in the Project panel to select them as well. Once you are finished highlighting the files, release the keyboard key.

Leave the sequence named Crime Scene Report unselected.

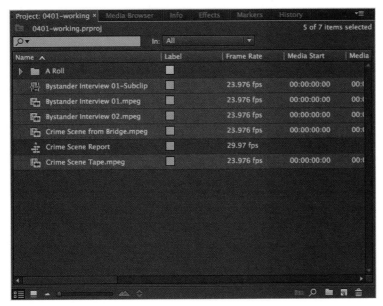

Selecting files in the Project panel is similar to selecting files on your hard drive.

5   In one motion, click on any one of the selected files and drag it to the New Bin button located at the bottom right of the Project panel. This creates a new bin and places all of the highlighted file inside of it.

Rename this new bin **B Roll**.

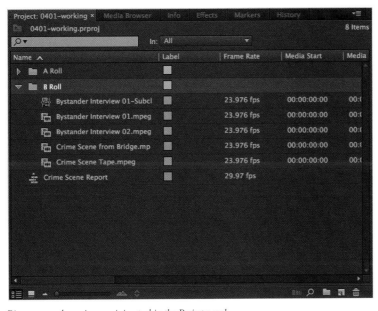

Bins serve as the main organizing tool in the Project panel.

6 Double-click the clip named **Bystander Interview 01–Subclip** to open it in the Source Monitor.

A. *Playhead Position.* B. *Select Zoom Level.* C. *Add Marker.* D. *Mark In.* E. *Mark Out.* F. *Go to In.*
G. *Step Back.* H. *Play-Stop Toggle.* I. *Step Forward.* J. *Go to Out.* K. *Insert Edit.* L. *Overwrite Edit.*
M. *Export Current Frame.* N. *Button Editor.* O. *In/Out Duration.* P. *Settings.* Q. *Select Playback Resolution.*
R. *Drag Audio Only.* S. *Drag Video Only.*

Depending on your monitor size and resolution, you may not be able to see all the controls available in the Source Monitor.

7 Click the Play-Stop Toggle button at the bottom of the Source Monitor to preview the file. This subclip was created in Prelude and is 12 seconds and 19 frames in duration. It involves the crime scene reporter interviewing a panicky bystander. This subclip was purposely created to have extra unneeded footage (called handles) at the beginning and end of the clip. We highly recommend that you shoot and capture footage with this extra padding so you do not accidentally finish with a clip that starts or ends right on the action or dialog you want to use. You may miss some really interesting and usable footage if you do.

Your first task is to remove this extra footage and trim the clip, as explained in the next step.

You can click the Play-Stop Toggle button or the spacebar on your keyboard at any time to start and stop the Monitor preview.

At around the 6-second mark, the interviewee starts moving around and gesticulating frantically. In the next part of this step, you will make this the beginning of the clip to exclude all previous footage from the Timeline.

8   Click the Playhead Position in the Source Monitor, change the value to 600, and press the Enter (Windows) or Return (Mac OS) key on your keyboard to move the playhead to the 6-second mark (00;00;06;00) on the Timeline.

When entering a time code location into the current time field, you do not need to include the semicolons between numbers, since the application does it automatically.

9   Click the Mark In button located at the bottom of the Source Monitor to set the In Point at the beginning of the clip and match the current position of the playhead.

Notice that the clip's duration has changed and the area between the playhead and the end of the clip changes color to indicate you have trimmed the clip.

The keyboard shortcut to set the In Point to the current position of the playhead is the I key.

10 Click on the Playhead Position field in the Source Monitor, change the value to **1710**, and press the Enter (Windows) or Return (Mac OS) key on your keyboard to move the playhead to the 17-second and 10-frame mark (00;00;17;10) on the Timeline.

11 Click the Mark Out button located next to the Set In Point button at the bottom of the Source Monitor to set the new end of the clip to match the current position of the playhead.

Notice that only the area between the current In and Out Points is highlighted. This is so you can quickly identify the active area of a clip.

The keyboard shortcut to set the Out Point to the current position of the playhead is the O key.

12 Click the Go to In button located at the bottom of the Source Monitor, to make the playhead jump to the In Point you set in an earlier step. Press the Play-Stop Toggle button to preview the clip and stop the preview when you are satisfied with your work.

The trimming you just completed is rough, so you will refine this edit later in the lesson. You can use the Source Monitor to perform rough edits, and then polish the clip after you add it to the Timeline to see how it integrates with the clips adjacent to it.

You can use the Transport controls, located in the center of the Source and Program Monitors to play, pause, and move forward or backward through video clips.

13 Choose File > Save or press Ctrl+S (Windows) or Command+S (Mac OS) to save these changes to your project.

Do not close this file; you will need it in the next part of the lesson.

Using multiple video tracks

You could keep all your clips on a single video track, but it might not always be a practical solution, especially when dealing with a complicated editing job. For example, you can easily create a cut-in or cut-away by placing a new clip containing B Roll footage on a track above the one containing an A Roll. Multiple tracks are also useful when you need to place graphics or titles above your video footage, or to compose multiple video clips to create a ghostly effect.

Adding and deleting tracks in the Timeline

When you create a new sequence in Premiere Pro, you can specify the number of audio and video tracks to include in the Tracks panel of the New Sequence dialog box. By default, the dialog box creates video and audio tracks for each new sequence based on the preset used, but you can add additional tracks or remove empty, unused ones. In this lesson's project, the Central Park Coverage sequence has only a single video track.

In this part of the lesson, you will add a new video track to the sequence so you can add the trimmed Bystander Interview 01 clip to it.

1   With the **pr0401-working.prproj** project still open, right-click (Windows) or Ctrl+click (Mac OS) in the empty space above the Video 1 track in the Timeline, and then choose Add Tracks to open the Add Tracks dialog box. Another option to open the Add Tracks dialog box is to choose Sequence > Add Tracks.

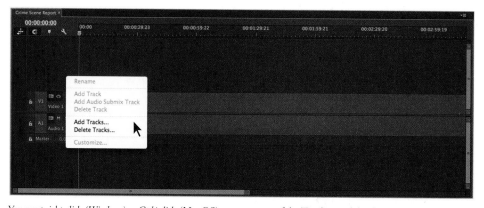

You must right-click (Windows) or Ctrl+click (Mac OS) an empty area of the Timeline track header to open the context menu.

2   If necessary, in the Video Tracks section of the Add Tracks dialog box, set the Video Tracks to add to 1; then, in the Audio Tracks section, set the number of audio tracks to add to 1.

The third section allows you to add a video sub mix track to the Timeline. By default, it should be set it to 0. You can specify where the new video and audio tracks are placed in relation to the current tracks on the Timeline. Confirm that the new video track is placed after Video 1 and the new audio track is placed after Audio 1. Confirm also that the new audio track is a Standard track.

3 Click OK to close the dialog box.

The Add Track dialog box allows you to add Video, Audio, and Audio Sub mix tracks to your Timeline.

To delete tracks, right-click (Windows) or Ctrl+click (Mac OS) a current track and choose Delete Track from the menu that appears. You can also open the Delete Tracks dialog box by choosing Sequence > Delete Tracks. In the dialog box that appears, choose whether to delete Audio and Video tracks by name or remove all empty audio and video tracks. Remember that the sequence needs at least one of each track type at all times; you cannot remove a track if it is the last of its kind left on the Timeline.

4 Double-click the empty space to the right of the Video 2 track's Toggle Track Output (◉) button. This expands the track's height to match that of Video 1. Repeat this for Audio 2 to expand this track as well.

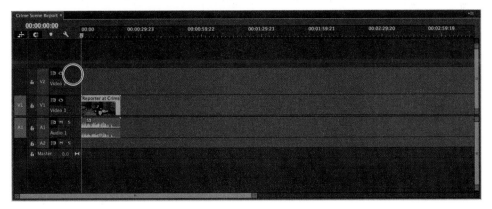

Expanding the height of tracks in the Timeline makes it easier to see your clips.

5   Expand the Audio 2 track by clicking the empty space to the right of its Solo Track (**🖪**) button.

6   Choose File > Save or press Ctrl+S (Windows) or Command+S (Mac OS) to save these changes to your project. Do not close this file; you will need it in the next part of the lesson.

Renaming tracks

By default, Premiere Pro names tracks in a sequential manner: Video 1, Video 2, Audio 1, Audio 2, etc. You can change the names to more easily identify which tracks hold specific types of content.

1   With the **pr0401-working.prproj** project still open and the Timeline panel active, right-click (Windows) or Ctrl+click (Mac OS) the track header for the Video 1 track and choose Rename from the menu that appears. Change the default name to **A-Roll** and press the Enter (Windows) or Return (Mac OS) key on your keyboard to exit the text editing mode.

2   Right-click the Video 2 track that you created in the previous exercise and again choose Rename from the menu that appears. Change the default name to **B-Roll** and press the Enter (Windows) or Return (Mac OS) key on your keyboard to exit the text editing mode.

3   Repeat this process for both audio tracks, renaming Audio 1 to **A-Roll** and Audio 2 to **B-Roll**.

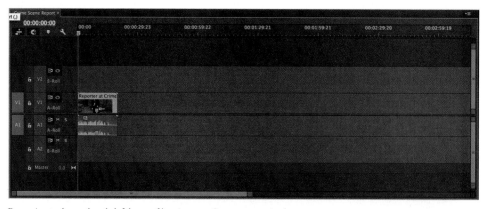

Renaming tracks can be a helpful way of keeping your Sequence organized.

4   Choose File > Save or press Ctrl+S (Windows) or Command+S (Mac OS) to save these changes to your project. Do not close this file; you will need it in the next part of the lesson.

Adding clips to the Timeline

You can add clips directly to the Timeline from the Project panel, Media Browser, or Source Monitor. In this lesson, you will add the clips that you trimmed in a previous exercise by dragging them from the Source Monitor and dropping them into an appropriate place on the Timeline.

1   With the **pr0401-working.prproj** project still open, if necessary, double-click the **Bystander Interview 01-Subclip.mpeg** in your Project panel to make it active and open it in the Source Monitor. This action also makes the Source Monitor active.

   Make sure you double-click the icon to the left of the clip name and not the name itself. Double-clicking the icon loads the clip into the Source Monitor, while double-clicking the name makes the name field editable.

   Notice the two icons located just below the video frame; one is similar to a film strip and the other is similar to an audio waveform. These icons indicate that the currently selected clip contains both an audio and a video track, and they also have another use. These icons can also be used to add only the audio or video portion of a clip to the timeline.

2   In the Timeline panel, move the playhead to the 9-second and 10-frame (00:00:09:10) mark. This is the timecode position of the marker that was added to the Reporter at Crime Scene clip on the Timeline. This will serve as the target destination when you add the **Bystander Interview 01-Subclip** to the timeline.

You can also move the playhead to the location of a timeline or clip marker by dragging it. To make the playhead snap to the position of a marker, press and hold the shift key on your keyboard while dragging it.

3   Press and hold the Ctrl (Windows) or Cmd (Mac OS) key on your keyboard, and then click the middle of the video frame in the Source Monitor and drag it to the A-Roll track on the Timeline. Drag the clip until your cursor lines up to the current position of the playhead; then drop the video at this point.

You have just completed an insert edit. This type of edit splits the clip that is already on the timeline at the position where you drop the new clip. This action extends the duration of the entire timeline to accommodate the added clip.

Pressing and holding the Ctrl (Windows) or Cmd(Mac OS) key while dragging a clip into the timeline creates an Insert Edit.

4   In the Timeline panel, move the playhead to the beginning (00;00;00;00) and press the spacebar on your keyboard to preview the clips in the Program Monitor.

You can start previews in the Timeline using keyboard commands or in the Program Monitor using the Transport controls.

    You can stop the Timeline playback at any time by pressing the spacebar again or by clicking the time ruler at the top of the Timeline panel. The time ruler is the area where the Timeline's time code appears.

5   Choose File > Save or press Ctrl+S (Windows) or Command+S (Mac OS) to save these changes to your project. Do not close this file; you will need it in the next part of the lesson.

When you previewed the file, you might have noticed that the edit point, where the shot of the reporter cuts to the bystander being interviewed, is rough. You will correct this in the next part of the lesson when you trim these clips in the Timeline panel.

Trimming clips on the Timeline

In this lesson, you began the editing process in the Source Monitor. There you trimmed your clips to eliminate excess and unnecessary footage. Once you add your clips to the Timeline, the true editing begins. The type of editing you do in the Timeline helps you judge how each clip relates to the other clips in your sequence, thus allowing you to refine the rough edits you make when trimming clips in the Source Monitor.

In this part of the lesson, you will trim the beginning and end of the **Bystander Interview 01–Subclip.mpeg** and the **Reporter at Crime Scene** clip to refine the project.

1   With the **pr0401-working.prproj** project still open and the Timeline panel active, move the playhead to the 18-second and 20-frame (00:00:18:20) mark on the Timeline. This is a good point in the clip at which to end it because it is a momentary pause in the character's rant; and since he is moving around, this pause point fits with the Cut on Action principle of continuity editing.

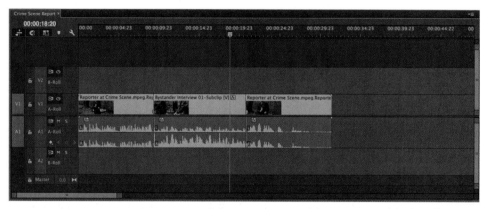

*Click the current time field in the upper-right side of the Timeline panel and type **1420** to jump to the 14-second and 20-frame mark on the Timeline.*

When working on your own projects, we strongly recommend that you play through the Timeline many times to determine the best edit point for your footage.

2   Press the + sign on your keyboard three times to cause the Timeline panel to Zoom
    In on the current position of the playhead. Notice the small graph on the audio
    track. This is called a waveform, and it displays the volume of a track over time. The
    playhead is currently positioned at a level point on the waveform, which represents a
    point of silence, when the speaker is quiet. This point is usually the best place to cut a
    clip, because it gives the illusion the speaker is taking a pause and has the most natural
    affect.

*You might want to adjust the number of times you zoom in on the timeline depending on your
monitor resolution. Additionally, you can adjust the height of a track by dragging the dividing
line in the track header that separates the A1 and A2 tracks.*

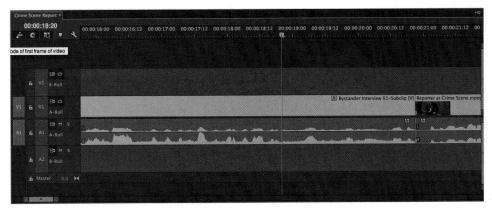

When trimming a clip, you must be careful to not cut too closely to where a person is starting or stopping while speaking.

3   Click the − sign on the keyboard until you can see all three video clips visible in the
    Timeline panel, and then confirm that the Selection tool is the active tool in the Tools
    panel. Position your cursor at the end of the **Bystander Interview 01–Subclip.mpeg**
    clip. Notice that the Selection tool changes to a Trim tool (⇥).

You can press the V key on your keyboard to activate the Selection tool.

4   Click the end of the clip with the Trim tool and drag it toward the playhead. The cursor automatically snaps to the playhead when it gets close. This trims the Out Point of the clip to match the current position of the playhead, but also leaves an empty space, called a gap, between the two clips.

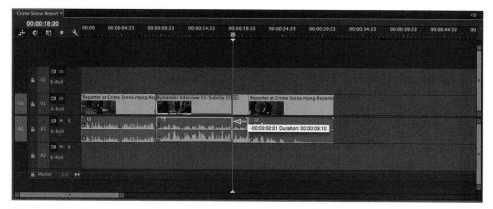

When trimming a clip, you must pay attention to the appearance of the cursor. This is how Premiere Pro tells you which tool variation you have active.

5   Right-click the gap between the clips and choose Ripple Delete from the menu that appears. This clears the gap and shifts all of the clips that are to the right to compensate for the gap's deletion.

6   Now you want to trim the beginning of the same clip. Move the playhead to the 10-second and 5-frame (00:00:10:05) mark on the Timeline. There is a little bit of hesitation in the beginning of the bystander's rant, and it will make a better edit if we remove it.

You can move your playhead on the Timeline manually by dragging it, but to move it precisely one frame at a time, press the left and right arrow keys on your keyboard.

You could use the Selection tool to trim the beginning of the clip, but as you learned previously, this would leave a gap between the two clips that you would then have to remove. In the next step, you will use a tool that automatically removes gaps as it trims your clips.

7   Click the Ripple Edit tool on the Tools panel to activate it. If the Tools panel is not visible, select Window > Tools.

Move the tool to the beginning of the **Bystander Interview 01.mpeg** clip and click and drag it to the playhead to perform a ripple edit to the clip. Make sure the Ripple Edit tool is facing the Playhead Position line before you begin to click and drag.

The keyboard shortcut to activate the Ripple Edit tool is B.

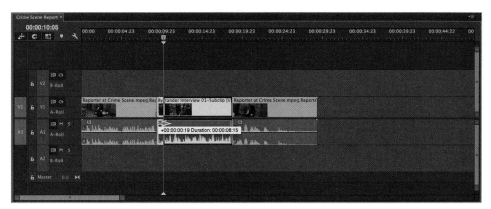

The tool appears to do nothing at all; but in fact, the entire clip moves automatically to the left to remove the gap created by trimming the clip.

8   Press the Home key on your keyboard or manually move the playhead to the beginning of the Timeline, and then press the spacebar to preview the edits in the Program Monitor.

9   Move the playhead to the 1–second and 4–frame (00:00:01:04) mark on the Timeline.

Click and drag from the beginning of the clip toward the playhead to perform the Ripple Edit. If you find this difficult, you can zoom in on the Timeline to make it easier to position the tool.

Again move the playhead to the beginning (00;00;00;00) of the Timeline and preview the edits in the Program Monitor by pressing the spacebar on your keyboard.

The edits seem more refined.

11 Click on the Selection tool in the tools panel to make it active and deactivate the Ripple Edit tool.

12 Choose File > Save or press Ctrl+S (Windows) or Command+S (Mac OS) to save these changes to your project. Do not close this file; you will need it in the next part of the lesson.

Using the Razor tool

You can use the Razor tool to shorten the duration of a clip or remove footage from the middle of a clip on the Timeline.

1 With the **pr0401-working.prproj** project still open, move the playhead to the 21-second and 20-frame (00:00:21:20) mark on the Timeline.

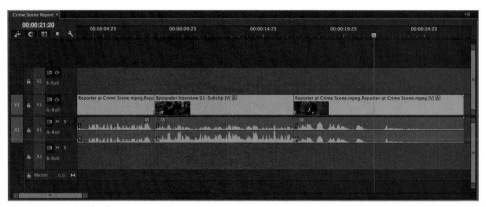

When viewing clips on the Timeline, we recommend you zoom in and out frequently to have a better sense of how your clips relate to each other.

You can zoom out on the Timeline to see the beginning and end of the Timeline simultaneously by pressing the − key, while pressing the + key zooms in on the Timeline.

2 Click the Razor tool in the Tools pane to activate it. You can use the Razor tool to cut or split clips to isolate the parts you want to keep.

Move the Razor tool to the playhead and click the **Reporter at Crime Scene.mpeg** clip to cut it.

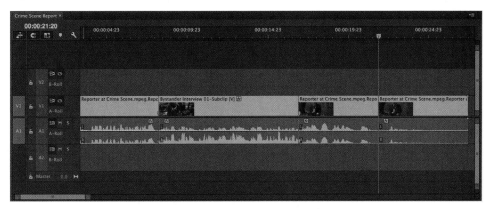

The Razor tool cuts through the audio and video of a clip on the Timeline.

You can also cut a clip on the Timeline using both a menu command and a keyboard shortcut. Choose Sequence > Add Edit or press Ctrl+K (Windows) or Command+K (Mac OS) to cut the clip on the active track at the current position of the playhead.

3   Click the Selection tool in the Tools panel to activate it, and then click the second Reporter at Crime Scene clip, the one that was just created at the position of the Playhead.

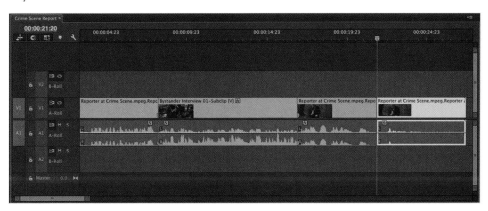

The Razor tool is used to split a clip and will automatically snap to the position of the playhead.

4   Press the Backspace (Windows) or Delete (Mac OS) key on your keyboard to delete the selected clip.

5 Press the Home key on your keyboard or manually move the playhead to the beginning of the Timeline, and then press the spacebar to preview the edits in the Program Monitor.

Choose File > Save or press Ctrl+S (Windows) or Command+S (Mac OS) to save these changes to your project. Do not close this file; you will need it in the next part of the lesson.

Making an Insert edit

An Insert edit allows you to add a clip currently previewed in the Source Monitor to the Timeline, while simultaneously moving the clips already on the timeline to accommodate the new one. You completed a manual Insert edit earlier in the lesson by dragging footage onto the timeline; now you will do it again, this time using a button or keyboard shortcut. You can use an Insert edit to add a new clip to the Timeline at the beginning, end, or middle of clips currently on the Timeline. When you perform an Insert edit in the middle of an existing clip, the command splits that clip and moves all adjacent clips to the right.

1 With the **pr0401-working.prproj** project still open, double-click the **Crime Scene Tape.mpeg** clip in the B Roll bin in the Project panel to preview it in the Source Monitor.

This clip is a just over nine seconds long; you will trim it down to use only the five seconds that include a left to right camera pan.

2 In the Source Monitor, move the playhead to the 6-second mark (00;00;06;00) and click the Set In Point button or press the I key on your keyboard to mark the clip's new In Point at 6 seconds.

3 Still in the Source Monitor, move the playhead to the 11-second mark (00;00;11;00) and click the Set Out Point button or press the O key on your keyboard to mark the clip's new Out Point.

The color change in the Source panel lets you know that you have created In and Out points in your video clip.

4 Once you have set the In and Out points for your Source clip, you must prepare the Timeline to receive it

Click the Timeline panel to activate it, and then, if necessary, move the playhead to the beginning (00;00;00;00) of the Timeline.

Notice the V1 and A1 labels to the left of the A Roll audio and video tracks. These are called Source Track Indicators and correspond to the video and audio tracks of the clip that is active in the Source Monitor.

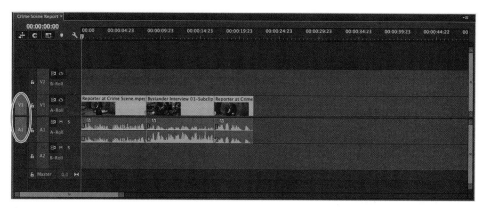

The Source Track Indicators appear when a clip is active in the Source Monitor.

Specifying the destination of clips with track targeting

*A. Source Track Indicators. **B.** Track Headers. **C.** Clips.*

In a Premiere Pro Sequence, the number of audio and video tracks you start with is determined by the Sequence Preset you choose in the New Sequence dialog box, but you can have any number of separate audio and video tracks in a single sequence, provided that your computer system has enough available RAM to support them. To add tracks to the Timeline using keyboard shortcuts, the controls in the Source Monitor, or the copy and paste commands, you must specify a destination track. This is process is known as track targeting.

When you add clips to the Timeline panel by dragging them from the Source Monitor, the Project panel, or the Media browser, you automatically target a track by dropping the clip onto that track. However, when you use the Source monitor controls, keyboard shortcuts, or copy and paste, you must specify a target track in advance. The placement of the Video and Audio target track selector in the Track Header area (where the track names are) indicates that a specific track is targeted and ready to receive clips. Depending on the properties of the clip in the Source monitor, you can have more than one audio and video track targeted at a time, or specify only a single audio or video track for targeting. For precise placement of content from the Source Monitor, you can map the tracks of the clip currently active in the Monitor to specific tracks on the Timeline by dragging the Source Track Indicators present to the left of the Track Headers.

5   The video from the clip in the source monitor will be placed in the B-Roll track. Click the V1 Target Track selector and drag it to the V2 track, the one you earlier renamed B-Roll.

Click the A1 Target Track selector to disable it. This will allow you to insert only the video from the clip in the Source monitor.

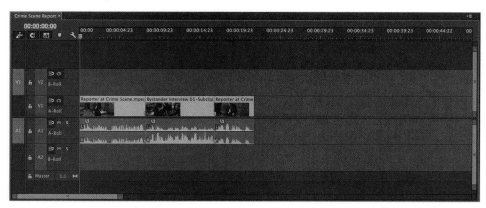

You must target video and audio tracks on the Timeline when using the Insert and Overwrite commands.

6   With the Timeline panel still active, click the Insert button (█) on the Source Monitor or use the , (comma) shortcut key to perform an Insert edit. Notice that the clip is added to the B-Roll track at the current position of the playhead and all the footage on the Timeline shifts to the right to accommodate it.

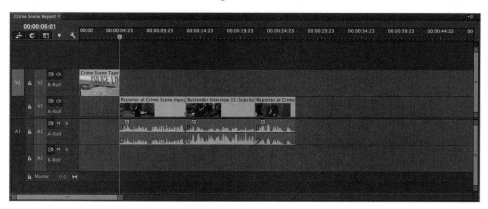

By using an Insert edit, you can increase the overall duration of the Timeline.

7   Press the Home key on your keyboard or manually move the playhead to the beginning of the Timeline, and then press the spacebar to preview the edits in the Program Monitor.

8   Choose File > Save or press Ctrl+S (Windows) or Command+S (Mac OS) to save these changes to your project, and then close the file.

Congratulations, you have completed this lesson.

Self study

Use the footage included in this project file to add the second Bystander interview to the Timeline. You can place it before or after the interview currently on the Timeline to practice trimming clips and making the Insert edit.

Review

Questions

1 What is B Roll and how is it used?

2 What is the difference between a cut-in and a cut-away?

3 Why is it important or necessary to trim clips in the Timeline and not just in the Source Monitor?

Answers

1 B Roll footage is the secondary footage shot and used in video and film productions. During the editing process, B Roll is used to add or enhance the meaning of the main footage or to cover the removal of unwanted or error-ridden material.

2 A cut-in is a cut that shifts from the main subject (A Roll) to an event occurring inside the same scene; a cut-away is a cut away from the main action to an event that occurs simultaneously.

3 The trimming done to clips in the Source Monitor usually results in rough edits. To refine an edit, you should see your clips on the Timeline to judge how each clip relates to the other clips in your sequence. It is easier to edit clips in the Timeline due to the specialized editing tools, such as the Ripple Edit tool, that can be used there.

What you'll learn in this lesson:

- To add video transitions between clips on the Timeline

- To create a slideshow from still images

- To adjust preferences to set the default transition type and duration

Adding Transitions to Video

The cuts-only editing approach from the previous lesson is the standard for dramatic television and film editing; however, you can use the transitions approach when you want to create a seamless blend from one video clip to another.

Starting up

In this lesson, you will work with the project files from the pr05lessons folder. Make sure that you have loaded the prlessons folder onto your hard drive from the supplied DVD. The Starting up section at the beginning of this book provides detailed information about loading lesson files, resetting your workspace, locating missing media, and opening the files in CC. If you have not already done so, please review these instructions before starting this lesson.

When opening the Premiere Pro project files used in this lesson you may experience a missing media message. You must locate any missing media before trying to proceed through the lessons. Please refer to the "Locating missing media" in the Starting up section of this book.

See Lesson 5 in action!

Use the accompanying video to gain a better understanding of how to use some of the features shown in this lesson. The video tutorial for this lesson can be found on the included DVD.

Understanding video transitions

A transition is a change or passage from one state or position to another. There are transitions for audio and video clips, but video transitions offer the greatest variety. In modern non-linear video editing applications, such as Adobe Premiere Pro, you can add transitions between video and audio clips to ease the change from one image to another or from one situation to another. Premiere Pro offers many different types of transitions, including dissolves, wipes, and fades. Using a transition instead of a straight cut, as shown in the previous lesson, is often a stylistic choice to make the viewer more aware of the video, and draw them out of the story.

In high-end film and television work, transitions are often avoided and cuts are are used in their place to move from one shot to another. However, even in this type of work, some transitions can be found. The three most commonly used transitions in this field are dissolves, wipes, and fades.

Dissolves

The most popular type of dissolve is the Cross Dissolve, also called a Cross Fade. The effect this type of dissolve produces is to fade out one video image as the next one fades in and it is often used to aesthetically convey a sense that a long time or a great distance is passing.

Wipes

 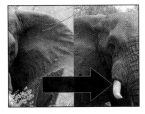 

Premiere Pro includes many different types of wipes, such as iris wipes, gradient wipes, and push wipes. Wipes are often used to convey a sense of movement from one location to another, such as when a scene changes from an exterior to an interior shot. The "invisible wipe," created while shooting, usually occurs when the camera follows the movement of an actor through a scene: when the camera passes in front of a wall, tree, or another figure, the editor can wipe to any other matching shot of the scene.

Fades to black or white

Fades to color are one of the most familiar transitions seen by viewers. A fade is created when the opacity of the video image is reduced to reveal a solid color (usually black or white) behind it. Fades are often used as a stylistic tool or to signify a major change; for example, a fade to black is often used to signify the end of a scene or film and transition into the credits.

Adding transitions to video clips

You can add a transition to any pair of video clips on the same track, but we strongly recommend you add them to trimmed clips because transitions extend beyond the end of the first clip and begin before the beginning of the second clip. If the beginning and end of the respective clips are not trimmed, the transition automatically creates a freeze frame.

In this part of the lesson, you will work with an existing project: you will prepare a pair of files to receive a transition, add them to the Timeline, and then add a Cross Dissolve transition between them.

All the media for this exercise can be found in the Media Library. It is located in the Video sub-folder of the Travelogue–Boston folder.

1 With Premiere Pro open, chose File > Open Project. Navigate to the pr05lessons folder that you copied to your hard drive and locate the **pr0501.prproj** file. Double-click the file to open it.

If you are at the Premiere Pro welcome screen, you can simply choose the Open Project link.This project contains one sequence named Working with Transitions and two pieces of media: **Bunker Hill Memorial Bridge.MTS** and **Cars on Bridge.MTS**.

The default Editing workspace and the modified one you created in an earlier exercise are both geared toward adding clips to the timeline and editing them there. Because you will be working primarily with adding and editing clip transitions in this lesson, a change is in order.

2 Choose Window > Workspace > Effects to change your current workspace to the preset Effects workspace built into the application.

If you have previously used this workspace, it may appear different than its default configuration; you can correct this by resetting the workspace.

To reset this workspace, choose Window > Workspace > Reset Current Workspace and choose Yes when prompted to proceed.

The default Effects workspace.

3   Choose File > Save As. In the Save Project dialog box, confirm that you are still in the pr05lessons folder, rename your file to **pr0501-working**, and then click the Save button.

Preparing a clip to receive transitions

As mentioned previously, for the best effect when using transitions, clips should have trimmed beginning or end points. This is why we recommend that you include handles when capturing footage. Handles are extra footage at the beginning and end of the clip or scene with which you want to work. Many videographers begin recording before the action they want to capture begins, and continue the recording until after it is over just to make sure they will have handles.

In this section of the lesson, you will trim the two clips in the Source Monitor to prepare them for the dissolve you will add later.

1   With the **pr0501-working.prproj** project still open, double-click the **Bunker Hill Memorial Bridge.MTS** clip in the Project panel to open it in the Source Monitor.

This clip is currently 9 seconds long. There is footage that you don't need at the beginning of the clip, which is used to establish the shot. There is also footage towards the end of the clip, where the camera work gets a little shaky. Trimming this clip will accomplish two goals: it will make the shot tighter and more succinct, and it will provide us with the trimmed clips that make transitions run more smoothly.

2 Move the Source Monitor playhead to the 2-second (00;00;02;00) mark on the time ruler; click the Mark In button at the bottom left of the Source Monitor to set the In Point of the clip to the current position of the playhead. Since this is a static shot of the bridge, removing the first couple of seconds will eliminate some redundant footage.

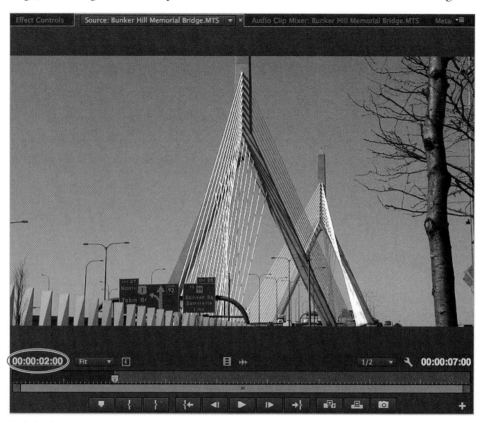

The playhead position can be set by dragging it, typing in the playhead position field, or using keyboard shortcuts.

To move the playhead to an exact location on the time ruler, click the Playhead Position field to make it active, type the time code location where you want to position the playhead, and then press the Enter (Windows) or Return (Mac OS) key on your keyboard. If you do not want to type the time code location, you can type the numerals of the location without the semicolons; for example, **300** is equal to the 3-second (00;00;03;00) mark on the Timeline, while **10** is equivalent to the 10th frame (00;00;00;10) mark.

3   The camera begins to get a little shaky slightly after the 7-second (00:00:07:00) mark on the timeline, so this will be a good point to end the clip.

Click the Playhead Position field in the Source Monitor to make it active, replace the current time (00:00:02:00) with the number **700**, and then press the Enter (Windows) or Return (Mac OS) key on your keyboard to jump the playhead to the 7-second (00:00:07:00) mark on the clip's time ruler.

It isn't necessary to include the colons when typing a time value into the Playhead Position field. The application will automatically assume the proper breaks for frames, seconds, minutes, and hours.

4   Click the Mark Out button (it is located right next to the Mark In button in the Source Monitor). This sets the Out point of the clip to the current position of the playhead.

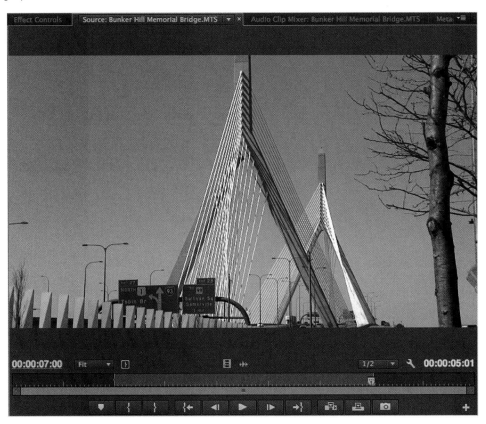

In and Out points can also be set using the "I" and "O" keys respectively.

5 With the Timeline Playhead located at the origin position (00:00:00:00), click the Insert button located on the lower-right area of the Source Monitor panel. This adds the trimmed clip to the Timeline in the V1 and A1 tracks.

The Timeline playhead automatically moves to the end of the clip when you perform an insert or overwrite edit.

Since this is the first clip you add to the Timeline, it doesn't matter whether you use an insert or overwrite edit here. Both would have the exact same result.

6 In the Project panel, double-click the video icon to the left of the **Cars on Bridge.MTS** clip to load it into the Source Monitor.

7 This clip is a shot of the same bridge, but offers more focus on the automobiles that are on the roadway. Like the previous clip, it has some redundant footage at the beginning and is a bit shaky towards the end.

Click in the Playhead Position field to make it active, and type **200** to replace the current value. Press the Enter (Windows) or Return (Mac OS) key on your keyboard; this moves the playhead to the 2-second (00:00:02:00) mark on the clip's time ruler.

8 Click the Mark In button in the Source Monitor, and then move the playhead to the 11-second (00:00:11:00) mark on the time ruler. Click the Mark Out button to set new In and Out Points for this clip.

Trimming a clip in the Source Monitor is often necessary when working with clips that have been shot with extra footage at the head or tail.

9   With the Timeline Playhead still located at the end of the
Bunker Hill Memorial Bridge.MTS clip you added earlier, click the Insert button
in the Source Monitor to insert the trimmed clip at the current position of the
Playhead.

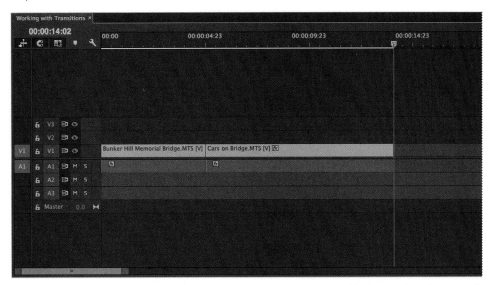

*If there are no In and Out Points currently set on the Timeline, Insert and Overwrite edits add your source clip at the position of
the playhead.*

10   Choose File > Save or press Ctrl+S (Windows) or Cmd+S (Mac OS) to save these
changes to your project. Do not close this file, you will need it in the next part of the
lesson.

Adding a transition between clips

You can easily add a transition between clips on a Timeline after trimming them, but you
must remember that the clips must be adjacent to each other and on the same video track.

1   With the **pr0501-working.prproj** project still open, click the Timeline panel to
make it active.

2   You might find it necessary to adjust the magnification of the Timeline panel to see
your clips and how they relate to each other more clearly. The controls to zoom in or
out on the Timeline panel are integrated into the panel's horizontal slider. Simply click
and drag on either button located at the ends of the slider.

3   Click and drag on either end of the slider to set the Timeline's magnification to a level that is comfortable to you. For this lesson, you will need to be able to see the ends of both clips and the edit line between them.

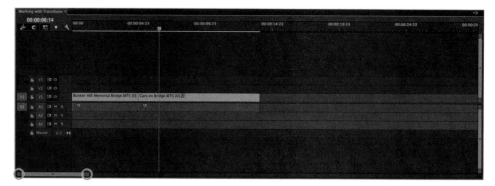

The horizontal slider in the Timeline panel can be used to change the magnification of the panel.

The keyboard shortcuts to zoom in and out on the Timeline panel are the plus (+) and minus (-) keys located at the top of a standard keyboard.

4   You can adjust the default track display to suit your preferences. Position your cursor in the Track header between the V1 and V2 tracks. When you hover over the dividing line between them, the cursor becomes a double-headed vertical arrow (‡). Click and draw with this arrow to enlarge the height of the V1 Track until it is approximately twice its original size.

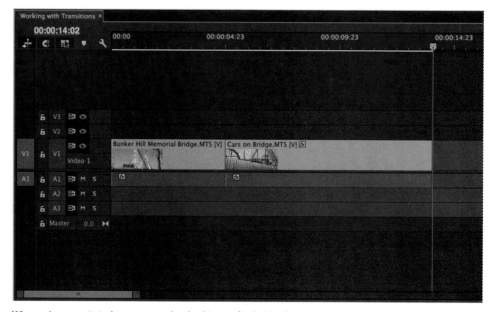

When tracks are maximized, you can see a thumbnail image of each video clip.

5   If necessary, click the tab for the Effects panel to make it active and visible.

Since you are still in the default Effects workspace, this should be grouped with the Project panel in the upper-left of the application's interface.

Since you are still in the default Effects workspace, this should be grouped with the Project panel in the upper-left of the application's interface.

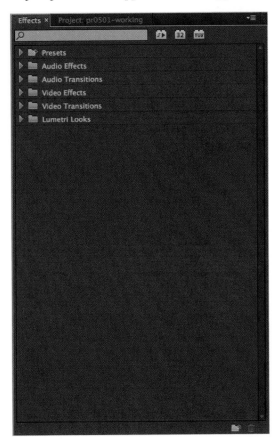

If you have closed the Effects panel, you can open it by choosing Window > Effects or using the keyboard shortcut Shift+7 (Windows and Mac OS).

6   In the search field at the top of the Effects panel, type the word **cross**.

Typing a word in the search field reveals every effect and transition with that word in its title; in this case, the Cross Dissolve and Iris Cross transitions are revealed.

The search field is helpful when you know the name or part of the name of the effect you want to use.

The list of effects may vary slightly on the Windows and Mac OS platforms.

7 Click the Cross Dissolve transition and drag it to the edit line between the two clips on the Timeline. When your cursor is hovering on the edit line between two video clips, the area becomes highlighted to indicate you can release the transition at that location.

You must carefully place the transition on the Timeline to ensure you position it at the edit line between the clips.

You can place a transition at the end of the first clip, at the beginning of the second clip, or in between the clips on the edit line. Each of these three areas becomes highlighted when you try to position the transition and each produces a different result in the final appearance of the project.

Notice the small red bar that appears at the top of the Timeline above the transition. It indicates that the transition must be rendered in order to preview at full quality in real time.

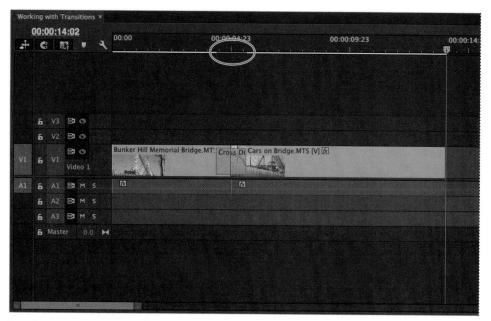

Depending on your system configuration, you will find that most of the effects and transitions you add to the Timeline must be rendered to preview at full quality.

8   Press the Enter (Windows) or Return (Mac OS) key on your keyboard to render all areas of the Timeline that need rendering. When the rendering is done, the application automatically shows a preview of the Timeline.

Timeline effects can also be rendered by choosing Sequence > Render Effects in Work Area or Render Entire Work Area.

9   Choose File > Save or press Ctrl+S (Windows) or Command+S (Mac OS) to save these changes to your project. Do not close this file; you will need it in the next part of the lesson.

In the next section of the lesson, you will adjust the transition's settings to slow it down and create a more gradual blend between the two video clips.

Editing transition settings

When a transition is applied to clips, it is applied with the transition's default settings; however, you can adjust the properties of all transitions to achieve the effect you want. All transitions have certain unique properties, but all share position and duration attributes.

1   Continuing with the **pr0501-working.prproj** project from the previous lesson, drag the playhead to the cross dissolve transition, on the edit line between the two clips.

Press and hold the Shift key while dragging the playhead to force it to snap to the edges of clips and transitions.

Depending on your monitor resolution, you might need to zoom in on the Timeline to enlarge the clips and make the transition easier to see. Remember that when you zoom in on the timeline, the application focuses the zoom on the playhead location.

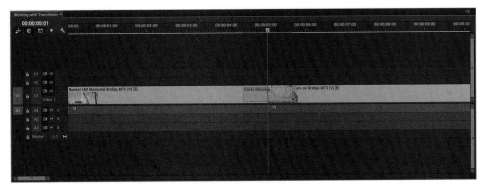

The current zoom state of the Timeline does not use a numerical value; you must adjust it until you are comfortable with how you see the clips.

2 Click the Cross Dissolve transition icon to highlight it. You will find it located between the two video clips on the Timeline.

Click the Effect Controls panel tab to bring it forward, allowing you to access the properties of the highlighted item. You will find the Effect Controls panel tab located in the same panel group as the Source Monitor.

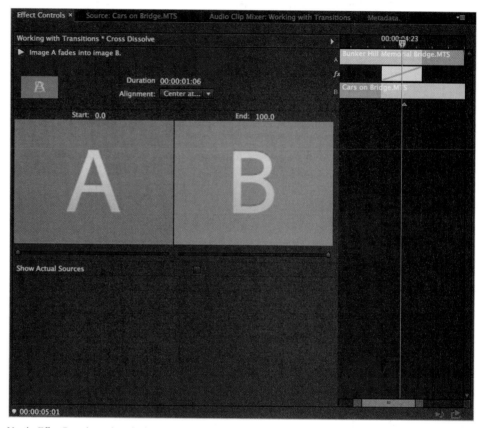

Use the Effect Controls panel to edit the properties of clips and transitions on the Timeline.

3   The Cross Dissolve has four sets of properties: Duration, Alignment, and Start and End blending amount.

Select the Show Actual Sources check box at the bottom of the properties to change the generic A and B icons in the Start and End fields and show the actual video from the clips you are using.

All transitions have Duration and Alignment properties; however, each can have other unique properties.

The Effect Controls panel is divided in two sections: the left side of the panel shows the properties of the transition with which you are working; the right shows a mini-Timeline view to let you see the effect of any changes. The display of the Timeline view shows the first clip on the track above and the second clip on the track below, in an older A/B track display. Both tracks are separated by a third transition track holding the Cross Dissolve. The display is a legacy of older editing systems and is now rarely seen in Premiere Pro or any other modern non–linear editing application.

4 In the Effect Controls panel, click the Duration value, change the current duration to **200**, and then press the Enter (Windows) or Return (Mac OS) key on your keyboard to set the transition's new duration to 2 seconds (00;00;02;00).

Any change you make to the properties of a transition is immediately visible in the Timeline view of the Effect Controls panel.

The other two properties available to you with a Cross Dissolve are Alignment and the Start and Ending blend. The Alignment property lets you change the transition to the end of the first clip, the beginning of the second clip, or centered on the edit line. Each produces different effects in how the two video images blend together. By default, this transition begins with the first clip fully visible and ends with the second clip fully visible to create the impression that one image fades into the next. However, you can change this effect by adjusting the Start and End blending amounts so the starting or ending images of transition are a blend of the two clips.

If you just want to edit the duration of a transition without viewing its other properties, double-click the transition in the Timeline. This will open a Set Transition Duration dialog box for your editing convenience.

5   Notice the red line indicating the transition must again be rendered to preview correctly.

Press the Enter (Windows) or Return (Mac OS) key on your keyboard to render all areas of the Timeline that need rendering.

When the rendering is done, the application automatically shows a preview of the Timeline.

Every time you change the properties of a transition or effect, re-render the video sequence to preview it properly.

6   Choose File > Save or press Ctrl+S (Windows) or Command+S (Mac OS) to save these changes, and then close this file by choosing File > Close Project.

Creating an image slideshow

You can create slideshows that combine a series of different images or videos together for artistic or educational purposes and even set them to music. In Premiere Pro, you can rapidly add a sequence of images to the Timeline and automatically insert a transition between each. To create the slideshow, you will set the default video transition and then use a command named Automate to Sequence to add the images to the Timeline.

In this section of the lesson, you will work with the **pr0502.prproj** project file. A series of still images you can use in the slideshow have already been imported and an NTSC format sequence has been created. The image files for completing this exercise can be found in the Safari folder located inside the Media Library folder.

1   Choose File > Open Project, navigate to the pr05lessons folder that you copied to your hard drive, and then open the **pr0502.prproj** project file.

You should now be in the Editing workspace. If necessary, reset this workspace to its default configuration by choosing Window > Workspace > Reset Current Workspace.

When you want to create a slideshow like this, we recommend that you organize the images or videos you want to use in the Project panel first, and then add them to the Timeline in a batch. This speeds up the slideshow creation process and also allows you to transition between each slide automatically.

2   In the Project panel, double-click the folder icon to the left of the Safari Images bin to open the bin in its own floating panel. You might need to resize the new panel so you can see all the images in the bin.

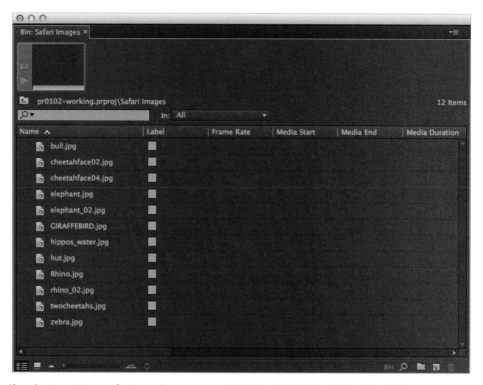

If you do not want to open a floating panel, you can press and hold the Alt (Window) or Option (Mac OS) key on your keyboard while double-clicking the bin icon to replace the Project panel.

3   At this point, the floating panel uses the same list view display that the Project panel did. This view, while helpful in some situations, does not let you organize media outside of a rigid hierarchical format and isn't appropriate if you want to visually sort your clips.

Click the Icon View button located at the bottom left corner of the bin's floating panel. Again, you might need to resize the panel to accommodate all of the clip thumbnails.

In the icon view, you can resize the panel to view more thumbnails.

The Icon View is used to arrange your clips based on their content so you can quickly assemble a rough edit that you can fine tune later in the Timeline. This type of display is also known as a storyboard view.

When working with the Project panel in the Icon View display mode, you change the order of clips by clicking on them and dragging the clip to a new location.

4 Locate the clip named **hut.jpg** and drag it to the first position in the icon display. A gray dividing line appears as you drag the clip in the panel; this line shows where you will position the clip.

In Icon View, you can manually position each piece of media, thus allowing you to quickly arrange a sequence of images or video clips.

5   Adjust the position of the clips so they are in the following order: **hut.jpg, cheetahface02.jpg, elephant_02.jpg, hippos_water.jpg, bull.jpg, elephant.jpg, twocheetahs.jpg, GIRAFFEBIRD.jpg, rhino_02.jpg, zebra.jpg, Rhino.jpg, cheetahface04.jpg**.

The order of your images should match this figure.

6   Close the Bin:Safari Images window. This will not undo the changes you have just made, it merely hides the bin.

7   Choose File > Save As. In the Save Project dialog box, confirm that you are still in the pr05lessons folder, rename your file to **pr0502-working**, and then click the Save button. Do not close this file; you will need it in the next part of the lesson.

Now that the images have been arranged, you will set the default transition you want, and then add all the images and transitions to the Timeline in the next steps.

Setting the default video transition

In Premiere Pro, the Cross Dissolve is assigned as the default video transition. A complete list of all the transitions available in the application can be found in the Adobe Premiere Pro help files, available by choosing Help > Adobe Premiere Pro Help or by pressing the F1 key on your keyboard. Please note that some video transitions are only available on the Windows platform.

1   With the **pr0502-working.prproj** project still open, click the Effects panel to make it active. You will find this panel on the lower-left side of the application interface, in the same group as the Project panel.

     The Effects panel is divided into several different sub-groups; each sub-group is then divided again to arrange the various effects and transitions based on similarity.

2   Click the Reveal triangle to the left of the Video Transitions label to show the application's transition groups.

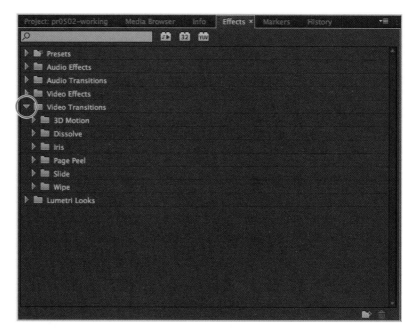

If you have text in the search field, delete it before manually searching through the Effects and Transitions.

The list of effects may vary slightly on the Windows and Mac OS platforms.

3   Click the Reveal triangle next to the Slide label to show the transitions in this group.

4   Right-click (Windows) or Ctrl+click (Mac OS) the Push transition and choose Set Selected as Default Transition from the menu that appears. That's all it takes to set a new transition as your default.

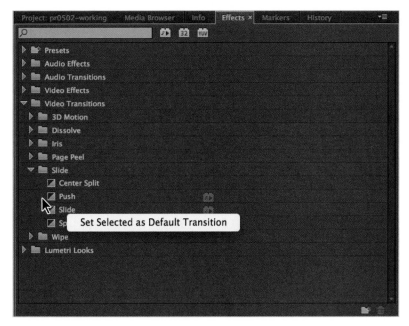

Set Selected as Default Transition is the only item on the menu that appears when you right-click (Windows) or Ctrl+click (Mac OS) a transition in the Effects panel.

5   Choose File > Save or press Ctrl+S (Windows) or Command+S (Mac OS) to save these changes to your project. Do not close this file; you will need it in the next part of the lesson.

Automatically adding clips to the Timeline

To review, you have prepared the clips by ordering them in the project panel for the Safari Images bin and assigned a new default transition; you can now add the images to the Timeline.

1   With the **pr0502-working.prproj** project still open, choose Window > Workspace > Reset Current Workspace. Click Yes on the dialog box that appears to complete the reset process. If necessary, move the playhead to the beginning (00;00;00;00) of the Timeline.

Double-click the Safari Images bin in the Project panel to again open it as a new floating panel. Please note that you might have to adjust the size of the panel to see all the images.

2   Click the first file in the bin hut.jpg, press and hold the Shift key on your keyboard, and then click the last file in the bin **cheetahface04.jpg** to select all images between them.

Pressing and holding Shift allows you to select a group of sequential files; pressing and holding the Control (Windows) or Command (Mac OS) key allows you to select multiple files that are non-sequential.

3   Choose Clip > Automate to Sequence to open the Automate to Sequence dialog box.

The dialog box controls the options used when you add the selected images to the Timeline.

Ordering: you can set this property to Sort Order or Selection Order. The Sort Order option uses the arrangement of clips in the bin to control how they are placed on the Timeline. Selection Order requires that you select each clip individually using the Control (Windows) or Command (Mac OS) key on your keyboard to control the order in which you add them to the Timeline.

Placement: you can set this property to Sequentially or At Unnumbered Markers. If you created unnumbered markers and added them to the Timeline, the latter choice will be active; this option is helpful for controlling the placement of the footage items. Without markers, the Sequential Placement option positions the different footage items next to each other on the Timeline, starting with the first one at the current position of the playhead.

Method: specifies whether to use an Overwrite or Insert edit to add the footage items to the Timeline. The option is irrelevant if there are no other clips present on the Timeline.

Clip Overlap: specifies the duration to overlap each clip you are adding to the Timeline. The value for Clip Overlap is applied at the beginning and end of each clip and shortens the clip's duration.

Still Clip Duration: allows you to specify how still images are treated when added to the Timeline. You can either use the specified In/Out Range of the clips, or override it by settting a specific number of frames to assign as the duration for each image.

There are also two sets of options that allow you to control whether the default audio and video transition are applied between each clip and whether you would like to ignore the audio or video sections of the selected clips.

4   Set the following values in the Automate To Sequence dialog box:

Ordering: Sort Order

Placement: Sequentially

Method: Overwrite Edit

Clip Overlap: **30** Frames

Still Clip Duration: Us In/Out Range

Confirm that the check boxes for applying the default audio and video transitions are enabled and that the check box to ignore video is disabled.

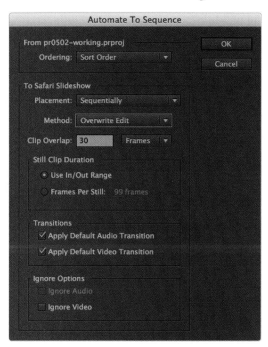

The Automate To Sequence command is the quickest method for creating image or video slideshows.

Click the OK button to add the selected images to the Timeline.

Close the Bin:Safari Images panel.

5 Notice the small red bar that appears at the top of the Timeline and above the entire sequence transitions. It indicates that all the content on the Timeline must be rendered in order to preview in real time and at full quality.

Click the Timeline panel to make it active, and then press the Enter (Windows) or Return (Mac OS) key on your keyboard to render all areas of the Timeline that need rendering.

When the rendering is done, the application automatically shows a preview of the Timeline.

You must always render images that you add to video sequences in Premiere Pro before you can preview them in real time and at full quality.

6 Now that you have added the images to the Timeline, notice that each image and transition is separate and individual from each other. You can now edit the transitions separately; you can even substitute one transition for another by simply dragging it from the Effects panel until it overlaps the current one on the Timeline.

You might need to zoom in on your Timeline to see the clips and transitions more clearly.

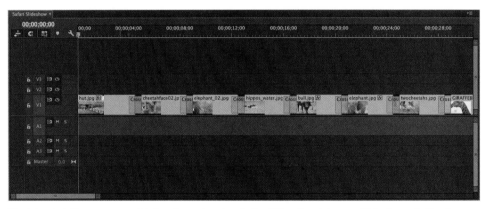

The Automate to Sequence command is the only way to automatically add transitions between multiple clips on the Timeline.

7 Choose Window > Workspace > Reset Current Workspace to return to the default Editing workspace with which you started the project.

8 Choose File > Save or press Ctrl+S (Windows) or Command+S (Mac OS) to save these changes to your project. You can now close this project.

Self study

Create an image slide show using your own photographs. You can assign a new default transition and vary the settings in the Automate to Sequence dialog box to achieve a unique look.

Review

Questions

1   What is the purpose of applying a transition between clips in the Timeline?

2   Where are transitions placed?

3   When using the Automate to Sequence command, what is the purpose of the Ordering property?

Answers

1   Transitions are added between video and audio clips to ease the change from one image to another or from one situation to another. They are often used as a stylistic choice that makes the viewer more aware of the video they are watching.

2   Transitions are placed between a pair of adjacent clips on the Timeline. Transitions can be positioned at the end of the first clip, at the beginning of the second clip, or centered on the edit line between the clips.

3   You can set the Ordering property to Sort Order or Selection Order. The sort order option uses the arrangement of clips in the bin to control how they are placed on the Timeline. Selection Order requires that you select each clip individually using the Control (Windows) or Command (Mac OS) key on your keyboard to control the order you add them to the Timeline.

Lesson 6

What you'll learn in this lesson:

- To create text using Premiere Pro
- To create a rolling title sequence for use as end credits
- To import and animating a Photoshop file

Working with Graphics

Text and titles are an integral part of many video projects. In this lesson, you will learn to use the native tools in Premiere Pro to create titles and to work with imported Photoshop files.

Starting up

In this lesson, you will work with the project files from the pr06lessons folder. Make sure that you have loaded the prlessons folder onto your hard drive from the supplied DVD. The Starting up section at the start of this book provides detailed information about loading lesson files, resetting your workspace, locating missing media, and opening the files in CC. If you have not already done so, please review these instructions before starting this lesson.

When opening the Premiere Pro project files used in this lesson you may experience a missing media message. You must locate any missing media before trying to proceed through the lessons. For more information refer to "Locating missing media" in the Starting up section of this book.

Use the accompanying video to gain a better understanding of how to use some of the features shown in this lesson. The video tutorial for this lesson can be found on the included DVD.

Creating titles in Premiere Pro

You can create three types of titles using the tools built into Premiere Pro: stills, rolls, and crawls. Still titles consist of static text and graphics, and as such, they are the simplest titles to create. Once you have created static titles using the title tools in Premiere Pro, you can animate them on the Timeline as you would any imported graphic.

Rolling titles consist of blocks of text that extend past the bottom of the video frame, and are commonly used for ending credits. Rolling titles animate automatically when you place them on the Timeline.

Crawling titles consist of long text blocks that extend past the right and left edges of the video frame. This type of title is commonly used in specialized cases, for example, news programs, or to simulate stock or news tickers.

Using the Titler

In Premiere Pro, the term Titler refers to the group of interrelated panels you can use to create text and titles. The panels you can use to create titles are: Title Actions, Title Designer, Title Properties, Title Styles, and Title Tools.

A. Title Actions. B. Title Tools. C. Title Designer. D. Title Properties. E. Title Styles.

Title Actions: this panel contains the commands to align and distribute the text and graphics you create in the Titler. The Align command becomes active when you simultaneously select two or more objects; the Distribute command becomes active when you select three or more objects.

Title Designer: this is the central panel of the Titler, and it is the panel where you can add and manipulate the text and graphics for your title. The Title Designer automatically displays the video frame at the current position of the playhead in the Timeline panel.

Title Properties: this panel displays the properties of the object currently selected in the Title Designer. Depending on what type of object you have selected, this panel will give you different sets of options. The Title Properties panel is used to review and edit item properties and is one of the main areas of focus when using the Titler.

Title Styles: this panel contains the library of text styles you can access in the Titler. Use this panel to apply any of the preset styles available for Premiere Pro. You can also save custom styles from the text you format in the Titler.

Title Tools: this panel contains tools you need to create the text and graphics for your titles. The panel contains a variety of text tools, as well as tools for creating both simple and complex shapes.

Understanding the safe zones

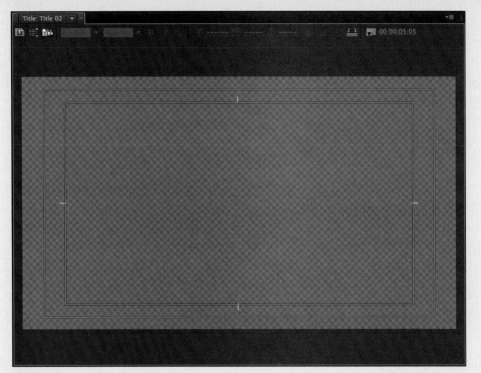

The safe zone margins are enabled by default; you can disable them from the context menu of the Title Designer.

There are two sets of margins that define the safe zones in the Title Designer panel: the inner gray rectangle designates the title-safe margin, while the outer gray rectangle indicates the action-safe margins of the video frame.

Safe zones are useful when you edit video or produce graphics that will be displayed on a television screen. Most television sets perform a function called over scanning on the video frame. As a result of this over scanning process, the outer edges of the picture could be placed outside the viewable area of the screen. Since the amount of over scanning is not consistent between different devices, the safe zones are a general guideline to help ensure that all the important information in a video frame is visible. We recommend you keep all text inside the title safe margin, since it represents the center 80% of the video frame. You can keep other important elements inside the action safe margin, which represents the center 90% of the available screen space.

Creating a lower third

The purpose of Lower Thirds is to add on-screen text that explains some aspect of the video. The most common use of lower thirds is to introduce individuals or settings in documentary-style projects. As the name suggests, lower thirds appear in the lower third of the video frame.

The media for this project can all be found in the Media Library. The video files (**Central Park–NYC–Fountain Scene.AVI** and **Central Park–NYC–Lake Scene.AVI**) used here are located in the Travelogue-New York folder while the audio file (**Classical Background Music.mp3**) is located in the Audio folder.

In this part of the lesson, you will create a lower third to introduce a setting changed in a documentary-style travelogue.

1 With Premiere Pro open, chose File > Open Project. Navigate to the pr06lessons folder that you copied to your hard drive, and locate the **pr0601.prproj** file. Double-click the file to open it.

This project contains a sequence with clips on the Timeline and a background audio track. You need a lower third to establish the setting for the clips. If necessary, move the playhead to the beginning (00;00;00;00) of the Timeline.

2 Choose Title > New Title > Default Still. Even though you are creating a still image title, it still has to be assigned a duration. All titles you create in the Titler are assigned the default still image duration; 150 frames. Keep in mind you can change this value in the General category of the Preferences dialog box at any time, though it will only affect titles created after the change is made.

In the New Title dialog box that appears, confirm that the settings of the new title conform to those of the project:

Width: 1280

Height: 720

Time base: 23.976 fps

Pixel Aspect Ratio: Square Pixels (1.0)

You can change the default still image duration in the General category of the Preferences dialog box.

3 Rename the default name of the title to **Lower Third–Central Park**. Click OK to create the title and open the Titler.

When you create a new title, its properties default to match the settings of your current sequence.

  Once you click OK, the title you have just created immediately appears as a new item in the Project panel.

4 If necessary, expand the Titler by dragging its lower-right corner to see all five panels simultaneously. If you prefer, you can also expand the Titler to full screen size using the buttons at the top of the panel.

5 Choose File > Save As. In the Save Project dialog box that appears, confirm that you are still in the pr06lessons folder, rename your file to **pr0601-working**, and then click Save.

Keep the file open; you will need it in the next part of this lesson where you will add text and graphics to create your lower third.

Adding text to the Titler

Titles can contain any combination of text, graphics, and images; however, text generally is the most important element. Working with text in the Titler is similar to working with text in other graphics applications, such as Photoshop and Illustrator.

In this part of the lesson, you will add the text to the default still title that you created in the previous part of the lesson.

1 With the **pr0601-working.prproj** project still open, confirm that the playhead is at the origin (00;00;00;00) point of the Timeline.

  If necessary, move the Titler to another location on your computer screen to view the Timeline panel.

In the Titler, click the Type tool in the Title Tools panel to activate it.

There are six tools in the Titler you can use to create text:

A. Type Tool.
B. Vertical Type Tool.
C. Area Type Tool.
D. Vertical Area Type tool.
E. Path Type tool.
F. Vertical Path Type tool.

Type tool & Vertical Type tool: the Type Tool creates horizontal lines of text you can read from left to right; the Vertical Type tool creates vertical lines of text you can read from top to bottom. To use these tools, you do not need to create a boundary text frame, just click the drawing area where you want the text to appear, and then type the text.

Area Type tool & Vertical Area Type tool: unlike text created with the Type tools, the text created with the Area and Vertical Area Type tools is constrained to a boundary text frame. To create the boundary text frame, click and drag these tools where you want the text to appear, and then type your text. The text automatically wraps to form new lines when it reaches the boundary of the text box.

Path Type tool & Vertical Path Type tool: the Path Type tools allow you to create a curved path to then create the text that follows it. Using these tools is very similar to using the Pen tool in graphics applications such as Photoshop and Illustrator. To create the curved path, click the drawing area at the point you want your text to start. Then click and drag to create the second point and continue clicking until you have created the path you want. Once you have completed the path, type your text and it will automatically conform to the contour of the path.

2 With the Type tool still active, place your cursor in the Title Designer panel, and then click the left side of the video frame just above the two people in the boat to create a text box.

The easiest way to create a text box is to simply click in the Title Designer and begin typing.

3 After you create the text box, the menus at the top of the Title Designer that control the Text properties become active, as do the menus in the Text Properties panel.

In the Text properties panel to the right, locate the Font Family property and change it to **Georgia**.

Use the Title Properties panel to edit the properties of the object that appears selected in the Title Designer panel.

4   Click the Text box you previously created in the Title Designer panel to make it active, and then type **Central Park**.

Press the Enter (Windows) or Return (Mac OS) key on your keyboard to create a second line of text and then type **New York City, NY**.

Working with the Titler is very similar to working with text in many popular graphics applications.

5   Choose File > Save or press Ctrl+S (Windows) or Command+S (Mac OS) to save these changes to your project.

Do not close this file; you will need it in the next part of the lesson.

In the next section of this lesson you will format the newly created text.

Formatting text boxes

Creating text in the Titler is just the beginning. Once you have the text, you can use the tools and panels found here to edit and style the title to fit your specific project's needs.

1   With the **pr0601-working.prproj** project still open, click the Selection tool in the Title Tools panel to activate it. Click the text box in the Title Designer panel to confirm it is selected.

2 Using the Selection tool, drag the text box until its lower-left corner is positioned at the left edge of the title safe margin.

The Selection tool is used to select and move objects in the Title Designer.

3 With the text box still selected, click on the value of the Font Size property in the Title Properties panel and change it to **90**. Notice that all the text changes. When you select a text box with the Selection tool, any change to the text properties is global. Confirm that the text box has the following property settings:

Font Family: Georgia

Font Style: Regular

Font Size: 90

Aspect: 100%

Leading: 0.0

Kerning: 0.0

Tracking: 0.0

Baseline Shift: 0.0

Slant: 0.0°

Small Caps: disabled

Small Caps Size: 75%

Underline: disabled

4   Locate the Fill property group in the Title Properties panel and set the Fill Type to Linear Gradient. This will add several new properties that specifically deal with the properties of this type of gradient to the fill group.

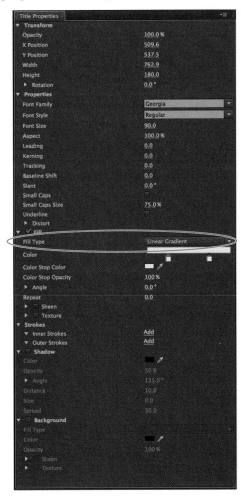

Each Fill Type in the Fill Property group has specific properties associated with it.

5   Located right below the Fill Type menu, the Color property has changed from a simple color swatch into a gradient slider. The two color boxes at the bottom of the slider are called gradient color stops.

Drag each so the first color stop is on the absolute-left of the slider and the second is on the absolute-right.

6 Double-click the first color stop to open a color picker and set the RGB values to R:**80**, G:**80**, B:**80** to produce a dark gray color; click OK to close the color picker and set the value of this color stop.

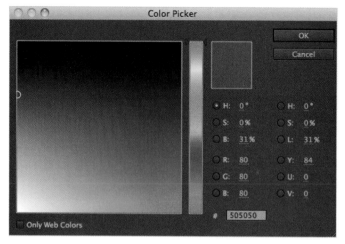

Graphics and Titles for video are always created in the RGB color mode.

The Color Picker in Premiere Pro is similar to that used in other Adobe applications. You can input color values in a variety of different color modes: HSB (Hue Saturation Brightness), HSL (Hue Saturation Lightness), RGB (Red Green Blue), YUV, and Hexadecimal code. You can also set color manually by selecting a Hue (color) from the vertical slider and then clicking the square color selector to set a saturation and brightness for the new color.

7   Located below the Fill property group, the Stroke property group allows you to specify an outline for the text and graphics you create. Multiple strokes can be applied to the outside or inside of the elements of your title.

Click the Add Label to the right of the Outer Stroke property to add a new Outer Stroke to the text, and set the following value for the Stroke:

Type: **Edge**

Size: **20.0**

Fill Type: **Solid**

Color: **Black** (R:0, G:0, B:0)

Opacity: **100%**

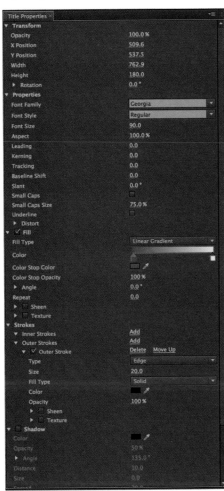

While you only add one in this exercise, text and graphics in the Titler can have multiple strokes applied to them.

8 Choose File > Save or press Ctrl+S (Windows) or Command+S (Mac OS) to save these changes to your project. Do not close this file; you will need it in the next part of the lesson.

Formatting text

You can format entire text boxes at once for convenience, but for greater control and creativity, you have the power to control the formatting of individual letters, words, and lines of type.

1 With the **pr0601-working.prproj** project still open, if necessary, click the Selection tool in the Title Tools panel to activate it.

2 With the Selection tool active, double-click the text box in the Title Designer panel. This selects the text frame automatically and activates the Type tool so you can select and edit individual text elements.

Using the Type tool in this way is similar to creating text in a word processing application. You can click inside the text box to move the text cursor, double-click to select a word, and click and drag to select a range of text.

3 Click and drag the Type tool to select the second line of text.

When used inside a text box, the Type tool functions in much the same way as a mouse cursor in a word processing program such as Microsoft Word.

4   In the Text Properties panel, change the Font Size property to **60**. Since you have highlighted the second line of text only, this is the only line affected by the change in the property's value.

Selecting individual areas of type allows you to edit their properties individually.

5   With the second line of text still selected, locate the Fill property group, and then change the Fill Type property to **Solid**.

Click the swatch to the right of the Color property to open the Color Picker panel and change the color value to R:**0**, G:**0**, B:**0** to produce a solid black; click OK to confirm the color change.

When choosing the appearance of a font, pick fill and stroke colors that complement each other.

6   Remove the black stroke around the text to make the text easier to read.

Locate the Strokes property group, and then click the Delete label to the right of the Outer Stroke that you applied in the previous section of the lesson. Select the first line of text. Notice that the Fill and Stroke properties now reflect the appearance of this text. These setting will become the appearance settings for the next object you create.

Be careful when applying a stroke to text. It can sometimes make the text more difficult to read.

7   Click the Selection tool in the Title Tools panel and then click anywhere in the Title Designer panel to remove the highlighting around the second line of text.

Notice that this line of text is difficult to read because the black is too close to the colors in the background video. You will fix this in the next step by adding a color box behind the text.

Choose File > Save or press Ctrl+S (Windows) or Command+S (Mac OS) to save these changes to your project. Do not close this file; you will need it in the next part of the lesson.

Creating shapes

Text placed directly on top of an image is often very difficult to read, whether the image comes from video or is a still image. To compensate, we recommend you place a color field behind the text to help make it more readable.

1   With the **pr0601-working.prproj** project still open, click the Rectangle tool in the Title Tools panel to make it active.

2   With the Rectangle tool, click and drag from the left side of the screen to create a rectangle that covers the lower third of the video frame. This covers the text that you created in the previous parts of this lesson. The appearance of the rectangle you have just created will be taken from appearance settings of the last object you had selected in the Titler. So depending on the text you selected when you used the Rectangle tool, you could end up with a black box or a box with a gradient fill.

When you work in the Titler, any new object you create is always placed in front of the other objects in the Title Designer panel. New objects also take on the appearance of the last object you created.

We recommend you extend the rectangle outside the Video Frame in the Title Designer panel to guarantee the color field extends to the absolute edge of the video screen, even on devices that do not use over scanning, such as computer monitors.

3   With the Rectangle still active, set the fill type in the Title Properties panel to Solid, click the Color property's swatch, and in the Color Picker, set the fill color to R:**101**, G:**97**, B:**188** to produce a cool blue tone.

Click OK to close the Color Picker dialog box.

You will want to vary the color you use in your graphics to find something that works with your specific projects.

4   Locate the Outer Stroke property group and click the Delete label next to the Outer Stoke to remove it.

New objects will inherit the appearance of the last object that was created, so you may have to spend a little time deleting extraneous properties.

5 Right-click (Windows) or Ctrl+click (Mac OS) the Blue rectangle in the Title
Designer panel, and from the menu that appears, choose Arrange > Send to Back.
This moves the rectangle behind every other object that is in the panel so the text is
visible above the color field.

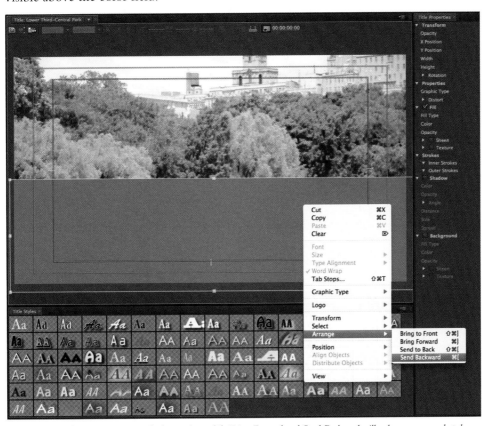

*Send to Back and Bring to Front are absolute settings while Bring Forward and Send Backward will only move your selected
object forward or backward one level at a time.*

6   Locate the Opacity property in the Fill property group of the Title Properties panel. Set the Opacity property to **50%**.

Making the color field semi-transparent makes the text easier to read without obscuring the video frame.

7   Choose File > Save or press Ctrl+S (Windows) or Command+S (Mac OS) to save these changes to your project. Do not close this file; you will need it in the next part of the lesson.

In this part of the lesson, you created a rectangle to use as a colored background to make reading the text for this lower third easier. There are other shapes you can create to enhance your titles, such as ellipses, rounded or inset cornered rectangles, as well as a variety of lines.

Adding images to a title

Your title can contain images in addition to text and graphics. In this part of the lesson, you will learn to add images to a title.

1   With the **pr0601-working.prproj** project still open, click the Selection tool in the Title Tools panel to make it active.

2   Right-click (Windows) or Ctrl+click (Mac OS) any empty area of the Title Designer panel, and from the menu that appears, choose Graphic > Insert Graphic.

In the Insert Image as Logo dialog box that appears, navigate to the Media Library, open the Images folder, and double-click the file named **NYState Motif.png** to import it.

You can insert any standard image format into a title using the Insert Logo command.

This graphic is an image of the state of New York with a marker in the approximate location of New York City. It is a PNG (Portable Network Graphic) file that allows it to have transparency and a high quality color display.

3   With the Selection tool still active, click the center of the image and drag it into toward the bottom of the video frame so it is adjacent to the text.

Any object selected in the Title Designer panel has a rectangular bounding box around it that you can use to transform (move, rotate, or scale) the selected object.

4   With the image still selected, move your mouse cursor to just outside the upper-right corner of the image's bounding box.

The mouse cursor changes from an arrow to a double-headed curved arrow (↳) when you place it just above the control point (the small dark square). This tool indicates that you can rotate the selected object.

To rotate the image counter-clockwise, click and drag the tool slightly to the left.

When working in Premiere Pro, the cursor is context sensitive. It changes appearance to show you it can perform a new function.

If you want to rotate an object by a specific amount, you can set a value for the Rotation property of any selected object in the Title Properties panel.

5   Choose File > Save or press Ctrl+S (Windows) or Command+S (Mac OS) to save these changes to your project. Do not close this file; you will need it in the next part of the lesson.

Saving a title style

You can save title styles you have created using the Title Styles panels. This helps you create consistent and reusable text.

1   With the **pr0601-working.prproj** project still open and the Selection tool active, double-click the text frame to select it; this automatically switches you to the Type tool.

2   With the Type tool now active, click and drag the Central Park text to select it.

Double-clicking any text box with the Selection tool automatically switches to the Type tool.

3   In the Title Styles panel, click the panel menu (•≣) button and choose New Style from the menu that appears.

Saving a Title style allows you to create consistent-looking text without the need to fill in multiple property options.

4   In the New Style dialog box, change the default style name to **Location Title** and click OK to save the new style.

Premiere Pro creates a new style based on the properties of the currently highlighted text.

The new style appears as the last entry in the Title Styles panel.

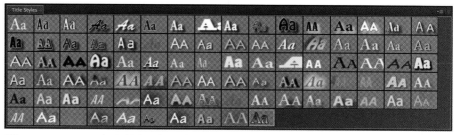

When you create a new style, the Title Style panel automatically scrolls to the bottom of the listed styles.

To apply your new style or any other style from the Title Styles panel, select your target text, and then click the style you want.

5   Choose File > Save or press Ctrl+S (Windows) or Command+S (Mac OS) to save these changes to your project. Do not close this file; you will need it in the next part of the lesson.

Creating a title overlay track

You can insert or add your title to the Timeline after you have created it. If you add it to the Video 1 track, you could only place it before or after the video clips; for this exercise, you will add your title to one of the video tracks above so the title appears superimposed on the video image.

1   With the **pr0601-working.prproj** project still open, close the Titler: on a computer running the Mac OS, click the red circle on the upper-left of the Titler panel group; on a computer running Windows, click the small x on the upper-right of the panel group.

2 If necessary, click the Timeline panel to make it active, and then press and hold the Ctrl (Windows) or the Command (Mac OS) key while you press the equal sign key (=) repeatedly until you can see the names of the track headers.

Track heights can be adjusted using a keyboard shortcut. Ctrl (Windows) or Command (Mac OS) + = (equal sign) enlarges the track height, while Ctrl (Windows) or Command (Mac OS) + - (hyphen) contracts it.

3 Once the track names become visible, right-click Video 3 and choose Rename from the menu that appears. Once the name field becomes editable, change it to **Lower Thirds**.

Press the Enter (Windows) or Return (Mac OS) key on your keyboard to commit the name changes to the track.

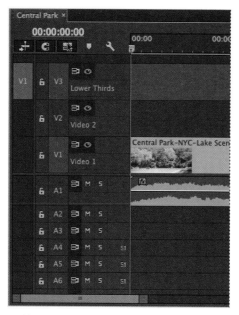

By default, sequences have three individual video tracks and two audio tracks, but they can have up to 99 of each.

4 You will now add to the Timeline the title you created in the earlier portion of this lesson.

In the Project panel, click the Lower Third–Central Park title and drag it onto the Lower Thirds track. Position it at the beginning (00;00;00;00) of the Timeline.

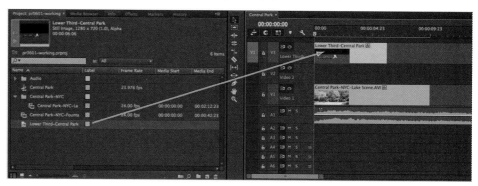

As is the case with clips, you can add titles directly to the Timeline through clicking and dragging.

5 Notice the red bar above the title indicating that you must render the title to preview it in real–time and at full quality.

Press the Enter (Windows) or Return (Mac OS) key on your keyboard to render all areas of the Timeline that need rendering.

Premiere Pro automatically previews the Timeline after rendering is done.

The playhead continues to play after the video is done previewing. This is because the background music track extends to the 30–second (00;00;30;00) mark on the Timeline.

To stop the playhead at any time after the video goes black, press the spacebar and then press the Home key to return the playhead to the beginning of the Timeline.

If you do not have a Home key on your keyboard, click the playhead and drag it back to the beginning of the Timeline.

6 Choose File > Save or press Ctrl+S (Windows) or Command+S (Mac OS) to save these changes to your project. Do not close this file; you will need it in the next part of the lesson.

Saving a title for later reuse

You can save titles to reuse later. This is helpful when you must create a title to share between multiple video projects, such as a serialized production for Television or the Web.

1 With the **pr0601-working.prproj** project still open, click the Lower Third-Central Park title in the Project panel to select it.

2 With the title selected, choose File > Export > Title.

Title export is only an option when you have a title selected in the Project panel.

3 In the Save Title dialog that appears, navigate to the pr06lessons folder on your hard drive and click the Save button. The title file is saved using the name of the title.

You can import titles into a Premiere Pro project using the Import command as you would other pieces of media.

4 Choose File > Save or press Ctrl+S (Windows) or Command+S (Mac OS) to save these changes to your project, and then close the project.

Creating an ending credit roll

As mentioned earlier in this book, you can create more than simple, still titles. Rolling Titles are often used to create the ending credits you see in film and television programs. While the first rolling titles were created by painting text onto panes of glass and moving them past a camera vertically, you can now accomplish the same effect much easier using Premiere Pro.

1   With Premiere Pro open, chose File > Open Project. Navigate to the pr06lessons folder and double-click the **pr0602.prproj** file to open it.

This project contains a sequence named End Credits that contains a single audio clip, named **Classical Background Music.mp3** that has already been added to the Timeline. The background audio is intended to accompany the end credits you will create. This file can be found in the Media Library in the Audio folder.

2   Choose File > Save As. In the Save Project dialog box that appears, confirm that you are still in the the pr06lessons folder, rename your file to **pr0602-working**, and then click the Save button.

3   Confirm that you are in the Editing workspace, and then choose Window > Workspace > Reset Current Workspace to return to the default Editing workspace. Just to be on the safe side, the application will ask you to confirm that you do indeed want to reset the workspace. In the dialog box that appears, click OK to the query: "Are you sure you want to return to the original workspace?"

4   Choose Title > New Title > Default Roll to open the New Title dialog box.

Leave the Video Settings at their default configuration and change the title's name to **Rolling End Credits**.

Click the OK button to open the Titler.

The default settings of a new title are set to match your current sequence.

5   If necessary, enlarge the Titler window until you can view all the individual panels.
    Click the Type tool to activate it and use it to draw a text box that covers the entire
    Title Safe area of the Title Designer panel.

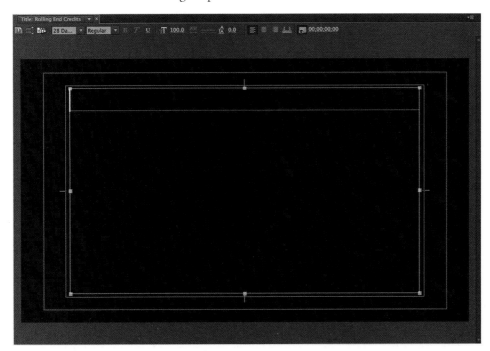

You can use the Type tool to define a text box as you would with the Area Type tool.

6   In the Title Properties panel, set the Font Family menu to **Georgia**, the Font Size
    property to **90**, and the Leading property to **50**.

7   With the Title tool active, click inside the text box in the Title Designer panel to make it active again. Use your keyboard to type the following text:

Artist [press the Enter (Windows) or Return (Mac OS) key]

Jeff Jacobs [press the Enter (Windows) or Return (Mac OS) key]

Album [press the Enter (Windows) or Return (Mac OS) key]

Enjoy the View [press the Enter (Windows) or Return (Mac OS) key]

Director [press the Enter (Windows) or Return (Mac OS) key]

Kurt Zisa [press the Enter (Windows) or Return (Mac OS) key]

To control when text breaks to form a new line, press the Enter (Windows) or Return (Mac OS) key on your keyboard.

After you add the last line of text, you will be at the end of the text box. To continue, you must enlarge the text box to give you more vertical space to add the remaining text.

8   In the Title Tools panel, click the Selection tool to activate it, and then place it over the bottom-middle control point of the text box.

You can use the Selection tool to select, move, and transform objects in the Titler.

9   The Selection tool becomes a double-headed vertical arrow when you place it over the control point.

Click and drag toward the bottom of the Title Designer panel to enlarge the text box.

Do not release your mouse button until you reach the bottom of the Title Styles panel. Notice that the scroll bar on the right side of the Title panel automatically gets bigger as you enlarge the text box.

When you create a roll, the Title panel automatically creates additional space as you add content vertically.

10 Double-click the text box with the Selection tool to switch to the Type tool and add the following text:

Camera [press the Enter (Windows) or Return (Mac OS) key]

Joe DeFelice [press the Enter (Windows) or Return (Mac OS) key]

Segment Producer [press the Enter (Windows) or Return (Mac OS) key]

Tom Madrigal [press the Enter (Windows) or Return (Mac OS) key]

Editor [press the Enter (Windows) or Return (Mac OS) key]

Joe Cap [press the Enter (Windows) or Return (Mac OS) key]

As you add text to the rolling title, the scroll bar on the right becomes active. You can use this scroll bar to view the available area of the text box if necessary. If you have a scroll wheel, you can use it to control this scroll area.

11 Click the Selection tool in the Title Tools panel to make it active and enlarge the text box to make room for the final bit of text:

Line Producer [press the Enter (Windows) or Return (Mac OS) key]

Eric Newman [press the Enter (Windows) or Return (Mac OS) key]

Technical Director [press the Enter (Windows) or Return (Mac OS) key]

John Vincennes [press the Enter (Windows) or Return (Mac OS) key]

Visit us on the web [press the Enter (Windows) or Return (Mac OS) key]

http://jeffjacobsmusic.com/ [press the Enter (Windows) or Return (Mac OS) key]

Use the scroll bar on the right side of the Title Designer panel to view your title after you are done.

12 Close the Titler and choose File > Save or press Ctrl+S (Windows) or Command+S (Mac OS) to save these changes to your project. Do not close this file; you will need it in the next part of the lesson.

Controlling the speed of a title roll

All titles you create in the Titler are assigned the default still image duration; 150 frames (5 seconds at 30 fps). Keep in mind you can change this value in the General category of the Preferences dialog box at any time, though it will only affect titles created after the change is made. This effect is not retroactive; changing this particular preference will only affect titles created and still images imported after you have made the change. When working with a credit roll, the speed of the title's movement is based on the duration of the title itself.

In this section of the lesson, you will add the credits you created previously to the Timeline, and then adjust their duration to match the length of the audio clip that is already there.

1   With the **pr0602-working.prproj** project still open, click the Rolling End Credits title in the Project panel to select it. Drag the title to the Timeline panel and place it at the beginning (00:00:00:00) of the Timeline on the V1 track. The title will have a duration of 150 frames.

When new titles are created they are added to the Project panel just like imported media. They must then be added to Sequences on the Timeline similar to video and audio clips.

2   Notice the red bar that appears above the title; it indicates a section of the Timeline needs to be rendered.

    Press the Enter (Windows) or Return (Mac OS) key on your keyboard to render all areas of the Timeline that need rendering. Premiere Pro automatically previews the Timeline when the rendering is done. Press the spacebar on your keyboard to stop the playback after the title finishes playing. Notice that the title rolls by too quickly to read the text.

3   Click the Home key or click on the playhead and drag it back to the beginning of the Timeline. The reason the text is unreadable is because the speed of a rolling or crawling title is based on the duration of the clip on the Timeline.

    Confirm that the Selection tool is active in the Tools panel at the top of the Premiere Pro interface and place it at the end of the Rolling End Credits clip on the Timeline.

4   When the Trim cursor (✛) appears, click and drag the end of the title clip to line up with the end of the audio clip. You may need to zoom out on the timeline to see the end of the audio clip.

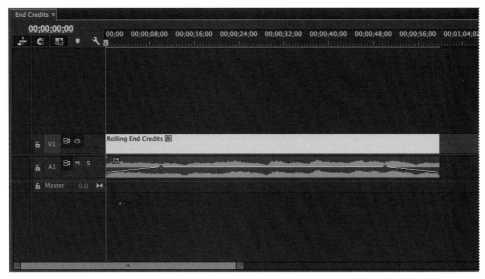

The Snap option of the application helps line up the start and end points of different clips.

When you reach the end of the audio clip, the mouse cursor snaps to it automatically. This is because the snap button is enabled on the Timeline. You can disable this by pressing the S key on your keyboard or by turning off the snap button located below the current time code display on the Timeline panel.

Notice the red bar that indicates a section of the Timeline needs to be rendered has appeared again.

5   Press the Enter (Windows) or Return (Mac OS) key on your keyboard to render all areas of the Timeline that need rendering. Premiere Pro automatically previews the Timeline when the rendering is done. Notice that the title moves much slower now.

6   Choose File > Save or press Ctrl+S (Windows) or Command+S (Mac OS) to save these changes to your project. Do not close this file; you will need it in the next part of the lesson.

In the next section of the lesson, you will learn to edit the title.

Editing titles

Titles created using the Premiere Pro Titler can be edited at any time. This offers you the flexibility to modify your titles quickly and easily without having to resort to opening another application such as Adobe Photoshop or Illustrator.

1   With the **pr0602-working.prproj** project still open, double-click the Rolling End Credits title in the Timeline panel to reopen it in the Titler.

2   Click the Selection tool in the Titler Tools panel to activate it, and then double-click the text box in the Title Designer to select it.

3   Press Ctrl+A (Windows) or Command+A (Mac OS) to select all the text in the text box.

An alternative to using the keyboard shortcut to select all the text in a text box is to click and drag over the text with the Type tool, much as you would in a word processing program.

4 Click the Center button located at the top of the Title designer panel.

You can align text to the Left, Center, or Right sides of the text box that contains it.

5 Click the Roll /Crawl Options (▤) button at the top of the Titler Designer panel to open the Roll/Crawl Options dialog box.

6 In the Timing section of the dialog box, turn on the checkboxes next to Start Off Screen and End Off Screen to enable them, and then click the OK button.

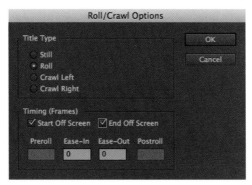

You can also use the Roll/Crawl Options dialog box to change one type of title into another, for example, when you want to convert a still title into a rolling one.

7   Close the Titler and return to the Timeline panel.

Notice the red bar that indicates a section of the Timeline needs to be rendered has returned. Any change to your title's appearance or properties has to be rerendered.

Click any area of the Timeline panel to activate it, and then press the Enter (Windows) or Return (Mac OS) key on your keyboard to render all areas of the Timeline that need rendering. Premiere Pro automatically previews the Timeline when the rendering is done. Notice that the rolling credits now start and end with the text off screen. Additionally, the speed of the overall title animation has been effected slightly.

You must rerender a title whenever you make a change to it.

8   Choose File > Save or press Ctrl+S (Windows) or Command+S (Mac OS) to save these changes to your project, and then close the project.

Working with Photoshop files

In some productions, it is common to display the production company's logo after the ending credits. In this section of the lesson, you are going to create your own logo by animating a layered Photoshop file.

All the media used in this section of the lesson can be found in the Images sub-folder of the Media Library.

1   With Premiere Pro open, chose File > Open Project. Navigate to the pr06lessons folder that you copied to your hard drive and locate the **pr0603.prproj** file. Double-click the file to open it.

This project contains a standard 1920 × 1080 high-definition sequence with a static image file already on the Timeline. You will import and animate a layered Photoshop file in the next subsections.

2   Choose File > Save As. In the Save Project dialog box that appears, confirm that you are still in the pr06lesson folder, rename your file to **pr0603-working**, and then click the Save button.

Don't close this file; you will need it to complete the rest of this lesson.

Importing layered Photoshop files

Photoshop has a layers feature that works in much the same way as the video track you see in Premiere Pro. Layers allow you to stack different images on top of one another, just as you created a lower-third and placed it above a video clip.

When working with layered Photoshop files, Premiere Pro can import a flattened composite image, or convert the file to a sequence and import each layer as an individual footage item. This type of import is helpful when you want to animate each layer individually, as explained in the next procedure.

1   With the **pr0603-working.prproj** project still open, choose File > Import, and in the Import dialog box, navigate to the Media Library folder located in the project files folder that you copied to your hard drive.

In the Media Library folder, locate the Images folder and double-click the **Bad Robot Productions.psd** file.

You can open the Import dialog box in several ways. The keyboard shortcut is Ctrl+I (Windows) or Command+I (Mac OS). You can also right-click (Windows) or Ctrl+click (Mac OS) the Project panel and choose Import from the menu that appears, or double-click any empty area of the Project panel to open the dialog box.

2   Importing a layered Photoshop file opens a secondary dialog box that you can use to set the options for how to import the file. In the Import As menu choose **Sequence**.

This imports each layer individually and adds them to a new sequence. The sequence feature is helpful in cases where all the elements in the Photoshop file are positioned where you need them.

Confirm that all the layer check boxes are selected and that the Footage Dimensions are set to Document Size. Click the OK button to import the layered file and create a new sequence to match its properties.

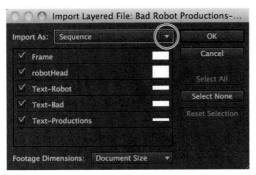

Importing a Photoshop file as a sequence allows you to work with each layer of the file individually.

The other choices in the Import As menu are helpful in different situations. The Merge All Layers option imports the layered Photoshop file as a flattened image and is very similar to importing a TIFF (Tagged Image File Format) or JPEG (Joint Photographic Experts Group) file. The Merged Layers option works almost as the first choice, but it allows you to specify which layers of the Photoshop file to merge together. Finally, the individual Layers option imports each layer as an individual footage item, but does not create a sequence for them.

3 When you click OK, a new bin appears in the Project panel. It contains the individual footage items for each layer and the sequence that was created to contain them. Click on the reveal triangle to the left of the new folder to see its contents.

The new sequence that was created when you imported the Photoshop Document is named Bad Robot Productions. Click this new sequence to select it. Notice that it has a duration of 5 seconds (00;00;05;00). The duration is caused by the fact that all the image layers in the sequence are set to be 5 seconds each. By default, this is the duration used for all imported still images.

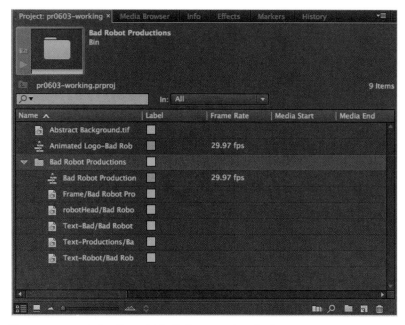

The new sequence and all media associated with it are grouped together for easy access.

4 Double-click the new sequence to make it active and open it in the Timeline panel. Then in the Bad Robot Productions Timeline, click either end of the Horizontal Slider at the bottom of the panel and drag it until you see the 5-second (00;00;05;00) mark visible on the Timeline. You will want to adjust the Timeline magnification until you can comfortably see both the beginning and end of the clips.

The amount you have to zoom in depends on your monitor's resolution.

5 Choose File > Save or press Ctrl+S (Windows) or Command+S (Mac OS) to save these changes to your project. Do not close this file; you will need it in the next part of the lesson when you animate the individual Photoshop layers on the Timeline.

Animating the position of clips

You can perform simple animation tasks in Premiere Pro by creating keyframes, which store property values at different positions on the Timeline. To create animation, you set two or more keyframes where a property's values are different, and the program automatically interprets the change in value. This interpretation, which is called interpolation, is how the majority of computer-based animation is created.

Please note that for more complex and detailed animation tasks you will want to use a dedicated video animation program such as Adobe After Effects.

1 With the **pr0603-working.prproj** project still open, confirm that the Bad Robot Productions sequence is active in the Timeline panel.

Double-clicking any sequence in the Project panel automatically opens it in the Timeline panel and makes it the active sequence.

2 The sequence consists of five video tracks each with one clip on it. If you expand the track headers, you will notice that each track name matches the name of the clip on that track. Both are taken from the original Photoshop layer name. The clips are stacked from top to bottom as follows (the list uses only the clip's layer names from Photoshop, not the full file address name assigned to each track):

Frame, robotHead, Text-Robot, Text-Bad, and Text-Productions

Click the clip second from bottom named Text-Bad to select it and make it active.

3 When a clip is selected, its properties become accessible through the Effect Controls panel.

Click the tab for the Effect Controls panel to make it active and bring it to the front of the panel display.

In the default Editing workspace the Effect Controls panels is grouped with the Source Monitor.

Notice that the clip has three inherent sets of properties: Motion, Opacity, and Time Remapping. For this clip, you will be working with the Motion property group.

The Effects Controls panel displays and edits the inherent properties of clips and the properties of any Effects attached to them.

4   Click the reveal triangle to the left of the Motion Property group to show the five properties: Position, Scale, Rotation, Anchor Point, and Anti-Flicker Filter.

The Effect Controls panel has two parts; the left side holds the effects you can edit while the right side is a mini-timeline view. You can adjust size of either side by placing your cursor over the barely visible dividing line between the two sections until it become a double-headed arrow. Drag the arrow cursor left or right to adjust the panel.

For this project, you will create a 2-second animation in which the text flies into view from the top of the screen. This requires you to animate the Position property of the clip. Since we already have the text in its final resting position, we will create the ending keyframe first and then create the keyframe where the clips is off-screen.

First, set the key frame that positions the text at the end of the 2-second animation:

In the Timeline panel, move the playhead to the 2-second (00;00;02;00) mark. This also moves the playhead in the mini-timeline view in the Effect Controls panel.

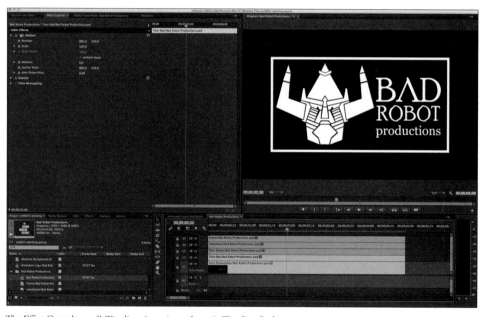

The Effect Controls panel's Timeline view mirrors the main Timeline display.

You should create the last key frame first because the graphic is imported as a sequence; therefore, all the content is already at the final position. It creates less work to set the final key frame first and then work back to create the animation and ensure you do not accidentally move the logo from its intended layout.

5   Click the Toggle Animation stopwatch icon to the left of the Position property to enable animation for this single property. This creates a key frame that stores the property's current value at the playhead's current position.

The Toggle Animation stopwatch automatically creates a keyframe where the playhead currently is.

6   Move the playhead back to the beginning (00;00;00;00) of the Timeline, and then in the Effect Controls panel, change the second value of the position property (this is the clip's vertical position) to **0.0** by clicking the current value to make it editable. This positions it at the top of the video frame outside of the visible area of the screen.

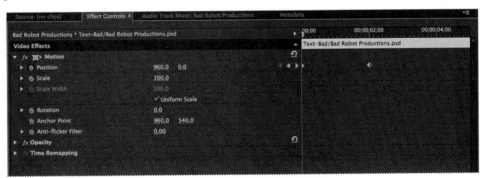

You can see any changes you make to the properties of a clip on the Timeline in the Program Monitor.

Press the spacebar on your keyboard to see the animation you have created play in the Program Monitor. You can press the spacebar again at any time to stop the playback.

7   Move the playhead to the 2-second (00;00;02;00) mark on the Timeline and click the Text–Robot clip to make it active so you can view its properties in the Effect Controls panel.

Again click the reveal triangle next to the Motion property group in the Effect Controls panel, and then click the Toggle Animation stopwatch next to the Position property to create the first key frame at 2 seconds and enable animation.

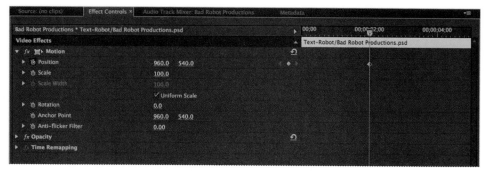

The Effect Controls panel shows you the properties for the selected and current clip.

8   Move the playhead back to the beginning (00;00;00;00) of the Timeline, and change the Position property's first value (this is the clip's horizontal position) to **1800** to move it outside the right boundary of the screen.

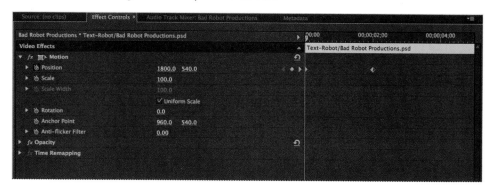

We strongly recommend you move the playhead to the correct time code position before changing a property value. Keyframes are created only at the current position of the playhead.

Press the spacebar on your keyboard to see the animation you have created play in the Program Monitor. Stop the playback when you are satisfied with what you have seen by pressing the spacebar again.

9   Once again move the playhead to the 2-second (00;00;02;00) mark on the Timeline, and then click the Text-Productions clip to make it active and reveal its properties in the Effect Controls panel.

Again click the reveal triangle next to the Motion property group, and then click the Toggle Animation stopwatch next to the Position property to create a key frame at 2 seconds and enable animation.

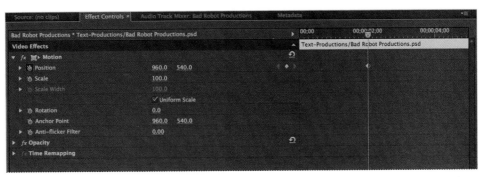

If you have your clips assembled in the correct position, it is often most efficient to create the final keyframe of the animation first.

10 Move the playhead back to the beginning (00;00;00;00) of the Timeline and change the position property's second value to **1000.0** to move it off the bottom boundary of the screen.

Press the spacebar on your keyboard to see the animation you have created play in the Program Monitor. Stop the playback when you are satisfied with what you have seen by pressing the spacebar again.

11 Choose File > Save or press Ctrl+S (Windows) or Command+S (Mac OS) to save these changes to your project. Do not close this file; you will need it in the next part of the lesson when you animate the opacity properties of the two remaining clips.

Animating the opacity of clips

You can animate any property of a clip. In the previous portion of this lesson, you animated the Position of the first three clips to create a fly-in animation where the text begins off-screen and flies on to reveal itself. You will now animate the Opacity property of the remaining two clips to complete the animated logo.

1 With the **pr0603-working.prproj** project still open, confirm that the Bad Robot Productions sequence is active in the Timeline panel.

2 Move the playhead to the 2-second (00;00;02;00) mark on the Timeline, and in the Timeline panel, click the robotHead clip to make it active and reveal its properties in the Effect Controls panel.

Click the reveal triangle next to the Opacity property group. This process is slightly different from what you have done previously because the Opacity property's Toggle Animation switch is already enabled by default so you don't have to turn it on.

Click the Add/Remove Key frame (◊) button located to the right of the property name. This adds a key frame for the current value of the Opacity property at the current position of the playhead.

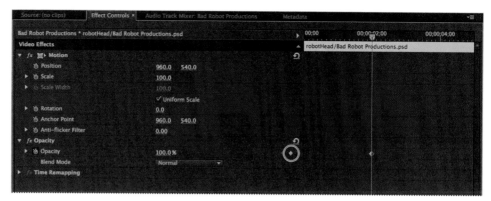

You can use the Add/Remove Key frame button to add or remove a key frame at the current position of the playhead.

3   Move the playhead back to the beginning (00;00;00;00) of the Timeline, and in the Effect Controls panel, change the Opacity property's value to **0.0%** to make it fully transparent.

Press the spacebar on your keyboard to see the animation you have created play in the Program Monitor. Stop the playback when you are satisfied with what you have seen by pressing the spacebar again.

4   The last animation you create is going to be different. The animation looks odd when the text flies over the white frame; since that frame is intended to enclose the entire logo, it should appear after every other part of the logo is already in place.

Once again move the playhead to the 2-second (00;00;02;00) mark on the Timeline, and then click the clip named Frame to make it active and reveal its properties in the Effect Controls panel.

Click the reveal triangle next to the Opacity property group and change the property's value to **0.0%**. This creates a key frame at the current position of the playhead, where the clip is completely transparent.

When the Toggle Animation switch is enabled for a property, any change to the property's value creates a keyframe at the current position of the playhead.

5   Move the playhead to the 3-second (00;00;03;00) mark on the Timeline, and in the Effect Controls panel, change the Opacity property's value to **100.0%** to make the frame around the logo fully visible.

Move the playhead back to the beginning of the Timeline and press the spacebar on your keyboard to see the animation you have created play in the Program Monitor. Stop the playback when you are satisfied with what you have seen by pressing the spacebar again.

6   In the Project panel, double-click the Animated Logo-Bad Robot sequence to make it the active sequence in the Timeline panel.

Drag the Bad Robot Production-NTSC sequence from the Project panel to the Video 2 track in the Animated Logo-Bad Robot sequence so it is placed above the abstract background already there.

You can add sequences to tracks in other sequences just as you would with other type of media.

7   Press the Enter (Windows) or Return (Mac OS) key on your keyboard to render all areas of the Timeline that need rendering.

Premiere Pro automatically previews the Timeline when the rendering is done. You can press the spacebar at any time to stop the preview.

8   Choose File > Save or press Ctrl+S (Windows) or Command+S (Mac OS) to save these changes to your project, and then close the project.

Working with motion graphics from After Effects

Adobe After Effects has long been a standard in the creation of motion graphics for television and video. In recent years, as bandwidth increased and the Internet gained better support for rich media, After Effects has also been used to create graphic intros and animation for the Web. Additionally, After Effects is now used to create content seen in presentation graphics and mobile devices. After Effects is a tool for storytelling, a way to create visually appealing motion graphics that can be integrated into any medium.

What is Adobe Dynamic Link?

One of the greatest time-consuming aspects of creating motion graphics and integrating them into your video project is the necessity of rendering your graphics files so you can import them into your NLE (Non-linear Editing System). Called intermediate renders, these video or image files require that you return to the original application that created them to edit or modify your graphics. To solve the problems of this intermediary system, Adobe created Dynamic Link. Running through various applications in the entire creative suite, Dynamic Link is a system designed to allow you to import native source files directly into application such as Premiere Pro, After Effects, and Encore. In Premiere Pro, you can use this system to import pre-existing After Effects compositions or create them from scratch to match the settings of your existing sequence. To use Dynamic Link, do one of the following:

Choose File > Adobe Dynamic Link > New After Effects Composition. This creates a new After Effects composition (the equivalent of a sequence), imports it into the Project panel, and then opens After Effects so you can create your graphics content.

or

Choose File > Adobe Dynamic Link > Import After Effects Composition to import a non-rendered, native After Effects composition into your Premiere Pro project.

Self study

To continue the topics that you learned in this lesson, you can create lower thirds and rolling credits for your own projects.

Review

Questions

1   When creating text and graphics for broadcast video, why are safe zones important?

2   What are lower thirds and where are they often seen?

3   When working in the Titler, what are the six Type tools and what does each of them do?

Answers

1   Most television sets perform a function called over scanning on the video frame. As a result of this over scanning process, the outer edges of the picture may be placed outside the viewable area of the screen. Since the amount of over scanning is not consistent on different devices, the safe zones are a general guideline to help ensure that all the important information in a video frame is visible.

2   Lower thirds are used to add on-screen text to help explain or illuminate some aspect of video. Often used in documentary style projects, lower thirds are commonly used to introduce an individual or setting.

3   **Type tool & Vertical Type tool**: The Type Tool creates horizontal lines of text you can read from left to right; the Vertical Type tool creates vertical lines of text you can read from top to bottom. To use these tools, you do not need to create a boundary text frame, just click the drawing area where you want the text to appear, and then type the text.

   Area Type tool & Vertical Area Type tool: Unlike text created with the Type tools, the text created with the Area and Vertical Area Type tools is constrained to a boundary text frame. To create the boundary text frame, click and drag these tools where you want the text to appear, and then type your text. The text automatically wraps to form new lines when it reaches the boundary of the text box.

   Path Type tool & Vertical Path Type tool: The Path Type tools allow you to create a curved path to then create the text that follows it. Using these tools is very similar to using the Pen tool in graphics applications such as Photoshop and Illustrator. To create the curved path, click the drawing area at the point you want your text to start. Then click and drag to create the second point and continue clicking until you have created the path you want. Once you have completed the path, type your text and it will automatically conform to the contour of the path.

What you'll learn in this lesson:

- To apply video effects to clips on the Timeline

- To adjust the tonality of clips on the Timeline

- To fix shaky footage with the Warp Stabilizer

- To apply quick color adjustments with Lumetri looks

Using Video Effects

You can apply effects to video clips on your Timeline, enhancing or correcting the video as necessary.

Starting up

In this lesson, you will work with the project files from the pr07lessons folder. Make sure that you have loaded the prlessons folder onto your hard drive from the supplied DVD. The Starting up section at the beginning of this book provides detailed information about loading lesson files, resetting your workspace, locating missing media, and opening the files in CC. If you have not already done so, please review these instructions before starting this lesson.

When opening the Premiere Pro project files used in this lesson you may experience a missing media message. You must locate any missing media before trying to proceed through the lessons. Please refer to "Locating missing media" in the Starting up section of this book.

See Lesson 7 in action!

Use the accompanying video to gain a better understanding of how to use some of the features shown in this lesson. The video tutorial for this lesson can be found on the included DVD.

What are video effects?

Video effects are processes you can apply to video clips on the Timeline. In Premiere Pro, effects are grouped into categories based on their use. There are two types of effects in Premiere Pro: fixed and standard.

Fixed effects are the pre-built effects automatically added to every clip on the Timeline. The fixed effects include: Motion, Opacity, Time Remapping, and Volume.

Standard effects add special qualities to your video, such as adjusted colors, blurriness, and noise. Premiere Pro includes several standard effects, but there are several third-party effects you can purchase from vendors such as Boris FX (*www.borisfx.com*), Digieffects (*www.digieffects.com*), and Synthetic Apperture (*www.synthetic-ap.com*).

Applying video effects

Effects are applied to clips on the Timeline instead of in between them, as is the case with transitions. All the video effects you can access in Premiere Pro are stored in the Effects panel, which is the library that contains all effects and transitions in the application. Effects are easy to apply: you locate the effect you want in the Effects panel using the search field or nested folder display and drag it to the clip you want in the Timeline. Once applied, you can edit effect properties in the Effect Controls panel when you select the clip in the Timeline.

Creating a Black & White effect

The Black & White effect de-saturates a color video clip and makes it appear as though it were shot on black-and-white film. Since modern camcorders only record in color, this effect is useful when you want to simulate an old-fashioned look on modern footage, or just create an artistic or dramatic effect.

In this part of the lesson, you will work with a pre-built Premiere Pro project and add the Black & White effect to a clip on the Timeline. The media for this section of the lesson can be found at Media Library > Travelogue-New York > video.

1   From the Premiere Pro Welcome screen, click the Open Project button, or with Premiere Pro already open, chose File > Open Project. Navigate to the pr07lessons folder you copied to your hard drive and locate the **pr0701.prproj** file. Double-click the file to open it.

This project contains a sequence called Lake Scene. In this sequence, the video from the **Central Park–NYC–Lake Scene.AVI** has been placed on the Timeline and divided into two parts. You will apply the Black & White effect to the first clip on the Timeline.

*The **Central Park–NYC–Lake Scene.AVI** clip on the Timeline was divided into two pieces using the Razor tool. After dividing the clip, the first part was dragged to the Video 2 track, and the Out Point of this clip was extended using the Selection tool to overlap the beginning of the second clip by 30 seconds.*

2   If you are still in the default editing workspace, you will find the Effects panel to the left of the Timeline. Click the Effects panel's tab to make the panel active and visible.

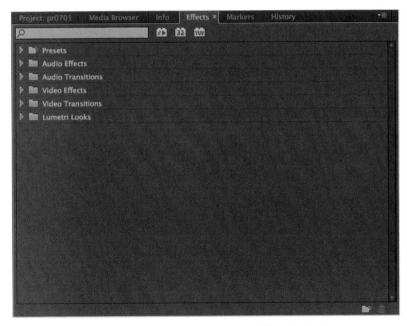

The Effects panel is the library for all the effects and transitions available in Premiere Pro.

3 Type the word **black** in the search field at the top of the panel. This limits the content of the panel so only folder names, effects, and transitions that have the letters *b l a c k* in their names appear.

The search field is helpful when finding specific effects or transitions.

4 Click the Black & White effect in the Effects panel, drag it to the Timeline panel and drop it onto the video clip on the Video 2 track. The clip in your Program monitor is now black-and-white.

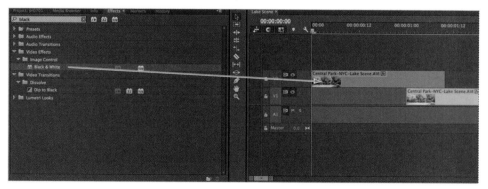

You can apply effects and transitions by dragging them from the Effects panel and dropping them onto clips in the Timeline.

5   Press the Enter (Windows) or Return (Mac OS) key on your keyboard to render all areas of the Timeline that need rendering.

When the rendering is done, Premiere Pro previews the Timeline automatically.

Notice that the black-and-white effect cuts out sharply when the clip ends; you will adjust this in the next part of the lesson by creating a transition from one clip to another.

6   Choose File > Save As. In the Save Project dialog box that appears, confirm that you are still in the pr07lessons folder, rename your file to **pr0701-working.prproj**, and click the Save button. Do not close this file; you will need it in the next part of the lesson.

Animating the opacity of clips

To create a natural, more aesthetically pleasing transition between the black-and-white clip and the color clip, you can have the black-and-white clip fade out to reveal the color clip on the video track below it. Opacity is one of the fixed effects available for all video clips that you can use to accomplish this.

In this section of the lesson, you will animate the Opacity effect of the clip that you added the Black & White effect to earlier in this lesson.

1   With the **pr0701-working.prproj** project still open, double-click the video clip on the Video 2 track to select it and open it in the Source monitor.

2   Click the Effect Controls panel tab next to the Source Monitor to make it active. The panel shows you all the Fixed and Standard effects currently applied to the selected clip. Notice that the panel is divided into two different areas. On the left you can see the effects and on the right you see a mini-Timeline view. This mini-Timeline view is used to animate effects.

The Effect controls panel shows the effects of any clip selected in the Timeline panel.

Remember you can adjust the width of the two columns in the Effects Controls panel by clicking and dragging on the dividing line between the two columns.

3   Click the reveal triangle to the left of the Opacity effect to reveal the Opacity effect's numerical value. This is where you will animate the clip's opacity.

The mini-Timeline display of the Effect Controls panel lets you animate effects.

4   In the Timeline panel, move the playhead to the 1-second (00;00;01;00) mark. Notice that the playhead in the mini-Timeline display of the Effects Controls panel also moves: both playheads are synchronized.

The clip on the Video 1 track begins at exactly the 1-second (00;00;01;00) mark on the Timeline. You can drag the playhead while holding the Shift key on your keyboard to force the playhead to snap to the beginning or end of the clips on your Timeline.

5   In the Effect Controls panel, notice that the Toggle Animation stopwatch to the left of the Opacity effect is already enabled. You can use this stopwatch to enable or disable animation.

Click the Add/Remove Keyframe button to the right of the Opacity effect to create a keyframe for the clip's Opacity at the current position of the playhead.

This provides a beginning point for the animation you will create. The beginning point stores the clip's Opacity at 100% (fully opaque).

You set a clip's opacity to any value between 100% (fully opaque) and 0% (fully transparent).

Keyframes are the basis for most computer-generated animation, and they store the property values of each effect. When you have two keyframes with different values, Premiere Pro automatically animates the change in value.

6   Hold the Shift key on your keyboard, and in the Timeline, drag the playhead to the end of the clip on Track 2. Holding down the Shift key forces the playhead to snap to the beginning and end of clips, as well as markers on the Timeline.

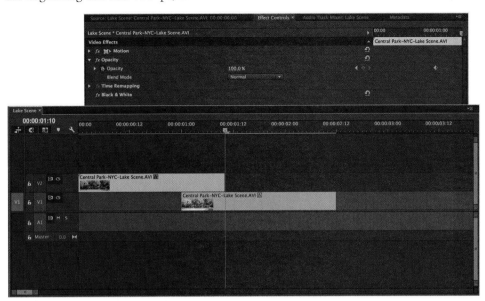

Notice that when you move the playhead in the Timeline, it also moves in the mini-Timeline display in the Effects Controls panel.

7   In the Effects Controls panel, change the value of the clip's Opacity to **0** (zero). This automatically adds a keyframe at the end of the clip where Opacity is 0. You now have a starting and ending value for the property that Premiere Pro can animate.

Since the mini-Timeline view only shows the duration of the active clip, keyframes at the very beginning and end of clips can be hard to see.

8   Press the Enter (Windows) or Return (Mac OS) key on your keyboard to render all areas of the Timeline that need rendering.

When the rendering is done, Premiere Pro previews the Timeline automatically. Notice that the Black & White clips fades out to reveal the full color one.

The contrast in the Black & White clip is weak; you will adjust this in the next part of the lesson.

9   Choose File > Save or press Ctrl+S (Windows) or Command+S (Mac OS) to save these changes. Do not close the file; you will need it in the next part of the lesson.

Adjusting the tonality of clips

Sometimes you want to use the effects available to you in Premiere Pro for artistic purposes, while at other times you can use them to correct or adjust footage that isn't perfect. You can use the Levels effect to enhance the tonality of your image, which is useful when correcting footage that has a lighting aberration or low contrast, or to create a dramatic or artistic effect. For this exercise, notice that after applying the Black & White effect to the first park video clip, it now appears washed out and dull. The problem occurred because the video has a very limited tonal range, so the darkest areas are not very dark and the lightest areas are not very bright. The variation between the lightest and darkest areas of an image is called the contrast, and you can adjust it using video effects.

In this section of the lesson, you will add an effect to the black-and-white clip to adjust its tonal variation and create a greater amount of contrast.

1 With the **pr0701-working.prproj** project still open, type the word **levels** in the search field of the Effects panel to reveal two video effects: Auto Levels and Levels. You can use these effects to adjust the tonal variation of a video clip. The Levels effect lets you control the amount of tonal adjustment; the Auto Levels effect adjusts the video clip to meet a set base standard.

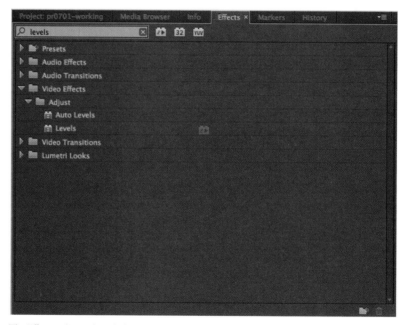

The Effect panel's search results become more refined when you add more letters to the search term.

2   Drag the Levels effect from the Effects panel and drop it on the clip on the Video 2 track. The red bar that indicates the video clip should be rendered appears.

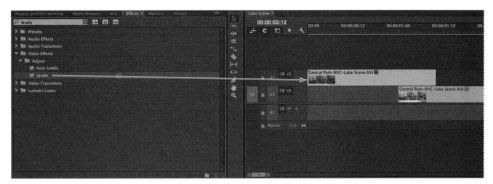

When you apply an effect to a clip, it automatically becomes active so you can edit its properties in the Effect Control panel.

Depending on your computer system configuration, every time you add an effect to a clip or change the properties of an existing effect, you need to render the Timeline again in order to see the results of your effect at full quality. The same applies when you edit the values of any effects properties.

3   Move the playhead to the 15-frame (00;00;00;15) mark on the Timeline panel so you can see the black-and-white clip in the Program monitor. Note that just applying the Levels effect produces no noticeable results because the default settings are neutral. In the next step, you will adjust the property values to enhance the video image.

4 In the Effect Controls panel, you may need to click the reveal triangle to the left of the Levels effect to see all the properties of the effect that you can edit and animate. Depending on your monitor resolution, you might not be able to read the property names because of a lack of space caused by the mini-Timeline displayed on the right of the panel.

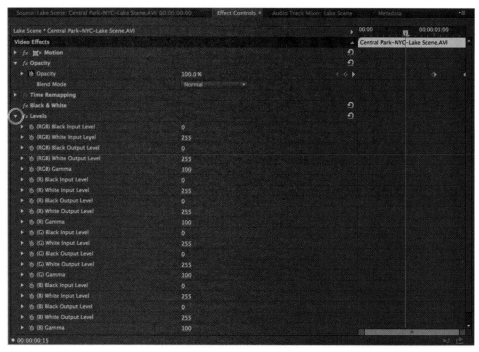

Some effects, such as Black & White, don't have any properties to edit, but many, such as Levels, offer a wide range of editable attributes.

5 Click the Show/Hide Timeline View to collapse the Timeline display and expand the property display to the full size of the Effect Controls panel. Now the full property names are visible.

You can collapse the Timeline view to provide a larger area to edit effect properties.

Controlling tonal variation with levels

In Premiere Pro, the Levels effect doesn't have graphs and sliders to control it as image editing applications such as Adobe Photoshop do. Instead, the Levels effect is controlled through numerical fields. This effect is used to regulate the contrast of a video clip by adjusting the black-and-white input and output levels and gamma of the clip. Changing the black or white input levels increases the amount of dark and light areas in the video, which increases the video's contrast. Changing the black or white output levels of a video clip reduces the dark and light areas of an image, reducing its contrast. If you overly reduce the output levels of an image, your result is a solid gray color. The gamma of a clip is its overall brightness value; adjusting it makes the mid-tone areas of an image darker or lighter.

You can use the Levels effect to adjust the composite image or any of the three individual color channels in the video clip. This allows you to edit the black-and-white input and output levels and the gamma of the Red, Green, and Blue color channels individually. Each of the properties that appear under the Levels effect has a Toggle Animation stopwatch. You can animate almost every effect property in much the same way as you animated the Opacity effect earlier in this lesson.

6   Change the value for the (RGB) Black Input Level to **20**, and then change the value of the (RGB) White Input Level to **240**. Adjusting the Input Levels of Black & White changes the minimum value for which pixels are considered black and white respectively, in the video clip. These new values will effectively increase the range of pixels that are assigned to Black and White in this clip. With a wider range of pixel value assigned to black-and-white, the contrast, which is the variation between the dark and light areas of the image are enhanced.

Click the *fx* button to the left of the Level effect to disable the effect and then view the video clip's appearance in the Program monitor with and without the effect. Do this a few times so you can compare the change effects on the clip's Levels. This is helpful to give you an idea of just how much of a change adding a simple effect can have.

Make sure you turn the effect back on before you advance to the next step in this lesson.

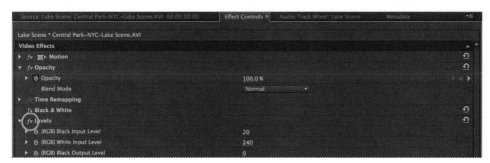

You can toggle effects on and off to easily compare and contrast the effects of your enhancements.

7   Press the Enter (Windows) or Return (Mac OS) key on your keyboard to render all areas of the Timeline that need rendering.

When the rendering is done, the application previews the Timeline automatically. Notice that the contrast of the black-and-white clip is much stronger now.

8   Choose File > Save or press Ctrl+S (Windows) or Command+S (Mac OS) to save these changes to your project.

You can now close this project; you have completed this section of the lesson.

Making quick color adjustments

The Lumetri Deep Color engine is an integrated feature in Premiere Pro that allows you to make quick and powerful color adjustments to video on your Timeline. The integration of the Lumetri engine into Premiere Pro allows you to quickly and easily apply a variety of looks to your footage.

You can find all the footage used in this section of the lesson in the Werewolves in Central Park folder from the Media Library folder.

1   From the Premiere Pro Welcome screen, click the Open Project button, or with Premiere Pro already open, chose File > Open Project. Navigate to the pr07lessons folder you copied to your hard drive and locate the **pr0702.prproj** file.

Double-click the file to open it.

Choose File > Save As. In the Save Project dialog box that appears, confirm that you are still in the pr07essons folder, rename your file to **pr0702-working.prproj**, and click the Save button.

This project contains a sequence called Reporter at Crime Scene. The sequence is composed of a number of different video clips that could all use a little color adjustment to be more visually striking. This is where the Lumetri Deep Color engine comes into play.

2 Choose File > New > Adjustment Layer. In the Adjustment Layer dialog box that appears, confirm that the width and height are set to **1920** and **1080** respectively, the Timebase is set to 23.976 fps, and the Pixel Aspect Ratio is Square Pixels (1.0).

Click OK to create the new Adjustment Layer.

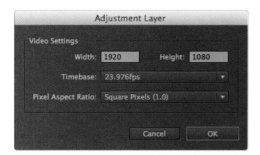

The Adjustment layers settings are based on the settings of the currently active Sequence.

Adjustment Layers are a great way to apply an effect to multiple video files, even if the clips are spread out over multiple tracks.

3 Drag the new Adjustment Layer you just created from the Project panel to the third video track (V3) on the Timeline.

Adjustment Layers are added to the timeline from the Project panel just like any other piece of footage.

4   Upon creation, Adjustment Layers are assigned the same duration as still images. With the selection tool active, place your cursor at the end of the Adjustment layer you just placed on the V3 track. The Selection tool becomes the Trim tool.

Use the Trim Tool (◄|) to lengthen the clip until it extends to the end of the last clip on the V1 track.

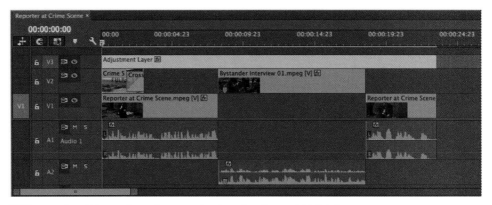

Still images, such as Adjustment Layers, have no set duration and can be extended infinitely.

5   Click the tab of the Effects panel to bring it forward and make it the active panel.

The Effects panel is a library of the effects and transitions available in Premiere Pro.

6   In the Effects panel, click the reveal triangle to the left of the Lumetri Looks folder, and then click the Cinematic folder to preview the available looks in this group.

The groups of looks included with Premiere Pro include Cinematic, Desaturation, Style, and Temperature.

7   Locate the Cinematic 2 effect and drag it onto the Adjustment Layer. Notice that the video displayed in the Program Monitor immediately changes. This particular effect enhances the contrast while dampening the brighter colors to produce a more muted look.

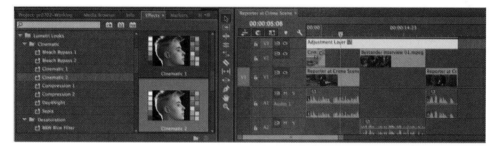

Since their effects are cumulative, multiple Lumetri looks can be applied to the same footage.

8   Choose File > Save or press Ctrl+S (Windows) or Command+S (Mac OS) to save these changes to your project.

You can now close this project; you have completed this section of the lesson.

Using the Warp Stabilizer

The Warp Stabilizer is used to remove jittery and shaky motion most often caused by camera movement. This effect allows the correction of handheld and shaky footage, turning it into a series of steady, smooth shots as if it had been captured using a tripod or dolly.

The media used in this portion of the lesson can all be found in the Media Library folder. All the footage can be found in the Jeff Jacobs Music Video folder.

1   From the Premiere Pro Welcome screen, click the Open Project button, or with Premiere Pro already open, chose File > Open Project. Navigate to the pr07lessons folder you copied to your hard drive and double-click the **pr0704.prproj** file to open it.

   This project contains a single sequence named Using the Warp Stabilizer. This sequence contains a file named Park Scene-Shaky.mpeg on the Video 1 track.

   Choose File > Save As. In the Save Project dialog box that appears, confirm that you are still in the pr07lessons folder, rename your file to **pr0704-working.prproj**, and click Save.

2   With the Timeline active and the playhead at the beginning (00:00:00:00), press the spacebar to preview the clip. This is a shot of two people walking in New York's Central Park. It is a hand-held shot with the camera operator walking behind the subjects. There are jerky movements of the camera which is quite distracting. Move the playhead back to the beginning of the timeline (00:00:00:00) when you have completed previewing the video file.

3   Click the Effects panel's tab to make it active and type the word **warp** into the search field. Drag the Warp Stabilizer effect onto the Park Scene-Shaky.mpeg footage in the Timeline.

The Warp Stabilizer is applied just like any other effect

4   Once applied, the Warp Stabilizer effect automatically runs. It acts as a background process so you are free to perform other actions while it is working on your footage.

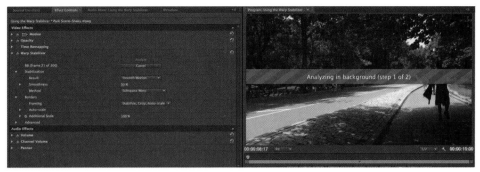

The time it takes to complete the Warp Stabilizer analysis will depend on your computer system.

The Warp Stabilizer Effect

There are several basic options that you should be familiar with when using the Warp Stabilizer:

Result: This property controls the intended results of the Warp Stabilizer effect. The only two options are Smooth Motion, which retains the original camera movement of the footage but attempts to make it appear smoother and less jerky, and No Motion which attempts to remove all camera movement from the video clip.

Smoothness: Controls how much of the original footage's camera motion is stabilized. Lower values preserve more of the camera's original motion while higher values produce a smoother result. Note that this property is only available when the Result is set to Smooth Motion.

Method: Specifies the highest type of operation the Warp Stabilizer attempts to perform on the footage;

Position tracking is based on the X and Y position of the content of your footage and is the simple type of stabilization that can be performed.

Position, Scale, and Rotation stabilization is based on all three of these properties and can provide a better result when the camera is moving through the scene.

Perspective tracking can better stabilize footage that may have perspective shifts.

Subspace Warp attempts to warp different areas of the video frame individually in order to attempt to stabilize the entire frame. If at any time the Stabilizer does cannot locate enough points to perform the selected stabilization, it will fall back to the preceding stabilization type.

Framing property specifies how the borders, (the moving outside edges of the video frame that result from the stabilization effect) appear when the stabilizing result is viewed.

(continues)

The Warp Stabilizer Effect (continued)

Method (continued)

Stabilize Only displays the entire frame including the moving edges. This is good when you want to see how much work is being done by the Warp Stabilizer.

Stabilize, Crop crops the moving Edges without scaling them up. This results in a stabilized video frame that is smaller in size than the original video frame that was stabilized.

Stabilize, Crop, Auto-scale is the default result of the Warp Stabilizer. This crops the moving edges and then scales up the resulting stabilized image to fill the entire size of the original video frame.

Stabilize, Synthesize Edges fills in the space created by the moving edges with content extrapolated from adjacent frames. Users of Adobe Photoshop may find it like a similar, tough, unrelated effect named Content Aware Fill.

5   Press the Enter (Windows) or Return (Mac OS) key on your keyboard to render all areas of the Timeline that need rendering. Rendering time will vary based on your system configuration.

Notice that while there is still camera movement in the footage, it is much smoother after the effect has been applied. When working with the Warp Stabilizer, you might find that the default settings will work in some situations without being adjusted. Such is the case with this footage; however, you might want to adjust properties such as Smoothness to remove a greater or lesser amount of camera shake based on the needs of your specific project.

6   Choose File > Save or press Ctrl+S (Windows) or Command+S (Mac OS) to save these changes to your project.

You can now close this project.

Congratulations, you have completed this lesson.

Self study

Using your own footage or the footage provided with this book, experiment with the different effects in the application and see how they can be used to enhance or alter your footage.

Just a thought about working with green or blue screens: While commercial green screens can be a bit expensive, there are ways to mitigate the costs. To make budget video shoots work filmmakers have been known to use regular fabric stretched on a rack or paint a wall with green or blue house paint and even colored poster board can be used to create quick, portable and cheap green screens. Remember, that with today's sophisticated software, your screens don't have to be the exact chroma key green or blue colors to be effective.

Review

Questions

1   What are the two types of effects that you have access to in Premiere Pro, and how do they differ?

2   In what type of situation might you want to use an effect to adjust the tonality of video footage?

3   What is the Warp Stabilizer used for?

Answers

1   The two types of effects available in Premiere Pro are Fixed Effects and Standard Effects. Fixed effects are the pre-built effects automatically added to every clip on the Timeline. The fixed effects include Motion, Opacity, Time Remapping, and Volume. Standard effects are used to add special qualities to your video, such as adjusted colors, blurriness, or noise. The Premiere Pro application includes several standard effects you can use.

2   Sometimes, you want to use the effects available to you in Premiere Pro for artistic purposes, while at other times you can use them to correct or adjust footage that isn't perfect.

3   The Warp Stabilizer is used to remove jittery and shaky motion most often caused by camera movement.

What you'll learn in this lesson:

- To apply Track Mattes to video clips to create custom transitions

- To create a garbage matte to simplify color keying

- To apply a color key to remove a green screen background

Video Compositing

You can combine video footage together to create a variety of visually appealing and engaging effects.

Starting up

In this lesson, you will work with the project files from the pr08lessons folder. Make sure that you have loaded the prlessons folder onto your hard drive from the supplied DVD. The Starting up section at the beginning of this book provides detailed information about loading lesson files, resetting your workspace, locating missing media, and opening the files in CC. If you have not already done so, please review these instructions before starting this lesson.

When opening the Premiere Pro project files used in this lesson you may experience a missing media message. You must locate any missing media before trying to proceed through the lessons. Please refer to "Locating missing media" in the Starting up section of this book.

See Lesson 8 in action!

Use the accompanying video to gain a better understanding of how to use some of the features shown in this lesson. The video tutorial for this lesson can be found on the included DVD.

Working with Track Mattes

Track Mattes, or Traveling mattes, is a technique used to hide or reveal specific areas of a video clip. This effect is achieved by using another video clip as the source of the track matte. You can use the source clip's alpha or luminance to identify the parts of the target clip that are visible. Alpha is the technical name for transparency; luminance is a measure of brightness of a video image.

A video clip or still image of text, or text created using the Titler, is a common source for track mattes. This technique, called clipping masks in programs such as Photoshop and Illustrator, allows the video or still image text clip to mask the layer below it so you can see an image or video inside the text shape. You can animate track matte sources by adding keyframes for any of the layer's fixed Motion effects.

Preparing the clip for a Track Matte

In this part of the lesson, you will use a 3-second (00;00;03;00) animation of the screen image transitioning from solid white to solid black. You will use this video clip to create a custom transition at the end of the clip on the Video 2 track using the Track Matte Key effect. Since the clip you will use as the source for the effect is only three seconds long, you can't use it on a clip longer than the target video. To fix this problem, you will split the Central Park-NYC-Fountain Scene.AVI so the final three seconds, the section that overlaps the Central Park-NYC-Lake Scene.AVI, form a separate clip. You will then apply the effect to this new split clip. You must prepare the clip this way so the rest of the clip does not become transparent.

The media used in this portion of the lesson can all be found in the Media Library folder. The video (**Central Park-NYC-Fountain Scene.AVI** and **Central Park-NYC-Lake Scene.AVI**) used is located in the video sub-folder of the Travelogue-New York media folder. The QuickTime file (**Animated Track Matte.mov**) used as the track matte here is located in the Graphics folder.

 Please note that users of the Windows operating system must have the free QuickTime player installed to import some video types.

1   From the Premiere Pro Welcome screen, click the Open Project button, or with Premiere Pro already open, chose File > Open Project. Navigate to the pr08lessons folder that you copied to your hard drive and locate the **pr0801.prproj** file. Double-click the file to open it.

   This file contains a single sequence called Applying a Track Matte.

2   In the Timeline panel, ensure the Video 1 and Video 2 tracks are active (highlighted light gray) and if necessary, move the playhead to the beginning of the Central Park-NYC-Lake Scene.AVI clip. This is located at the 15-second and 22-frames (00;00;15;22) mark on the Timeline.

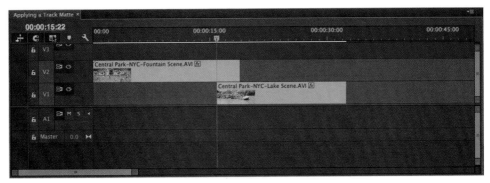

You can click a track label (V1, V2, etc.) to toggle that track to active or inactive; active tracks appear with a light gray highlight on the track label.

You can move the playhead to the beginning of the clip in several ways:

- *Type the destination time code in the Current Time text field in the upper-left corner of the Timeline panel.*

- *By dragging the playhead toward the clip while holding the Shift key on your keyboard so it snaps to the beginning and end of each clip.*

- *By pressing the Page Down key on your extended keyboard, you limit the playhead from one edit line to the next. The edit lines are the points where one clip ends and the next begins. The playhead must be on a track that's currently active so it can stop at a clip's edit line. Active tracks appear highlighted light gray; clicking a track toggles it from active to inactive.*

3 Click the Central Park-NYC-Fountain Scene.AVI on the Video 2 track to make it active and choose Sequence > Add Edit to cut the clip at the current position of the playhead. The reason you are cutting the clip now is so later, when you apply the Track Matte effect, the effect won't be applied to the entire clip's duration.

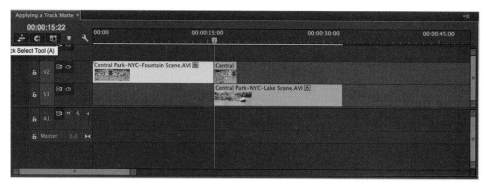

The keyboard shortcut to add an edit is Ctrl+K (Windows) or Command+K (Mac OS).

You can use the Razor Tool ( ) to cut the clip instead of the Add Edit command.

4 Choose File > Save As. In the Save Project dialog box that appears, confirm that you are still in the pr08lesson folder, rename your file to **pr0801-working.prproj**, and click the Save button. Do not close this file; you will need it in the next part of the lesson.

Now that you have separated the clip into two individual clips, the second clip is ready to receive the Track Matte Key effect, which you will add in the next part of this lesson.

Applying and editing the Track Matte Key effect

The Track Matte effect is added to the clip on your Timeline that you want as the target. You must place the source clip in a video track above it, and it should contain an alpha channel or be a high contrast image if you want to use its luminance value for the effect. In this portion of the lesson, you will work with a video file that is a high contrast black-and-white animation created in Photoshop and exported as a video file.

1 With the **pr0801-working.prproj** project still open, double-click the Animated Track Matte.mov in the Video bin of the Project panel to open it in the Source Monitor.

Preview the video by clicking the Play/Stop Toggle button in the Transport controls. Notice that this animation transitions from fully white to black when a series of black squares appear on screen in sequence over a 3-second (00;00;03;00) period. This will be the basis for the custom transition you will create using the Track Matte Key effect.

2 Click the Animated Track Matte.mov in the Project panel and drag it to the Video 3 track. Place it above the second clip on the Video 2 track. It will snap to the beginning of the playhead when you drag it into position.

The Program Monitor turns white when the animation is placed on top of the video clip.

3 Click the Effects panel tab, located in the same group as the Project panel, to make it active. Then in the Effects panel, type the word **track** in the search field. The Track Matte Key effect appears with its container folder, Keying, visible.

Drag the effect to the second Central Park-NYC-Fountain Scene.AVI clip on the Video 2 track.

If you don't use the search field, you can find the Track Matte Key by going to Video Effects > Keying > Track Matte Key in the Effects panel.

4 With the second Central Park-NYC-Fountain Scene.AVI clip selected, click the Effect Controls panel tab to make it active and visible. Since the second Central Park-NYC-Fountain Scene.AVI is currently active this clip's effects are listed in the panel.

Click the Show/Hide Timeline view button to hide the mini-Timeline, and if necessary, then click the reveal triangle to the left of the Track Matte Key effect to see its properties.

You have to double-click a clip to open it in the Source Monitor, but you only need to single-click on a clip to view its effects in the Effect Controls panel.

5   Change the Matte property to Video 3; this is where the animation you want to use as the source of the effect is located.

Change the Composite Using property to Matte Luma. Since this video file does not contain any transparent areas, the default Matte Alpha setting for this property would not produce a result.

6   Press the Enter (Windows) or Return (Mac OS) key on your keyboard to render all areas of the Timeline that need rendering.

When the rendering is done, the application previews the Timeline automatically.

The block animation has now become the transition between the two video clips.

7   Choose File > Save or press Ctrl+S (Windows) or Command+S (Mac OS) to save these changes to your project.

Close this file by choosing File > Close Project; you have completed this section of the lesson.

Using the Ultra Keyer

Chroma keying lets you composite two images together by removing a specific color from one of the images. You can use chroma keying when you shoot video of your subject in front of a blue or green screen and then replace the screen color with a different background. Some examples of using this technique, also called color keying, blue screening, or green screening, is weather reporting on television and films that use virtual backgrounds and set extensions.

Adobe Premiere Pro includes several standard effects used for keying video footage; you used one of these when you created a track matte. The Ultra Key effect combines several different keying effects into one and provides a single point of control for many keying tasks.

The Ultra Key Effect properties

The Ultra Keyer has many important properties that you can adjust to fine tune your chroma keying results. Some of the important, adjustable properties are explained below.

Matte Generation

Transparency: Sets the amount of transparency of the source footage. A value of 100 is fully transparent; a value of 0 is fully opaque.

Highlight: Sets the opacity of lightest areas of the source video footage. You can adjust this property to enhance the transparency of a color screen that lacks a single consistent tone. The available values of this property range from 0 to 100, with a default value of 50. A value of 0 has no effect on the source video.

Shadow: Sets the opacity of dark areas of the source video footage. Use this property to adjust the transparency of a dark element that has become transparent. The available values of this property range from 0 to 100, with a default value of 50. A value of 0 has no effect on the source video.

(continues)

The Ultra Key Effect properties (continued)

Tolerance: Filters out colors that have seeped into the foreground area from the background, such as those caused by color spill. Increase the tolerance to allow for a greater amount of variation from the chosen key color. The available values of this property range from 0 to 100, with a default value of 50. A value of 0 has no effect on the source video.

Pedestal: Filters out noise in a grainy image. Noise is often caused in video footage because of low light conditions. The available values of this property range from 0 to 100, with a default value of 10. A value of 0 has no effect on the source video.

Choke: Shrinks the size of the alpha channel matte created by the color key effect by tightening or contracting the matte following the contours of your foreground subject. The available values of this property range from 0 to 100, with a default value of 0.

Soften: Softens or blurs the edge of the alpha channel matte created by the color key process using a box blur filter (fractional kernel size). The available values of this property range from 0 to 100, with a default value of 0.

Contrast: Adjusts the contrast: the variation between the lightest and darkest areas along the edge of the matte. The available values of this property range from 0 to 100, with a default value of 0.

Mid Point: Sets the mid-point for the contrast property. The available values of this property range from 0 to 100, with a default value of 50.

Spill Suppression

Desaturate: Sets the saturation of the background color. Use this property to desaturate colors close to being fully transparent; for example, the color fringe at the edge of a foreground subject caused by a background color cast. The available values of this property range from 0 to 100, with a default value of 25.

Range: Sets the amount of color spill that is desaturated. The available values of this property range from 0 to 100, with a default value of 50.

Spill: Adjusts the amount of spill compensation. The available values of this property range from 0 to 100, with a default value of 50.

Luma: Restores the original luminance values of the source footage using the alpha channel created by the keying effect. The available values of this property range from 0 to 100, with a default value of 50.

Color Correction

Saturation: Sets the saturation: the intensity of the color values of the foreground subjects in the source video footage. The available values of this property range from 0 to 100, with a default value of 100.

Hue: Sets the hue: the color values of the foreground subjects in the source video. The available values of this property range from −180° to +180 ° with a default value of 0°.

Luminance: Sets the luminance or brightness of the foreground subjects in the source video. The available values of this property range from 0 to 200, where 0 is black and 100 is 4x the base luminance value. The default value of this property is 100.

Creating a garbage matte

The first step in the chroma keying process is to create a garbage matte to isolate the subject and the area immediately around it. A garbage matte is created quickly and doesn't need to be precise. It is usually just a rough shape that removes any extraneous areas of the video frame that do not need to be removed using a keying effect. When using a green screen, the important area is the one around your subject, especially if they are moving. You will often see parts of the set, such as a light stand, or the frame holding the screen at the edges of the video image; use the garbage matte to remove these areas.

There are three types of garbage mattes you can create in Premiere Pro, which are differentiated by the number of anchor points each has. You can use the 4, 8, and 16 point Garbage Mattes to quickly mask the unimportant areas of a video image before applying the Ultra Key effect.

The media used in this portion of the lesson can be found in the Media Library folder. All the footage can be found in the Jeff Jacobs Music Video folder.

1   From the Premiere Pro Welcome screen, click the Open Project button, or with Premiere Pro already open, chose File > Open Project. Navigate to the pr08lessons folder you copied to your hard drive and locate the **pr0802.prproj** file. Double-click the file to open it.

    This file contains a single sequence called Using the Ultra Keyer. There are two movie clips within this sequence: Central Park-Laura Walking.mpeg on the Video 1 track, and Jeff Jacobs-Greenscreen CloseUp.mpeg is above it on the Video 2 track.

2   Click the Effects panel's tab to make the panel active and to bring it to the front of the panel group. Then, in the search field, type the word **garbage** to reveal all the Garbage Matte effects in Premiere Pro.

    Drag the Four Point Garbage Matte effect to the
    Jeff Jacobs-Greenscreen CloseUp.mpeg clip on the Video 2 track.

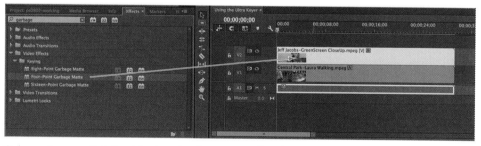

Garbage mattes come with 4, 8, or 16 anchor points that you can use depending on the complexity of the shape you are trying to matte.

3   With the Jeff Jacobs-Greenscreen CloseUp.mpeg clip selected, click the Effect Controls panel to reveal it and make it active. The properties of the effect applied to the **Jeff Jacobs–Greenscreen CloseUp.mpeg** clip are visible in the panel.

Click the Show/Hide Timeline view button to hide the mini-Timeline.

Adding an effect to a clip automatically selects that clip so its properties are immediately accessible in the Effect Controls panel.

4   In the Effect Controls panel, click the effect called Four-Point Garbage Matte to reveal the matte's control points in the Program Monitor.

If necessary, click on the reveal triangle to the left of the Four-Point Garbage Matte effect to view its properties. The matte has a property to set each of the individual corner's control points. Each property has two values: the X (Horizontal) position and the Y (Vertical) position. In the Effect Controls panel display, the first value for each control points property is its X position while the second value is the point's Y position. The idea behind using a garbage matte is to limit the area that the keyer will have to calculate without accidentally removing any part of your subject. A garbage matte is also used to remove any background content that may exist outside of the area you want to key out.

By default, the Four-Point Garbage Matte's control points are positioned at the corners of your clip. Make the following changes to the Properties:

Top-Left: Change the value of the X position (the first value) to **655** and leave the second value as is.

Top-Right: Leave this property as is.

Bottom-Right: Leave this property as is.

Bottom-Left: Change the value of the X position (the first value) to **105** and leave the second value as is.

A small portion of the background clip is now visible because you moved the garbage matte's corner points. Since the subject (the guy singing, Jeff Jacobs) is moving constantly; we have to be very loose with the matte.

Scrub (drag backward and forward on the timeline) the playhead to make sure the matte is not too close to him and avoid removing a part of his body.

The garbage matte need not be perfect since its purpose is to remove extraneous areas.

5   Choose File > Save As. In the Save Project dialog box that appears, confirm that you are still in the Lesson 8 folder, rename your file to **pr0802-working.prproj**, and click the Save button. Do not close this file; you will need it in the next part of the lesson.

Now that the garbage matte is in place, you will apply the Ultra Key effect to the clip in the next step.

Applying the Ultra Key

The Ultra Key effect contains a series of effects to generate color keys quickly and efficiently. All the tools that you need to generate the alpha (transparency) matte by removing the background green color, adjust the edges of the matte to eliminate color spill from the background and even color correct the foreground footage itself are all located in a single location.

1   With the **pr0802-working.prproj** project still open, type the word **ultra** in the search field at the top of the Effects panel to reveal the Ultra Key.

You do not need to capitalize words when using the panel search field.

2   Drag the Ultra Key effect to the Jeff Jacobs-Greenscreen CloseUp.mpeg clip on the Video 2 track.

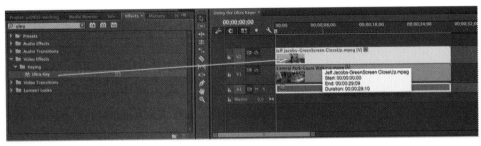

All effects are applied by dragging and dropping them onto clips on the Timeline.

3   If necessary, click the Effect Controls panel to reveal it and make it active. The properties of the effect you applied to the Jeff Jacobs-Greenscreen CloseUp.mpeg clip are visible in the panel.

Again, if necessary click the Show/Hide Timeline view button to hide the mini-Timeline, and then click the reveal triangle to the left of the Ultra Key effect to see its properties.

4   Click the Key Color eyedropper to activate it, and then click the slightly darker green area to the left of the subject's shoulder. The green background is removed, making the background video visible.

The Ultra Key effect removes areas of an image that match the selected Key Color.

5   The area where the Ultra Key effect removes the green screen appears different from the area revealed by the garbage matte, because the screen wasn't a single continuous tone; it had some darker and lighter areas. Some of these areas are still slightly opaque, causing the overlay effect, you. You can see this if you look closely at the Program Monitor.

Click the reveal triangle to the left of the Matte Generation group to view the properties contained there. If necessary you can hide any other revealed properties such as those of the Four-Point Garbage Matte to give yourself more room in the Effect Controls panel.

Change the value of the Pedestal property to **49** to remove the remaining white overlay.

The other properties in this group should be set as follows;

Transparency: **40**   Highlight: **10**

Shadow: **50**   Tolerance: **50**

The Ultra Key is sometimes a one-click solution; however in this case, you have to adjust it to produce optimal results

6 Click the reveal triangle to the left of the Matte Cleanup property group. Change the value of the Choke property to **9** and the value for Soften to **17**.

This completes the adjustments to the effect.

You can animate almost every property in the Ultra Key effect. While not often used for simple greenscreen removal, animating the effect's properties allows to you create special effects such as custom wipes and dissolves.

7 Press the Enter (Windows) or Return (Mac OS) key on your keyboard to render all areas of the Timeline that need rendering. The process could be long because of the complexity of the Ultra Key effect.

When the rendering is done, the application previews the Timeline automatically.

The green screen has been completely removed by the effect.

8 Choose File > Save or press Ctrl+S (Windows) or Command+S (Mac OS) to save these changes to your project. Do not close this project, you will use it in the next part of this lesson.

Spill Suppression and Color Correction

The power of the Ultra Keyer doesn't stop at simply removing the green screen from your video footage. One of this effect's greatest strengths is that it can also be used to adjust the color of your subject; a process that used to require you to add several additional effects. When you shoot video of a subject in front of a green or blue screen, it is very common for some of the screen's color to spill onto your subject. This is especially the case if the subject is too close to the screen itself. Another problem that you may encounter is caused by the different types and strengths of lighting in the subject and background video. Luckily, the Ultra Keyer provides tools that allow you to correct both of these issues.

1   With the **pr0802-working.prproj** project still open and the Jeff Jacobs-Greenscreen CloseUp.mpeg selected in the Timeline panel, locate the Ultra Key effect in the Effect Controls panel. Click on the reveal triangle to the left of the Spill Suppression property group to see the Desaturate, Range, Spill, and Luma properties. You may need to hide other property groups to avoid having to scroll up/down in the panel.

2   Set the Desaturate value to **80**. You should be able to see the color of the video in the Program monitor change: The green tint that his skin and edge of clothing had is now gone.

The Spill Suppression property group removes the tint of the set Key Color.

3   Notice that the foreground figure appears much darker than the background. This is due to the different lighting set-up used in each scene. Click the reveal triangle next to the Color Correction property group in the Effect Controls panel to view the Saturation, Hue, and Luminance properties.

4   Change the Luminance property to **125**. This makes the foreground video brighter and closer to the brightness of the background footage.

5   Choose File > Save or press Ctrl+S (Windows) or Command+S (Mac OS) to save these changes to your project.

You can now close this project; you have completed this part of the lesson.

Self Study

Create your own green screen footage and experiment with replacing it using Premiere Pro. If you don't have a green screen, you can try a green poster board or even a solid blue or green wall as a background.

Review

Questions

1 What is Track Matte used for and what two properties of a source video can be used to create one?

2 What is the purpose of a Garbage Matte?

3 What is chroma keying and what is it used for?

Answers

1 Track Mattes, also called Traveling mattes, is a technique used to hide or reveal specific areas of a video clip. You can make a track matte based on the source clip's alpha (transparency) or luma (brightness) channels.

2 A Garbage Matte removes any extraneous areas of the video frame that do not need to be removed using a keying effect.

3 Chroma keying is a technique used in film and television that lets you composite two images together by removing a specific color from one of them. Chroma keying is used most often when you shoot video of your subject in front of a blue or green screen and then replace the screen color with a different background image or video.

What you'll learn in this lesson:

- To animate the audio level of a file to change volume over time
- To remove audio from a video file to create an independent audio file for editing
- To improve and clean up audio files in Premiere Pro

Working with Audio

Premiere Pro lets you edit audio tracks and audio files. You can add background music, add a narrative track, and clean up background noise to enhance the overall quality of your project.

Starting up

In this lesson, you will work with the project files from the pr09lessons folder. Make sure that you have loaded the prlessons folder onto your hard drive from the supplied DVD. The Starting up section at the beginning of this book provides detailed information about loading lesson files, resetting your workspace, locating missing media, and opening the files in CC. If you have not already done so, please review these instructions before starting this lesson.

When opening the Premiere Pro project files used in this lesson, you may experience a missing media message. You must locate any missing media before trying to proceed through the lessons. Please refer to "Locating missing media" in the Starting up section of this book.

See Lesson 9 in action!

Use the accompanying video to gain a better understanding of how to use some of the features shown in this lesson. The video tutorial for this lesson can be found on the included DVD.

Understanding digital audio

Digital audio is composed of analog sound waves that are captured and converted into a digital file, and its quality is determined by sample rate and bit depth.

The process that converts analog sound into a digital file doesn't actually capture the entirety of the analog source verbatim. Instead it samples the original signal in order to create a digital representation of it. The sample rate is the number of samples that are made in a given time span; usually a second. The higher the sampling rate of a digital file, the greater the quality and clarity. A commercially available audio CD has a sample rate of 44 kHz or 44,100 samples per second.

The bit depth of a file measures the amount of data each sample contains. The greater the bit depth of a digital audio file, the greater its possible dynamic range will be. For example, recordings with a limited dynamic range sound hollow and of low quality, while those with a higher range can better reproduce the natural sound of a range of musical instruments and other audio sources. A commercially available audio CD has a bit depth of 16 bits.

A standard digital camera usually records audio at 48 kHz, or 48,000 samples per second at 16 bits.

Understanding audio tracks

In Premiere Pro you can add audio to your sequences, edit it and also add effects to it. In this application, there are three types of audio files you can come into contact with; mono, stereo and 5.1 surround.

Stereo audio

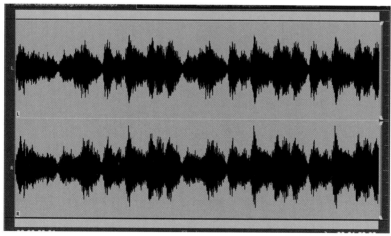

Most on-camera and studio microphones record stereo sound.

A Stereo sound file contains a left and right audio track. In true stereo applications, these two tracks contain different audio signals to create the illusion of directionality; in many cases, the same sounds are duplicated on both channels. Most stock audio, along with audio captured from a camcorder's onboard microphone, as well as audio ripped from compact disks, will be stereo.

Mono audio

Many external mics that can be attached to cameras, record mono audio.

A Mono audio signal contains a single audio track. Many external microphones that you can attach to video camcorders record mono sound.

5.1 audio

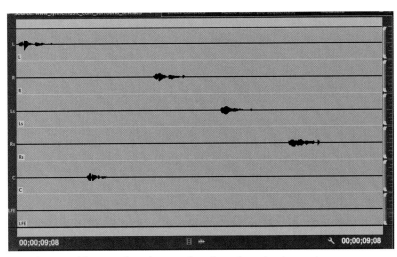

5.1 audio is one of the surround sound types used to enhance the movie going experience.

5.1 Surround Sound uses multiple speakers to surround listeners in a 360° bubble of sound to better simulate the way we perceive sound in a live environment. The 5.1 system uses five speakers and one sub-woofer to achieve this effect and it is the only type of Surround Sound currently supported on the Premiere Pro Timeline.

In Premiere Pro sequences, you can add as many tracks as your computer system's configuration will allow.

Premiere Pro can automatically detect and interact with the audio devices connected to your computer, but occasionally you might need to manually adjust the application's preferences to use a specific audio device. Set up the default audio device to use for input or output by choosing Edit > Preferences > Audio Hardware (Windows) or Premiere Pro > Preferences > Audio Hardware (Mac OS).

As there are different types of audio you can work with in a project, there are also different types of audio tracks you can create in your Premiere Pro sequence. The Standard audio track type can accommodate both Mono and Stereo audio clips, and it is the default track type in the application. The Mono track type only contains a single audio channel rather than the two available with Stereo tracks. If you add a stereo clip to a mono track it is automatically converted into a mono clip. The Adaptive track type can contain both mono and stereo tracks much like the Standard type can, but with adaptive tracks, you can map source audio to different output audio channels. And finally, 5.1 tracks can contain only 5.1 audio clips.

When creating audio tracks in a sequence you can either create a new regular audio track or a sub-mix track. Regular audio tracks are the standard, mono, adaptive and 5.1 options mentioned previously, while sub-mix tracks can be set as the output destination for multiple regular tracks. Sub-mix tracks are useful for managing audio mixes and effects. In this lesson, you will be working primarily with stereo audio files and the standard track type.

Stripping audio from a video file

Occasionally, you might choose to use your camera to record environmental or ambient sound, a particular sound effect, or voiceover because you don't have access to dedicated recording equipment. In such cases, you will need to separate the audio track from the video file you are working with. After you strip the audio from its associated video file, the audio track becomes a separate file that you can add to the Timeline independently or use it in other applications, such as Adobe Audition.

In this part of the lesson, you will extract the audio track from a video file so you can add it to an existing sequence. The file you will work with is a scenic shot from New York's Central Park. You will add it to a still image montage to incorporate environmental ambient sound and help establish a location and emotional feel. You can find the media for this project in the Travelogue-New York folder located in the Media Library folder, in their respective images and video sub-folders.

1 From the Premiere Pro welcome screen, click the Open Project button, or with Premiere Pro already open, choose File > Open Project. Navigate to the pr09lessons folder that you copied to your hard drive and locate the **pr0901.prproj** file. Double-click the file to open it.

This project contains a single video file called Central Park–NYC–Fountain Scene. AVI and a series of still images.

2 Choose File > Save As. In the Save Project dialog box that appears, confirm that you are still in the pr09lessons folder, rename your file to **pr0901-working**, and then click Save.

3 Click the reveal triangle to the left of the Video bin in the project panel to display the **Central Park–NYC–Fountain Scene.AVI** clip in the Project panel. Click this video clip to highlight it.

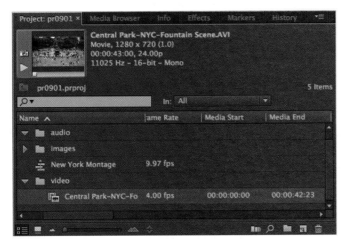

To strip the audio track from a video file, you must first select that file in the Project panel.

Depending on your screen resolution, you might have to scroll the Project panel to make the video bin visible.

4 With the video clip highlighted, choose Clip > Audio Options > Extract Audio to strip the audio track from the file. You do not need to specify any settings with this command. Premiere Pro creates a separate and independent audio file by ripping the audio from the original video clip, just as you would rip audio from a music CD. The new file is created in the same directory that contains your Premiere Pro project file, and then immediately imported into your project.

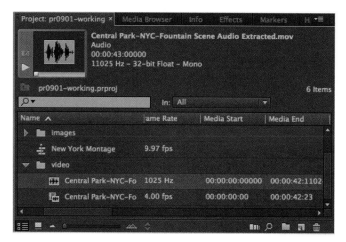

The new audio file is saved in the same bin as the video file from which it was extracted.

Recall that the original video clip stored in your hard drive remains intact. Premiere Pro creates the new audio file by copying the audio data from the original video file.

5 Click the new audio file to select it, then drag and drop it into the audio bin in the Project panel.

6 Right-click (Windows) or Ctrl+click (Mac OS) the new audio file and choose Rename from the menu that appears. Change the file name to **Environmental Sound** and press the Enter (Windows) or Return (Mac OS) key on your keyboard to exit the text editing mode.

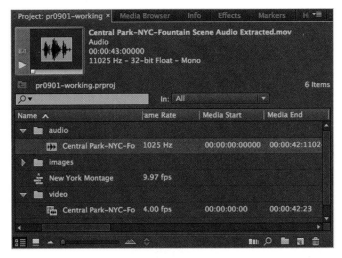

You can also rename a piece of footage by clicking on it when it is already highlighted.

7 Click the Environmental Sound audio file to select it. Drag the audio file to the Timeline panel and drop it onto the Audio 1 track.

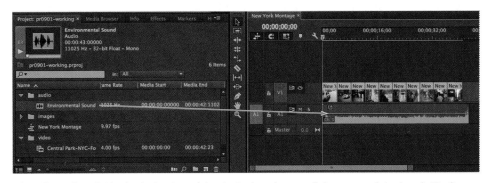

When adding a file to the Timeline by dragging and dropping it, always be aware of where you are placing it on the Timeline.

8   The audio file is a little too long and does not match the duration of the image montage on the Timeline. Activate the Selection tool and position it at the end of the Environmental Sound file on the A1 track. When the Selection tool becomes the Trim tool, click and drag the audio clip's end point until it is aligned with the end of the last image on the V1 track.

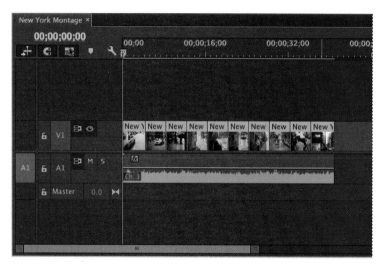

The Selection tool becomes the Trim tool whenever you are near the beginning or end of a clip.

9   Press the Enter (Windows) or Return (Mac OS) key on your keyboard to render all areas of the Timeline that need rendering. Premiere Pro automatically previews the Timeline after rendering; you'll hear the audio playing along with the still images.

10   Choose File > Save or press Ctrl+S (Windows) or Command+S (Mac OS) to save your changes to this file.

Close this file. You have completed this section of the lesson.

Audio channel mapping

Premiere Pro sequences require that you specify the type of track you want to create for audio. Some track types, such as Mono, only accept that type of audio clip while others, such as standard, allow you to mix different clip types together. Since video files could contain a single stereo or mono track, or dual mono tracks, it may sometimes be necessary to adjust how the application is treating an audio clip. Audio channel mapping is the feature in Premiere Pro that helps you perform the desired conversion.

In this part of the lesson, you will change the mapping of a mono audio clip to interpret it as a stereo clip and place it onto a stereo track on the Timeline.

1   From the Premiere Pro welcome screen, click the Open Project button, or with Premiere Pro already open, choose File > Open Project. Navigate to the pr09lessons folder that you copied to your hard drive and double-click the **pr0902.prproj** file to open it.

This file contains a series of audio and video clips already placed on the Timeline, so it does not need much work to complete the project. You can find the media for this project in the Media Library folder. The majority of the media in this project is located in Travelogue-Boston. The background music track called **Classical Background Music.mp3** is located in the Audio folder in Media Library.

2   In the Project panel, double-click the **Shawmut Tours-Booking.wav** file to make it active and open it in the Source Monitor. You will find this file in the Voice Overs bin inside the Audio bin. You might have to enlarge the width of the Name column in the Project panel to make the entire file name visible.

This file has a single waveform, indicating it is a mono audio file, thus containing sound only in one channel. You will remap this file into a stereo file that will duplicate the single channel to both sides, before you can add it to the Audio 1 track on the Timeline.

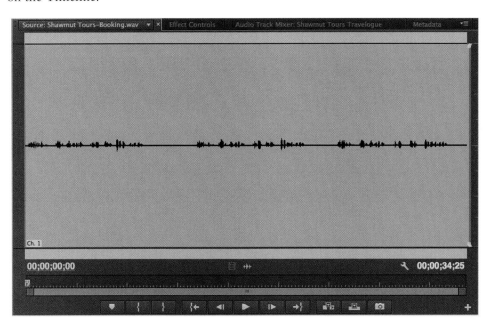

Many external microphones do not record audio as a stereo signal; instead, they create a single mono track.

3   With the Shawmut Tours-Booking.wav clip still selected in the Project panel, choose Clip > Modify > Audio Channels to open the Modify Clip dialog box.

4   In the Channel Format drop-down menu choose stereo. In the Source Channel drop-down that appears choose Channel 1. This will become the right channel when added to an audio track.

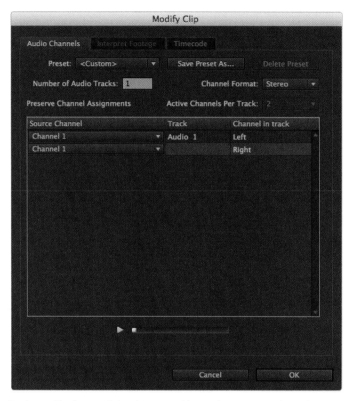

You do not affect the original clip when you modify its audio options; you change the way Premiere Pro interprets it.

You can save your setting in the Modify Clip dialog box by clicking the Save Preset As button and setting a preset name.

5 Click OK to close the dialog box and change the interpretation of the audio clip. The clip's display in the Source Monitor changes: it now has two audio channels, each an exact copy of the other.

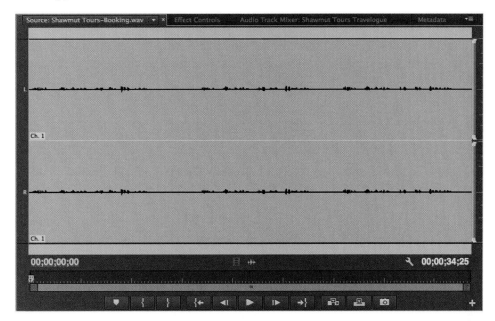

Remapping a tracks audio channels does not affect the original clip that resides on your hard drive.

6 If necessary, click the Source Monitor to make it active, and then press the spacebar on your keyboard to play the clip. The file contains three distinct sets of waveforms, each separated by a short pause.

You should always include multiple takes when recording voiceovers so the editor can choose the take to use. For this lesson, you will use the second take.

You must modify the audio channels of a clip before adding a clip to the Timeline.

7   In the Source Monitor, click the Playhead Position field, type **1303** and press the Enter (Windows) or Return (Mac OS) key on the keyboard to move the playhead to the 13-second and 3–frame mark (00;00;13;03) on the Timeline. This is just before the speaker begins the second voiceover. Press the *I* key on the keyboard or click the Mark In Point button on the lower-right of the panel to set the clip's In Point to the current position of the playhead.

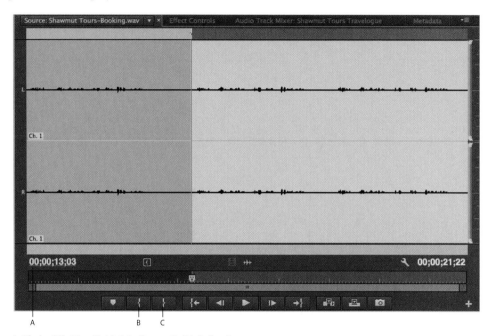

A. Playhead Position. B. Mark In Button. C. Mark Out Button.

8   Click the Playhead Position field, type **2213** and press the Enter (Windows) or Return (Mac OS) key on your keyboard to move the playhead to the 22-second and 13-frame mark (00;00;22;13) on the Timeline. This is just after the speaker finishes the second voiceover.

Press the *O* key on the keyboard or click the Mark Out Point button on the lower-right of the panel to set the clip's Out Point to the current position of the playhead.

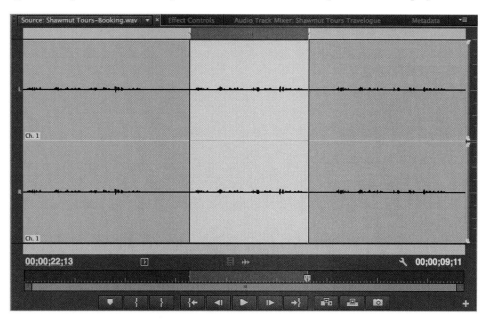

Remember that In and Out points are always set to the current position of the playhead.

9   Click and drag the Drag Audio Only button located below the Source Monitor's visual display to drag the clip onto the Audio 1 track on the Timeline, and position it so it is adjacent to Shawmut Tours–Locations.wav clip on the Timeline.

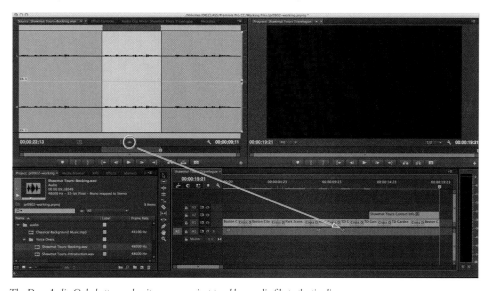

The Drag Audio Only button makes it very convenient to add an audio file to the timeline.

10 Press the Enter (Windows) or Return (Mac OS) key on your keyboard to render all areas of the Timeline that need rendering. Premiere Pro automatically previews the Timeline after rendering.

Choose File > Save As. In the Save Project dialog box that appears, confirm that you are still in the pr09lessons folder, rename your file to **pr0902-working**, and then click the Save button.

Don't close this file; you'll need it in the next part of the lesson.

Adding more audio tracks to the Timeline

You can define the number of audio and video tracks a sequence contains when you create a new one in Premiere Pro. In the process of working with your sequences, you might need to create additional audio tracks for voiceovers, sound effects, background music, or other types of incidental audio not linked to specific video clips. This is a situation where you need to create additional audio tracks.

In this section of the lesson, you will create a new audio track to hold background music for the Shawmut Tours Travelogue project.

1 With the **pr0902-working.prproj** project still open, locate the **Classical Background Music.mp3** clip in the Project panel, and then double-click it to make it active and open it in the Source Monitor. Press the spacebar on your keyboard to preview this file.

This is a two-minute audio clip created to be used as incidental or background music. In this lesson, you will use approximately 20 seconds of this footage as a background audio track for the Travelogue.

2 In the Timeline panel, right-click the empty space below the A1 Track header and choose Add Tracks from the menu that appears to open the Add Tracks dialog box.

When working in the Timeline panel, it matters where you click. Right-clicking in different areas results in different contextual menus appearing.

If you are using a single-button mouse device on the Mac OS platform, hold the Control key on your keyboard and click the mouse device to display the Context menu. Please note that the Mac OS does support the use of the multi-button mouse. If you are using an Apple mouse such as the Mighty Mouse or Magic Mouse, you can enable multi-button functionality by going to the Mac OS system preferences panel and clicking the mouse icon.

3   In the dialog box, set the number of video tracks to add to zero, confirm that the number of Audio Tracks to add is set to 1, and that the track type is set to Standard. You should also confirm that the placement of the track is set to After Audio 1.

You can create additional Audio, Video, and Sub-Mix tracks in the sequence using the Add Tracks dialog box.

Click OK to close the dialog box and create the new stereo audio track.

4   Choose File > Save or press Ctrl+S (Windows) or Command+S (Mac OS) to save these changes to your project. Do not close this file; you will need it in the next part of the lesson.

Making a Three-Point edit on the Timeline

In this exercise, you only need to add a section of the music clip to the Timeline, rather than the entire clip. For such a case, you can effectively use the Three-Point edit. This type of edit adds a portion of the clip in the Source Monitor to the Timeline by setting two markers on the Timeline that define the duration of the clip you want to add, and a single marker in the Source Monitor that defines the starting point of the source. When you add this clip to the Timeline, the two In Points become aligned, and you can then add footage to fill the destination area defined on the Timeline.

In this section of the lesson, you will add the **Classical Background Music.mp3** clip to the Timeline using a Three-Point edit.

1   With the **pr0902-working.prproj** project still open, click the Timeline panel to activate it and if necessary, move the playhead to the beginning (00;00;00;00) of the sequence.

Press the Home button on your computer's extended keyboard to automatically move the playhead to the beginning of the Timeline.

2   With the Timeline panel still active, press the *I* key on your keyboard or click the Mark In Point button on the Program Monitor to add an In Point to the Timeline.

3   Press and hold the Shift key on the keyboard and drag the playhead to the end of the last clip on the Timeline, this will be at the 19-second and 21-frame (00:00:19:21) mark. Press the O key on your keyboard or press the Mark Out button in the Program monitor to insert an Out Point at the end of the Timeline.

Holding down the Shift key while dragging the playhead forces it to snap to the beginning and end of clips on the Timeline. Press the End key on your computer's extended keyboard to automatically move the playhead to the end of the Timeline.

This completes the first part of the preparation for a three-point edit; the Timeline is now ready to receive the clip. Next you will prepare the source clip.

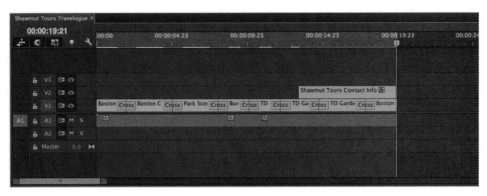

The area of the sequence inside the In and Out points you created is highlighted darker on the time ruler at the top of the Timeline.

4   If necessary, locate the Classical Background Music.mp3 in the Project panel and double-click it to make it active and open it in the Source Monitor. This is the clip you will add to the sequence, but first you must create an In point in the clip to sync with the In Point already on the Timeline.

In the Source Monitor, click in the Playhead Position field, type **2824** and press the Enter (Windows) or Return (Mac OS) key on the keyboard to move the playhead to the 28-second and 24-frame mark (00;00;28;24) on the Timeline.

5 Press the *I* key on the keyboard or click the Mark In Point button on the lower-left of the Source Monitor panel to set the clips In Point to the current position of the playhead.

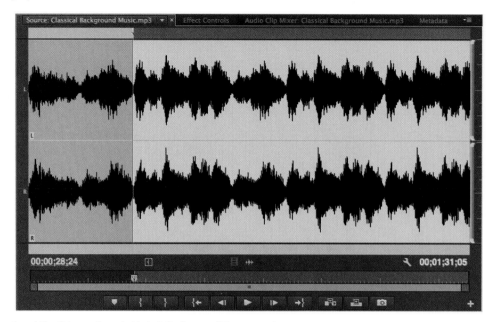

In and Out Points can be marked in both the Source and Program monitors.

6 In the Timeline panel, click and drag the A1 Source Track Indicator to move it to the A2 track.

The Track headers of highlighted and active tracks appear lighter in the Timeline than those that are not active.

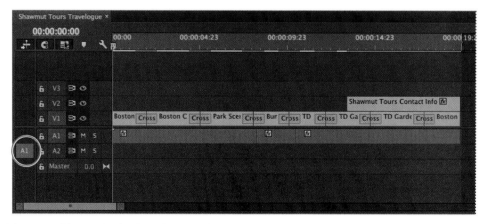

The position of the Source Track Indicator determines where your source material will be placed when you make Insert and Overwrite edits.

7 Press the period key (.) on your keyboard or click the Overwrite button on the bottom-right of the Source monitor to make a Three-Point Overwrite edit. Unlike an Insert edit, an Overwrite edit adds a clip to the Timeline on the selected track without increasing the overall duration of the sequence.

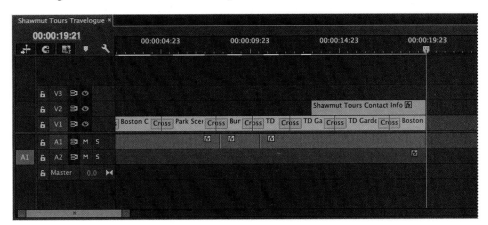

The In and Out Point markers are automatically removed from the Timeline after using an Insert or Overlay edit to add the source clip.

8 Click the Timeline panel to make it active, and then move the playhead to the beginning of the sequence. Press the spacebar on your keyboard to play the Timeline. You can no longer hear the voiceovers because the music is loud; you will correct this in the next few steps.

9 Double-click the Classical Background Music.mp3 clip on the Timeline to make it active and load it into the Source Monitor. This allows you to edit the clip's audio effects in the Effect Controls panel. Click the Effect Controls panel located behind the Source Monitor to make it active and visible.

10 In the Effect Controls panel, click the reveal triangle to the left of the Volume effect to display the Bypass and Levels properties. Changing the Levels property lets you control the volume of the clip.

Use the Levels property to increase or decrease the clip's loudness from a baseline value of zero.

You can animate the Audio Levels of a clip in Premiere Pro using the Effect Controls panel. Unlike most other properties, the toggle animation stopwatch is automatically enabled for all the Volume properties.

11 Click the Levels property Toggle Animation stopwatch to disable animation so you can set a global value that lasts for the entire duration of this clip. Click the Level's property value and change it to −40 to reduce the volume of the clip.

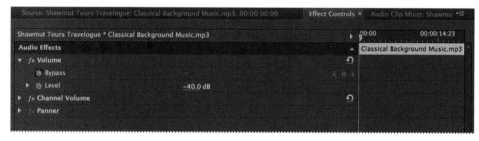

The volume of a clip is measured in decibels.

12 Click the Timeline panel to make it active and if necessary move the playhead to the beginning of the sequence. Press the spacebar on your keyboard to play the Timeline. The background music volume is now at a more manageable level.

13 Choose File > Save or press Ctrl+S (Windows) or Command+S (Mac OS) to save these changes to your project. Do not close this file; you will need it in the next part of the lesson.

Setting volume keyframes

When adding incidental audio to your Premiere Pro sequences, you may obscure other audio that is also on the timeline. Unlike when working with the video in your sequence, where only the top video layer is visible at any time, all audio files play simultaneously. This can make the sound in your video difficult to understand because the background music would play over the dialogue, or the sound effect would overpower the voiceover. This relationship between audio clips makes it extremely important that you are aware of the relative volume of each clip you are using. Premiere Pro can help you solve this issue by animating the volume of any audio clip on the Timeline.

In this section of the lesson, you will add keyframes to the volume property of an audio clip to animate a change in volume over time.

1   With the **pr0902-working.prproj** project still open, click the Timeline panel to activate it and if necessary move the playhead to the beginning (00;00;00;00) of the sequence.

    In the previous lesson, you lowered the volume of the **Classical Background Music.mp3** clip to hear the narration over it; now you will animate the end of the clip so the music fades.

2   In the Timeline panel, place your cursor at the bottom of the A2 track header. When your cursor becomes a double-headed arrow (⇕), click and drag down to enlarge the track height.

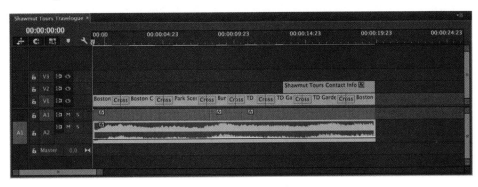

You must first expand a track to see the audio waveform of clips on that track.

3   Click the Playhead Position field located at the upper-left of the Timeline panel, type **1706** and press the Enter (Windows) or Return (Mac OS) key on the keyboard to move the playhead to the 17-second and 6-frame mark (00;00;17;06) on the Timeline.

4   If it isn't currently selected, double-click the **Classical Background Music.mp3** clip on the Timeline to make it active, and then if necessary, click the Effect Controls panel to reveal it once again. Notice that the right part of the panel contains a mini-Timeline view to help you animate clip effects.

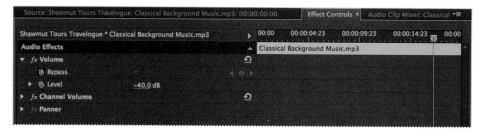

The playhead in the Effect Controls panels Timeline view is a mirror of the one on the Timeline.

You can adjust the size of the Properties and mini-Timeline view in the Effect Control panel by dragging the dividing line between them.

5   Click the Toggle Animation stopwatch to the left of the Level property to enable animation. A keyframe is created at the current position of the playhead.

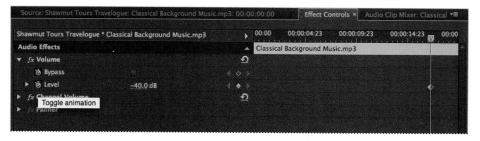

New keyframes are always created at the current position of the playhead when creating animation.

6   In the Timeline panel, press and hold the Shift key on the keyboard and drag the playhead to the end of the last clip, this will be at the 19-second and 21-frame (00:00:19:21) mark. You can also press the End key on your keyboard while the Timeline panel is active.

7   In the Effect Controls panel, change the value of the Level property to **−100**. This creates a new keyframe at the current position of the playhead on the Timeline, and the audio volume fades out toward the end of the clip.

Premiere Pro automatically animates changes when it detects a difference in the values of your keyframes.

8   Click the Timeline panel to make it active and move the playhead to the beginning of the sequence. Press the spacebar on your keyboard to play the Timeline.

9   Choose File > Save or press Ctrl+S (Windows) or Command+S (Mac OS) to save these changes to your project. Do not close this file; you will need it in the next part of the lesson.

Improving audio in Premiere Pro

You might often record audio that has extraneous sounds. For example, you might record voiceovers with background noise from your surroundings; or you might record a scene in a crowded room and pick up some of the surrounding conversations. Your audio could also be too low in volume due to your microphone settings or the speaker being far from the microphone.

In this part of the lesson, you will adjust the voiceover clips to raise the volume and remove the increased background noise created by doing so.

1   With the **pr0902-working.prproj** project still open, double-click the first voiceover clip on the A1 track on the Timeline to make it active. If you hover your cursor over this clip, you will see a pop-up tip that confirms that it is named **Shawmut Tours-Introduction.wav**.

    If necessary, click the Effect Controls panel tab located next to the Source Monitor to reveal it and make it active.

2   In the Effect Controls panel, locate the Level property in the Volume property group and click the Toggle Animation stopwatch to disable animation for this property. Click the value for Level and change it to **6**. This is the highest value to which you can raise the volume, without adding additional effects.

Always remember that 0dB is the baseline audio volume.

3   Press the spacebar on your keyboard to play the Timeline. Notice that the voiceover is now louder than before. Let the preview play into the second voiceover clip to really notice the difference in volume. Notice also that the background noise of the clip has also been increased by the volume change; we will adjust this in a later step.

4   You can add a Volume effect to the clip to increase it further if the initial volume change is not enough. Click the Effects panel to activate it and make it visible; locate the Volume effect by clicking Audio Effects > Volume. Once located, click the effect, then drag and drop it onto the Shawmut Tours-Introduction.wav clip on the Timeline.

You can add audio effects in much the same way as you add video effects.

You can also locate effects by typing either a full or partial name into the Effect panel's search field.

5   A new effect called Volume appears in the Effect Controls panel. If necessary, click the reveal triangle to the left of the new effect to reveal its properties. Change the value of the Level property to **6**.

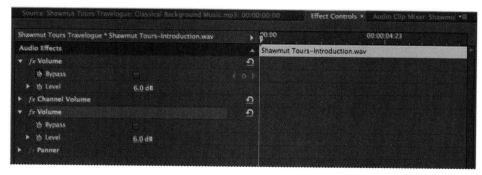

Remember that increasing the volume of a clip also increases the background noise of the clip.

6   Press the spacebar on your keyboard to play the Timeline. Again the voiceover's volume has been increased. Let the preview play into the second voiceover clip to really notice the difference in volume. Notice also that the background noise of the clip has also been increased by the volume change and is even more distracting than it was originally.

7   You can fix the increased noise by applying another filter: DeNoiser.

In the Effects panel, locate the DeNoiser effect in the Audio Effects folder by typing the word **DeNoiser** into the panel's search field. Drag this effect onto the **Shawmut Tours-Introduction.wav** clip on the Timeline.

The DeNoiser properties

The DeNoiser effect automatically detects background noise on a clip and removes it. The effect was designed to remove noise caused by digitizing analog recordings, but you can use it to reduce background noise and drone caused by an improperly sound-dampened recording environment. You can apply the effect to 5.1, stereo, and mono clips.

Reduction: Since the DeNoiser removes sound that is at a certain volume, use this property to set the amount of noise to remove within a range of −20 and 0 dB.

Offset: Sets an offset value between the automatically detected noise level and a value defined by the user. This is limited to a range between −10 and +10 dB. The Offset property allows greater control when the automatic noise detection is not enough.

Freeze: Stops the noise floor interpretation at the currently established value.

8   If necessary, click the reveal triangle to the left of the DeNoiser, and then click the reveal triangle next to Individual Parameters to reveal the Reduction property.

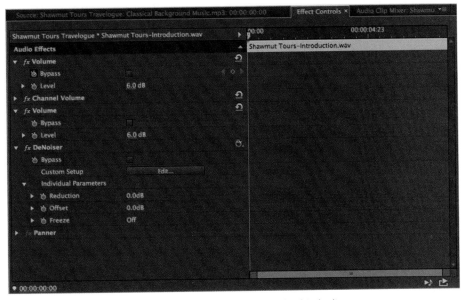

The Reduction parameter is used to set the volume of the sounds that are reduced in the clip.

9   Click the reveal triangle to the left of the Reduction property, and move the slider to the left until the property value reads **−10dB**.

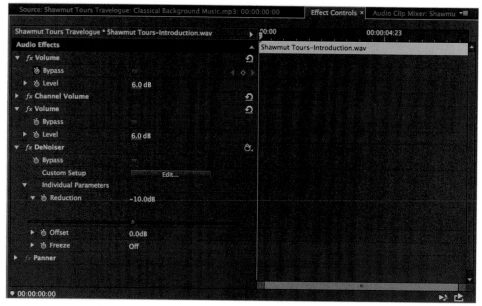

Your own clips will require you to adjust different properties.

10   If necessary, move the playhead to the beginning of the timeline (00:00:00:00) and press the spacebar on your keyboard to play the Timeline. Notice that the voiceover's noise has been significantly reduced. Depending on the specifics of your own clip, you may have to adjust different values.

Effects can be copied and pasted onto other clips by selecting them on your source clip; you can use the Control (Windows) or Command (Mac OS) key to select multiple effects and choosing Edit > Copy. Then select the destination clip or clips and choosing Edit > Paste.

11   Choose File > Save or press Ctrl+S (Windows) or Command+S (Mac OS) to save these changes to your project. Close the project; you have completed this lesson.

Self study

1   Add your own background music track to one of your projects.

2   Add keyframes to it to create multiple fade in and fade out effects.

Review

Questions

1   What are the four types of audio tracks that can be created in a Premiere Pro sequence?

2   How does a Three-Point Edit work?

3   What are the three Individual Parameters available in the DeNoiser effect and what do they do?

Answers

1   The four types of audio tracks that can be created in a Premiere Pro sequence are: Mono, Standard, Adaptive, and 5.1.

2   A Three-Point Edit works by adding a portion of the clip currently loaded into the Source Monitor to the Timeline. The editor then sets two markers on the Timeline to define the duration of the clip to add, and a single marker in the Source Monitor to define the starting point of the source.

3   Reduction: Since the DeNoiser removes sound that is at a certain volume, use this property to set the amount of noise to remove within a range of −20 and 0 dB.

    Offset: Sets an offset value between the automatically detected noise level and a value defined by the user. This is limited to a range between −10 and +10 dB. The Offset property allows greater control when the automatic noise detection is not enough.

    Freeze: Stops the noise floor interpretation at the currently established value.

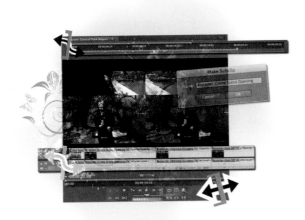

Lesson 10

What you'll learn in this lesson:

- To create subclips to increase your editing freedom

- To make a three-point edit

- To use the Rolling, Slip, and Slide tools

- To use time-remap video to speed up video

Advanced Editing Techniques

You can accomplish many tasks using the Selection and Razor tools, but you will want to understand the more advanced and task-specific tools of Premiere Pro for more complex and detailed editing.

Starting up

In this lesson, you will work with the project files from the pr10lessons folder. Make sure that you have loaded the prlessons folder onto your hard drive from the supplied DVD. The Starting up section at the beginning of this book provides detailed information about loading lesson files, resetting your workspace, locating missing media, and opening the files in CC. If you have not already done so, please review these instructions before starting this lesson.

When opening the Premiere Pro project files used in this lesson you may experience a missing media message. You must locate any missing media before trying to proceed through the lessons. Please refer to "Locating missing media" in the Starting up section of this book.

See Lesson 10 in action!

Use the accompanying video to gain a better understanding of how to use some of the features shown in this lesson. The video tutorial for this lesson can be found on the included DVD.

Creating subclips

An individual video file might contain several takes, shots, or scenes. To manage them more effectively, we recommend separating longer clips into smaller sections called subclips. Creating subclips does not affect the master clips stored on your hard drive because you are not creating additional physical clips. However, Premiere Pro treats subclips much like the master clips, so you can add them to the Timeline and gain greater freedom for assembling your edits.

You can easily make subclips using the Source Monitor: just set In and Out points on a master clip and then use the Make Subclip command.

You can find all the footage for this portion of the lesson in the Media Library within the Werewolves in Central Park folder.

1   From the Premiere Pro Welcome screen, click the Open Project button, or with Premiere Pro already open, chose File > Open Project. Navigate to the pr10lessons folder you copied to your hard drive and locate the **pr1001.prproj** file. Double-click the file to open it.

    This project contains a sequence called Central Park Report and links to videos you can use for A Roll and B Roll.

2   Locate the Reporter at Crime Scene clip in the Project panel. It will be in the A-roll bin, which is inside the Video bin. If necessary, enlarge the width of the panel's Name column to view more of the clip name.

    Double-click the clip to open it in the Source Monitor.

    This clip is about 20 seconds long and contains two distinct areas you can use: the crime scene report and the reporter's sign off. By dividing these two areas into individual subclips, you can experiment with the placement of the resulting clips to craft your scene.

3 To create a subclip, you must first set In and Out points on the master clip:

With the Source Monitor active, move the playhead to the beginning of this clip, and then press the *I* key on your keyboard or click the Mark In Point button in the transport controls area of the Source Monitor to mark the clip's In Point.

By default, a clip's duration is set to the beginning and end of that clip, but you can override this by setting In and Out points.

Notice that the Time Ruler area below the video frame changes color to indicate that you have marked an In point for the clip.

4   Move the playhead to the 9-second and 9-frame mark (00;00;09;09) on the Timeline. This point is in the middle of the pause the reporter makes before beginning her sign off.

Press the letter O key on your keyboard, or click the Mark Out button in the transport controls area of the Source Monitor to mark the clip's Out Point at the current position of the playhead.

You can use the Play In to Out button in the Controls area of the monitor to preview only the content between the clip's current In and Out points.

5   Choose Clip > Make Subclip and in the Make Subclip dialog box change the default name to **Reporter-Crime Scene Opening**. Click the OK button to create the subclip.

New subclips are added to the folder currently selected in the Project panel.

6   Now you will create the second subclip: with the playhead at the 9-second and
    9-frame mark (00;00;09;09) on the Timeline, press the *I* key on your keyboard, or
    click the Mark In button in the transport controls area of the Source Monitor to mark
    the second subclip's In Point at the current position of the playhead.

    This actually creates a clip that is a single frame in duration, but you will adjust this in
    the next step.

7   In the Source Monitor, move the playhead to the 15-second mark (00;0;15;00) on the
    Timeline, and then press the letter O key on your keyboard, or click the Mark Out
    button to mark the subclip's Out Point.

The active area of the subclip you are creating is denoted by the highlighted area of the time ruler.

8   Select Clip > Make Subclip, and in the Make Subclip dialog box that appears, change
    the default name to **Reporter-Sign Off**, and then click the OK button to add the
    subclip to the Project panel.

9   Choose File > Save As. In the Save Project dialog box that appears, confirm that you
    are still in the pr10lessons folder, rename your file to **pr1001-working**, and click the
    Save button. Do not close this file; you will need it later.

    In the next part of the lesson, you will use the subclips you created in this exercise and
    some of the B Roll footage to make a rough cut of the project.

Using Automate to sequence

In Lesson 4, you used the Automate to Sequence command to simultaneously add a series of still images to the Timeline. In this lesson, you will use the same command to add the subclips you created in the preceding part of the lesson.

1   With the **pr1001-working.prproj** project still open, click the reveal triangles for the A Roll and B Roll folders. On the Timeline panel, confirm that the playhead is at the beginning (00:00:00:00) position.

2   Press and hold the Control (Windows) or Command (Mac OS) key on your keyboard, and then click the following files in the order listed here to select them: **Crime Scene Tape.mpeg**, **Reporter–Crime Scene Opening**, **Bystander Interview 01.mpeg**, and **Reporter–Sign Off**.

The selection order of files can be used in the Automate to Sequence dialog box.

You might have to expand the Name fields header to see the full clip names.

3   Choose Clip > Automate to Sequence to open the dialog box that will allow you to add the selected files to your Timeline.

4   In the Automate to Sequence dialog box, confirm that the Ordering pull-down menu is set to Selection Order.

If necessary, set the Placement drop-down menu to Sequentially and the Method drop-down menu to Overlay Edit.

Set the Clip Overlay amount to **0** (zero).

Click the check box fields to disable the Apply Default Audio Transition and Apply Default Video Transition check boxes, and then click the OK button to add the clips to the Timeline.

Like many of the features of Premiere Pro, the Automate to Sequence command can be used in a variety of ways.

5   Click the Timeline panel to highlight it, and then press the = key on your keyboard multiple times until you have zoomed in sufficiently to see all the clips on the Timeline.

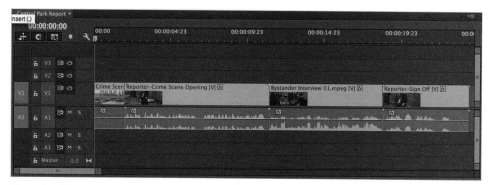

The number of times you need to press the key varies depending on your screen size and resolution.

You can also adjust the magnification of the Timeline with greater control by dragging the handles at the left and right of the Timeline's bottom scroll bar.

6   Choose File > Save or press Ctrl+S (Windows) or Command+S (Mac OS) to save these changes to your project. Do not close this file; you will need it in the next part of the lesson.

Making a Three-Point edit

A three-point edit is an editing technique used to insert a clip from the Source Monitor onto a destination track in the Timeline panel. You accomplish this task by setting a total of three edit points shared between the source and destination.

The three-point edit is a very flexible tool that all editors can utilize. While three point edits can make use of both the Source Monitor and Timeline panel, where you start is entirely up to you. If you have a set duration on the Timeline to fill, you will want to place the In and Out Points on your Timeline and then add an In Point to the clip in your Source Monitor. However, if you have a specific area of your Timeline you need to cover, you can set the In and Out Points in your Source Monitor to define a duration of the clip to insert and then add single point on the Timeline to set the destination for this clip. A good example of this type of Three-Point Edit is when you need to hide a jump cut by covering it with B Roll.

In this section of the lesson, you will create an In Point on the Timeline to set the destination point for the footage that you will insert. You will then create both an In and Out Point on the clip in the Source Monitor to set it's duration.

Setting an In Point on the Timeline

To complete this exercise, you will first set an In Point marker on the Timeline.

1   With the **pr1001-working.prproj** project still open, move the playhead to the 5-second mark (00;00;05;00) on the Timeline. This is where you will insert the new clip.

2   With the Timeline active, press the *I* key on your keyboard, or click the Mark In Point button in the transport controls area of the Program Monitor panel. Notice the time ruler at the top of the Timeline now shows a darker color to indicate you marked an In Point.

This point will become the destination for the clip you will add to the Timeline as part of the Three-point edit.

Three-point edits require a total of three In and Out Points split between the Timeline and Source Monitor.

You can remove an In or Out Point marker on the Timeline by right-clicking (Windows) or Ctrl+click (Mac OS) any area of the time ruler and choosing Clear Sequence Marker > In and Out, In or Out, depending on the type of marker you want to remove.

3   Choose File > Save or press Ctrl+S (Windows) or Command+S (Mac OS) to save these changes to your project. Do not close this file; you will need it in the next part of the lesson.

Setting In and Out Points on a clip

Now that you have added an In Point marker to the Timeline, you will add an In and Out Point marker to a source clip.

1   With the **pr1001-working.prproj** project still open, double-click the clip icon for Crime Scene from Bridge.mpeg in the Project panel to open it in the Source Monitor. You can find the clip in the B Roll bin.

2   In the Source Monitor, move the playhead to the 39-second mark (00;00;39;00) on the Timeline and then press the *I* key on your keyboard or click the Mark In Point button in the transport controls area of the panel to set the In Point of this clip.

A three-point edit requires a total of three markers to be shared between the Timeline and the Source Monitor.

3   In the Source Monitor, move the playhead to the 41–second and 14-frame mark (00;00;41;14) and then press the *O* key on the keyboard or click the Mark Out Point button located in the panel's transport controls area.

During this Three-Point edit, Premiere Pro automatically aligns the two In points.

4   Once you set the source clip's In and Out Points, you can add the clip to the Timeline: click the A1 target track indicator to deactivate it. This action disables the audio track so that only the video from the source clip will be added to the timeline.

Confirm that the V1 target track indicator is active and the V1 track is selected.

Keep in mind that both of these actions must be performed for this Three-Point edit to work properly.

Perform an Overwrite Edit by clicking the Overwrite button in the transport controls area of the Source Monitor, or by pressing the period (.) key on your keyboard.

An overlay edit is helpful when you want to overwrite or superimpose footage on the Timeline without increasing the length of your overall timeline.

5   Choose File > Save or press Ctrl+S (Windows) or Command+S (Mac OS) to save these changes to your project. Do not close this file; you will need it in the next part of the lesson.

Making Ripple and Roll Edits

You can use the Selection and Razor tools to perform many tasks in Premiere Pro; however, some tasks require more specialized tools. This section and the following two describe these specialized tools, beginning with the Ripple and Rolling Edit tools.

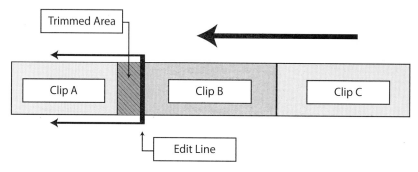

A Ripple edit.

The Ripple Edit tool is used to trim a clip while shifting the subsequent clips in the Timeline by the amount of the trim. A Ripple edit is useful when you want to trim a clip without leaving a gap, as happens when trimming clips with the Selection tool. When making a Ripple edit between two adjacent clips, the Program Monitor displays a different preview on the left and right of the monitor: the preview on the left shows the Out Point of the first video; the one on the right displays the In Point of the second video. The previews update dynamically as you adjust the edit line between the clips.

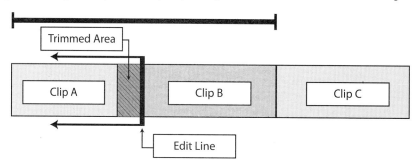

A Rolling edit.

The Rolling Edit tool is used to simultaneously trim an adjacent Out and In point by shifting the edit point between the two clips while preserving the overall duration of these adjacent clips. A Rolling edit is helpful when you need to adjust the edit point between a pair of clips to refine an edit. Just as with a Ripple edit, the Program Monitor displays a side-by-side preview of In and Out points as you change them.

In this part of the lesson, you will use Ripple and Rolling edits to refine the current sequence. In this and subsequent exercises within this lesson, you will use the playhead for convenience and consistency when setting a destination point for your trim. However, when you perform your own edits, you will likely use the Program Monitor previews to find match points, and then make your edit points based on those.

1   With the **pr1001-working.prproj** project still open, move the playhead to the 1-second and 1-frame mark (00;00;01;01) on the Timeline panel.

2   Click the Ripple Edit Tool (**+**) on the Tools panel to activate it, and then move your mouse cursor to the end of the first clip on the Timeline (the clip initially called **Crime Scene Tape.mpeg**). You may need to zoom in on the Timeline for your convenience.

You can activate the Ripple Edit tool by pressing the letter B on your keyboard.

3   When the cursor is properly positioned at the beginning or end of a clip on the Timeline, it automatically becomes the yellow Ripple Edit tool (⁺). Use this tool to click the end of the first clip and drag it to the playhead.

The Ripple Edit tool automatically snaps to the playhead when it is close enough.

As you perform a Ripple Edit, the Program Monitor displays two previews: the first is the changing End Point of the clip you are trimming; the second is the In Point of the clip that follows it. When you release your mouse cursor, all the clips to the right of the trim automatically shift positions to avoid creating a gap.

The Program Monitor preview helps you find a match point between the two clips.

4 In the Timeline panel, move the playhead to the 5-second mark (00;00;05;00) and then click the Rolling Edit tool in the Tools panel to activate it.

You can activate the Rolling Edit tool by pressing the letter N on your keyboard.

5 Move the mouse cursor to the edit line between the second and third clips, until the cursor becomes the Rolling Edit Icon (⌗).

6   Click and drag the Rolling Edit tool to the playhead.

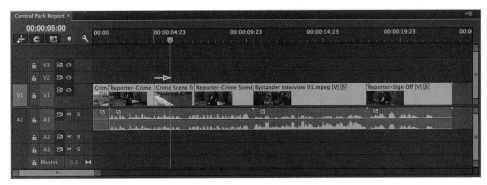

Just as the other editing tools, the Rolling Edit tool automatically snaps to the playhead when it is close to it. Ensure the Snap button is enabled on the Timeline.

The Program Monitor displays two video previews as you adjust the edit point with the Rolling Edit tool. The preview on the left shows the changing Out Point of the clip on the left side of the edit line; the preview to the right shows the changing In Point of the clip on the right side of the edit.

The Program Monitor preview helps you find a match point between the two clips, just as it does when you make a Ripple edit.

The combined duration of the two clips remains unaffected because the Rolling Edit changes the location of the edit point where the two clips join. For this exercise, the result is that the long shoot of the crime scene from the bridge is reduced.

7   Choose File > Save or press Ctrl+S (Windows) or Command+S (Mac OS) to save these changes to your project. Do not close this file; you will need it in the next part of the lesson.

Making Slip and Slide Edits

You will usually use the Slip and Slide edit tools with clips that are adjacent to one another in a sequence, but the tools will also work when used on a clip that has blank space on one side.

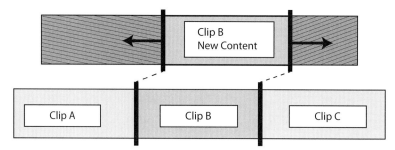

Slip Edit.

You can use the Slip tool to shift a clip's In and Out Points without affecting clips that are adjacent to it; an effect Premiere Pro accomplishes by changing the In and Out Points of the clip by the same amount without changing the overall duration of that clip. When using the Slip tool, the Program Monitor displays previews of the In and Out Points of the clip you are adjusting and of the fixed Out and In points of the preceding and following clips on the Timeline.

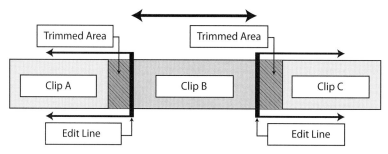

Slide Edit.

You can use the Slide tool to shift a clip along the Timeline while trimming adjacent clips to compensate for the move. Since you use the Slide tool on the clip's In and Out Points, the clip's duration does not change, but the Out Point of the clip to the left and the In Point of the clip to the right are trimmed by the amount of frames by which you slide the clip. When using the Slide tool, the Program Monitor shows a preview of the clip you are sliding, a preview of the changing Out Point of the preceding clip, and a preview of the In Point of the following clip.

1   With the **pr1001-working.prproj** project still open, move the playhead back to the beginning (00;00;00;00) of the Timeline since you do not need it in any particular position to make a Slide edit.

2 In the Tools panel, click the Slip tool (⟷) to activate it, and then position it on top of the third video clip in the Timeline, the one called **Crime Scene From Bridge.mpeg**.

You can activate the Slip tool by pressing the letter Y on your keyboard.

3 In this clip, there is a figure lurking on the bridge watching the crime scene report unfold. It might create a sense of drama to show him in the shot. To do this, you will perform a Slip edit.

Place the Slip tool over the **Crime Scene from Bridge.mpeg** clip and then click and drag it to the right to begin the edit.

Watch the Program Monitor as you are performing the edit. The two small previews at the top are the Out and In points of the preceding and following clips. The two large previews are the new In and Out points you are moving through as you Slip the clip. At the bottom-left of the Monitor there is a time code display; continue to adjust the clip until the display reads +00;00;03;10.

The Program Monitor Overlays will read 00:00:43:10 for the clip's new In Point and 00:00:45:00 for the clip's new Out Point.

The Program Monitor display lets you choose new match points for the beginning and end of the clip.

4 Move the playhead to the 3-second and 15-frame mark (00;00;03;15) on the Timeline, and then click the Slide tool (⟷) in the Tools panel to activate it.

You can activate the Slide tool by pressing the letter U on your keyboard.

5 You might have a better, more dynamic scene if the cut to the figure lurking on the bridge occurred sooner. To accomplish this, you will perform a Slide edit.

Using the Slide tool (↔), click the **Crime Scene From Bridge.mpeg** clip and drag it toward the playhead.

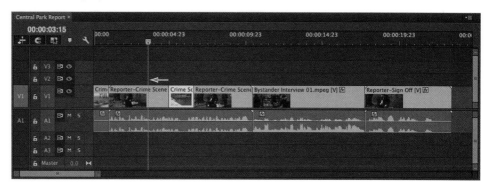

Similar to the other editing tools, the Slide tool snaps to the playhead automatically when the Snap button is enabled on the Timeline.

Notice that the Out Point of the preceding clip and the In Point of the following clip adjusted automatically as you slid the **Crime Scene From Bridge.mpeg** clip. Also notice that the Program Monitor previews the In and Out Points of the clip you are sliding and the new Out and In Points for the preceding and following clips.

We strongly recommend using the Program Monitor previews when using the Slide tool.

6 Move the Playhead to the beginning of the Timeline, and then press the spacebar to preview the edits you have just made.

7   Choose File > Save or press Ctrl+S (Windows) or Command+S (Mac OS) to save these changes to your project. Close this file; you have completed this section of the lesson.

Adjusting the clip speed

Video clips usually play back at the same frame rate at which they were shot. However, you can choose to speed up or slow down a clip to create different effects. For example, you could speed up a group of adjacent clips to show the passage of time or show movement from one place to another; or you could slow down adjacent clips to create a slow-motion effect.

You can find all the footage used in this section of the lesson in the Travelogue-New York folder in the Media Library.

1   From the Premiere Pro Welcome screen, click the Open Project button, or with Premiere Pro already open, chose File > Open Project. Navigate to the pr10lessons folder you copied to your hard drive, and then locate the **pr1002.prproj** file. Double-click the file to open it. This project contains a sequence called Adjusting Clip Speed that contains two clips for which you will adjust the speed.

Choose File > Save As. In the Save Project dialog box that appears, confirm that you are still in the pr10lessons folder, rename your file to **pr1002-working**, and click Save

2   If necessary, move the playhead to the beginning of the Timeline and then press the spacebar to preview the Sequence. Notice the speed at which the first video clip plays. You can stop the playback at anytime by pressing the spacebar again.

3   In the Timeline, move the playhead to the 30-second mark (00;00;30;00) and click the Rate Stretch tool (↔) in the Tools panel to activate it.

4   Move the cursor to the end of the first clip. The cursor becomes the Rate Stretch tool (↔).

5   Click the end of the clip and drag the tool to the playhead until it snaps to the playhead.

Use the Rate Stretch tool to slow down or speed up a clip's speed.

6   The Rate Stretch tool leaves a large gap between the two clips after you are done. Right-click in the gap and choose Ripple Delete from the menu that appears.

An alternative to using the Ripple Delete command is to manually select and drag the clips on your Timeline to remove gaps.

7   When you change the speed of video footage, this change can often result in the video acquiring a jerky motion. To correct this, you can enable Frame Blending, a technique that visually merges frames together to create a smoother transition between frames.

Right-click the first clip, and from the menu that appears, choose Frame Blend.

8   Press the Enter (Windows) or Return (Mac OS) key on your keyboard to render all areas of the Timeline that need rendering. Premiere Pro automatically previews the Timeline when the rendering is done.

Notice that the clip plays back faster. Click on the Selection tool in the Tools panel to make it active.

9   You can also adjust the playback speed of a clip on the Timeline with the Speed/ Duration dialog box:

In the Timeline panel, right-click the second clip and choose Speed/Duration from the menu that appears.

10 In the Speed/Duration dialog box, you can adjust the clip by setting a new Speed at which you want the clip to play, set a new final duration, or reverse a clip to play backward to forward on the Timeline.

Change the speed of this clip by clicking the current Speed value and changing it to **200**; click the OK button. The clip plays back at twice the original speed.

You can also adjust the speed of a clip by setting a new duration if you need to fit the clip to a specific point on the Timeline.

11 Right-click the second clip, and from the menu that appears, choose Frame Blend.

12 Press the Enter (Windows) or Return (Mac OS) key on your keyboard to render all areas of the Timeline that need rendering. Premiere Pro automatically previews the Timeline when the rendering is complete.

As you can see, both clips now play back considerably faster than normal. You can use such effects as transitions or to bridge gaps between points in space or time in a story.

When you adjust the speed of a video clip, the resulting motion can appear jerky. You can compensate for this by enabling the frame blending effect.

13 Choose File > Save to save the changes you have made to the file. You can now close this file. Congratulations, you have completed this lesson.

Self study

Use the tools described in this lesson along with the Selection and Razor tools to edit **pr1001-working.prproj** and create a more cohesive sequence.

You can also experiment with the options available to you with the Rate Stretch tool and Speed/Duration dialog box by adjusting the speed of your own video clips.

Review

Questions

1 A three-point edit is an editing technique used to insert a clip from the _____ onto the destination track in the _____ panel. You can accomplish this task by setting a total of _____ edit points shared between the source and destination.

2 Describe a Ripple Edit and a Roll Edit.

3 Describe how the Slip and Slide edit tools are used in Premiere Pro.

Answers

1 A three-point edit is an editing technique used to insert a clip from the <u>Source Monitor</u> onto the destination track in the <u>Timeline</u> panel. You can accomplish this task by setting a total of <u>three</u> edit points shared between the source and destination.

2 A Ripple edit is used to trim a clip while shifting the subsequent clips in the Timeline by the amount of the trim.

A Roll edit is used to trim an adjacent Out and In Point simultaneously by shifting the edit point between the two clips while preserving the overall duration of these adjacent clips.

3 The Slip tool is used to shift a clip's In and Out Points without affecting adjacent clips. It accomplishes this by changing the In and Out Points of the clip by the same amount without affecting the overall duration of the clip.

The Slide tool is used to shift a clip along the Timeline while trimming adjacent clips to compensate for the move. Since you use this tool on a clip's In and Out Points, its duration remains fixed, but the Out Point of the clip to the left and the In Point of the clip to the right are trimmed by the amount of frames you slide the clip.

What you'll learn in this lesson:

- To understand the different output formats
- To use the properties of video files
- To export a file for deployment to mobile devices

Outputting Your Video

After editing is completed, you will want to export the video for use in broadcast, on-line, or DVD. In this lesson, you will gain an understanding of options for deployment and factors that influence the quality of exported video.

Starting up

In this lesson, you will work with the project files from the pr11lessons folder. Make sure that you have loaded the prlessons folder onto your hard drive from the supplied DVD. The Starting up section at the beginning of this book provides detailed information about loading lesson files, resetting your workspace, locating missing media, and opening the files in CC. If you have not already done so, please review these instructions before starting this lesson.

When opening the Premiere Pro project files used in this lesson you may experience a missing media message. You must locate any missing media before trying to proceed through the lessons. For more information refer to "Locating missing media" in the Starting up section of this book.

See Lesson 11 in action!

Use the accompanying video to gain a better understanding of how to use some of the features shown in this lesson. The video tutorial for this lesson can be found on the included DVD.

Output for the Web and desktop

In recent years, the Internet has become a popular medium in which to display video projects, especially because bandwidth has increased and the Internet offers better support for rich media. In addition, and with the proliferation of corporate video, Premiere Pro can and has been used to create content for presentation graphics and mobile devices. However, Premiere Pro continues to be a tool for storytelling and a way of creating engaging video projects that you can deploy to any medium.

When you create video for the World Wide Web or for computer systems, you should be aware that there is no single standard for web and desktop video, and there are several types of video players, some of which are explained in the next subsections.

Flash video and the Flash player

Flash video is the native video format supported by the Adobe Flash platform and it is widely used in the delivery of online video content, which makes it the most ubiquitous video format on the Web. Flash video is widely used by companies and individuals for its ease of deployment and player customization.

Windows Media and the Silverlight player

Windows Media Video (WMV) is the video format created by Microsoft, the makers of the Windows operating system. A variation of WMV is used for Silverlight video, which has been used by companies such as NBC Sports for their live Olympics coverage and Netflix for delivering streaming video content. Windows Media is also a supported format on some multimedia players and mobile devices, such as the Zune and Windows-based phones.

QuickTime video and the QuickTime player

The QuickTime format is controlled by Apple computers and for years was the de facto standard for web-delivered video. The QuickTime player is freely available, it is compatible with MAC and PC operating systems, and it is required to view QuickTime movie files. QuickTime video format is also supported on some mobile devices, such as the Apple suite of iPods and iPads. In addition, you must have this player when using Premiere Pro on a computer running the Windows operating system.

HTML5 Video

HTML5 (Hyper Text Markup Language) includes features that let you play video without the need for a plug-in, such as Adobe Flash or Microsoft Silverlight. Currently there are two competing standards for native HTML5 video support: H.264 and OGG Theora. A disadvantage of native HTML5 video is that different browsers could choose to support one video standard over another. In addition to its use as one of the HTML5 video standards, H.264 video has also become a de facto format for desktop based distribution. Since it's tied to a single specific player like Windows Media or Apple QuickTime, you can play H.264 video using a wider variety of applications.

Understanding formats and codecs

The difference between codecs and video formats can be confusing. Most computer users are familiar with the term *format* when describing files. For example, people with a design or graphics background are familiar with files of different formats, such as JPEG or TIFF; casual computer users are familiar with formats such as Word documents or PowerPoint files. However, when you are working with video, you need to understand more than the format. Video formats such as QuickTime, AVI, Windows Media, and Flash Video are containers, much like a briefcase. The contents of the briefcase are written in a specific language that you need to understand. This is the relationship between formats and codecs: formats are the containers, and the codecs are the language the contents are written in.

Codec is a conjunction of the words *compressor* and *decompressor*. Codecs are mathematical algorithms used to reduce audio and video files to manageable sizes. Video files can be very large; for example, 20 minutes of NTSC DV video from a standard definition miniDV camcorder is over 4 GB in size, which is the capacity of one single layer DVD. Without codecs, you could not easily store and save video footage for archiving, and you could never watch video online, by e-mail, or on a mobile device. To view an audio or video file, you must have a player compatible with the format and you must have the same codec used to compress it available on your computer so you can decompress it.

For example, suppose a friend shoots a short video of his dog doing a back flip, edits it, adds background music and sound effects, creates a QuickTime Movie using the H.264 codec, and e-mails it to you. To view the video, you open the movie in the latest version of QuickTime Player, VLC Media player, or one of several other media players that support the playback of QuickTime files, and it plays without a problem: you are able to see the video because you have a player that is compatible with the QuickTime Movie format (.MOV) and you also have the H.264 codec installed on your computer. You probably didn't install the codec yourself: Your operating system comes with some codecs installed and many popular media players automatically add additional codecs when you install them.

When working with video editing and animation programs, you might encounter issues of format incompatibility that will not let you import or view specific file types; however, often the problems are caused by missing or unsupported codecs.

Understanding temporal and spatial compression

There are two types of compression that video codecs use to reduce file sizes: temporal and spatial. Some formats use one or the other compression type, but most formats use both types to reduce audio and video files to manageable sizes.

Spatial compression is very similar to the compression used in image formats such as JPEG and GIF. This image compression is usually lossy, works on each frame in a video file individually, and it is sometimes called intraframe compression.

Temporal compression, also called interframe compression, compares a video frame to the one preceding it and only saves the data that is different between the two frames. This type of compression can become problematic if the original frames are removed or damaged.

As mentioned above, codecs can use either or both types of compression. Codecs that only use spatial compression, such as the DV codec, are preferable for editing because frames can be independent from each other. Codecs that use temporal compression, such as MPEG-2, offer better compression ratios, but can be problematic for editing because of the interrelationship between frames.

Understanding bit rate

Bit rate is the amount of data allocated to each second of video, and it is a major determinant of file quality. Usually the bit rate value is displayed as kbps (kilobytes per second); for example, the average bit rate of DVD video is 5,000 kbps. In general, the higher the bit rate of a video file, the better the quality will be. These are some comparative examples: Standard Definition DV 25 (mini DV) footage is approximately 25,000 kbps; DVD quality video is approximately 5,000 kbps; VHS video has a bit rate of approximately 1,200 kbps. Understanding the relationship between a file's bit rate and its quality can help you determine the best export settings for your video project.

Understanding frame rate and resolution

Video is a series of individual images shown in quick succession. The frame rate of video is measured by the number of frames it contains each second, and it is usually denoted as fps. Different video standards have different frame rates; some support a variety. American television is broadcast at 30 fps, PAL is 25 fps, and film uses a frame rate of 24.

In design, resolution is a term that refers to pixel density: the number of pixels in a given amount of space, usually an inch, and denoted in ppi (pixels per inch). For example, images created for high-quality magazines are usually 300 ppi; images created for the Web usually have a resolution of 72 ppi. In the field of video and digital photography, resolution refers to the pixel dimensions of an image; in other words, the number of horizontal and vertical pixels that compose the image. In this field, ppi is not used to address resolution.

When creating or optimizing graphics in pixel-based programs, such as Photoshop, the default resolution for video graphics is 72ppi, as it is for web graphics. Vector-based applications, such as Illustrator, don't use pixels and only let you set the pixel dimensions of your project file.

Understanding aspect ratio and pixel aspect ratio

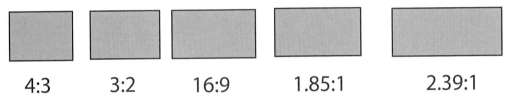

4:3   3:2   16:9   1.85:1   2.39:1

Different devices and camera formats can often have radically different aspect ratios.

Aspect ratio and pixel aspect ratio can be confusing when working with video formats. The aspect ratio, also called image aspect ratio, is the proportion of the width of an image to its height. This value is usually expressed as two numbers separated by a colon; for example, 4:3 or 1.85:1. Sometimes, aspect ratio can be referred to in more generic terms, such as standard and widescreen mode. In videography, the two most common aspect ratios are 4:3 (sometimes denoted as 1.33:1) for standard definition display and 16:9 (sometimes denoted as 1.78:1) for widescreen or high definition formats. Film uses different aspect ratios than video and broadcast television; two well-known ones are 1.85:1 and 2.39:1, which accommodate a wider vista and can better simulate human vision.

The differences in aspect ratio become apparent when video is displayed on a television screen with an aspect ratio different from that of the video itself. For example, when displaying widescreen video (16:9, 1.85:1, 239:1) on a 4:3 television or computer monitor, the video covers the full width of the screen, but two black boxes appear at the top and bottom of the screen in a technique called letterboxing. You can see this effect when you play a film transferred to DVD on a television or computer monitor. Footage that is created using a 4:3 aspect ratio, and then displayed on a widescreen device might appear with black bars to each side in a technique called pillarboxing. You can also have a video image that is displayed with simultaneous letterboxing and pillarboxing; this scenario is called windowboxing.

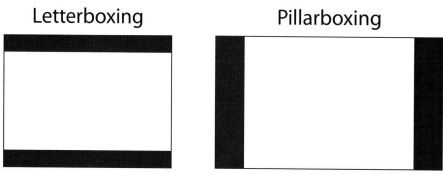

Letterboxing and pillarboxing are how display devices cope with video that does not match the device's own aspect ratio.

Pixel aspect ratio is the proportion of the width of the pixels that compose a video or still image to their height. A pixel is the smallest individual unit of a digital image; pixels can be of different shapes and sizes. The pixels used by a computer monitor are square in shape and have a pixel aspect ratio (par) of 1:1 (1.0); many of the standard video formats have rectangular pixels. For example, standard definition D1/DV NTSC footage has a par of 0.9 : 1 (.9); widescreen NTSC footage has a par of 1.21:1 (1.21); and high–definition HDV 1080 and DVCPro HD 720 have a par of 1.33:1 (1.33).

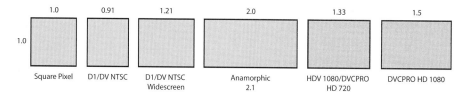

Pixel aspect ratio is the reason that NTSC and NTSC widescreen have the same pixel dimensions, but different aspect ratios.

When footage is interpreted incorrectly, it can appear squashed or stretched, causing circular objects on screen to appear ovular. Graphics programs such as Photoshop create content using square pixels, but they have presets and previewing modes for video projects that provide a good representation of the graphics as they might appear on a television monitor. When creating graphics in Photoshop and Illustrator, we highly recommend you use their video presets and choose one that matches your Premiere Pro sequence.

Progressive display vs. interlacing

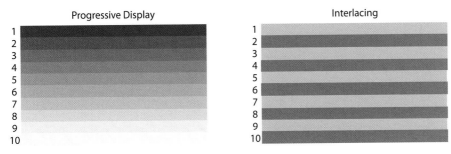

Progressive Display	Interlacing
1	1
2	2
3	3
4	4
5	5
6	6
7	7
8	8
9	9
10	10

Most modern televisions and other electronic display devices are progressive displays.

The two methods of displaying images on a video screen are Progressive display and Interlacing. In the United States, and before changing to a digital broadcasting system, televised images were sent as interlaced signals in which every frame of video was made by combining two half-images called fields.

Before the advent of high-definition LCD and Plasma screens, televisions were made by wrapping a plastic or wooden frame around a large glass device called a Cathode Ray Tube (CRT). These CRT television screens were composed of a series of even and odd numbered lines called scan lines, and each frame of video was displayed by illuminating these lines starting at the top of the screen. Interlacing was created to display video signals on this type of TV set and worked by illuminating one set of lines first (even or odd numbered), and then moving back to the top of the display to illuminate the other set. In this way, the display would show the second set of lines when the first set began to fade; the result was a complete picture for the viewer. This process occurred 60 times a second with NTSC broadcast television. Unlike Interlacing, Progressive display illuminates the scan lines sequentially from top to bottom.

Most modern televisions can display in interlaced and progressive mode, and the ATSC (American Television Systems Committee) includes broadcast standards for both, while all computer monitors use progressive display only. The difference between the two display methods occurs in video camera formats as well; older NTSC or PAL cameras can only shoot interlaced video, but many newer cameras let you choose between interlaced and progressive shooting modes, for example, 50i (25fps), 60i (30fps), 30p (30fps) or 24p (24fps).

Exporting an H.264 file for mobile devices

The H.264 format contains presets to produce video for a wide variety of mobile devices and online distribution services. Some examples of supported services and devices are Apple TV, YouTube, Vimeo, TiVo, the iPod, and mobile phones.

In this section of the lesson, you will export a Premiere Pro sequence in a variety of formats.

You can find all the files used in this project in the Werewolves in Central Park folder in the Media Library. The Reporter at Crime Scene.avi file is located in the A Roll folder; the remaining footage is located in the B Roll folder.

1 From the Premiere Pro welcome screen, click the Open Project button, or with Premiere Pro already open, chose File > Open Project. Navigate to the pr11lessons folder that you copied to your hard drive and locate the **pr1101.prproj** file. Double-click the file to open it. This project contains a single sequence called Reporter at Crime Scene.

2 Click the Timeline panel to make it active. The reason you want to make sure the Timeline is active is because you can use the Export command to export whatever is selected; the Source Monitor, a clip in the Project panel or the Timeline.

3   Choose File > Export > Media to open the Export Settings dialog box.

The keyboard command to export media is Ctrl+M (Windows) or Command+M (Mac OS).

The settings in the Export Settings dialog box default to the export settings you used last.

4   In the Export Settings dialog box, choose H.264 from the format drop-down list on the right to set the choices available in the Preset drop-down list.

From the Preset drop-down list, choose Apple iPad 2, 3, 4, Mini; iPhone 4S, 5; Apple TV 3 – 1080P 23.976. Setting the preset fills in all the menus and switches to produce video files optimized for display on this device.

This specific preset is designed to create a file that is compatible with the current generation of Apple devices. It preserves the high-definition size and quality of the footage, along with its framerate. Depending on your intended output destination, you will want to choose a preset that best represents your own needs.

5   Click the name of the file adjacent to the Output name field to open the Save As dialog box. Change the name of the file to **Reporter at Crime Scene–iPad version**, then navigate to the pr11lessons folder on your hard drive and click the Save button.

By default, the exported file is saved into the same directory as the last file you exported, and the file's name is automatically set to the name of the sequence you are exporting.

6   Click the Export button to begin the export process and the Encoding Status panel opens. This panel provides a status bar and a counter to show the estimated time remaining until the completion of the encoding process.

When exporting, the application renders or encodes a video file with the settings you specified and saves it to your hard drive. Creating a video file from your Premiere Pro sequence can be both a time-intensive and processor-intensive process. The duration of the encoding process depends upon the footage being encoded, the specific codec used, and the speed of your computer.

The dialog box closes once the process is complete.

7   To preview the file, minimize the Premiere Pro application and navigate to the folder on your hard drive where you saved your file. Double-click the **Reporter at Crime Scene–iPad version.mp4** file to preview it in your default video application.

8   Return to Premiere Pro and choose File > Save As. In the Save Project dialog box that appears, confirm that you are still in the pr11lessons folder, rename your file to **pr1101-working**, and click the Save button.

Do not close this file; you will need it in the next part of the lesson.

Understanding the Export Settings dialog box

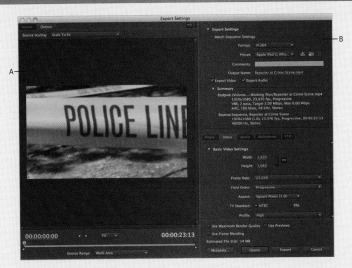

A. Source and Output monitors. B. Export settings.

Source and Output Monitors: Use the Source and Output monitors to preview the sequence or clip you want to export. Use the work area bar at the bottom of this area to preview and trim the source you are exporting. Drag the handles at either end of the bar and click the Set In Point or Set Out Point buttons to change the duration of the exported file. Use the Source and Output tabs at the top of this section to switch the preview area from your original source footage and the anticipated exported result.

Export Settings: Use the Export Settings area of the dialog box to specify settings ranging from the format and compression used in the exported file to the name and location to use when saving on your hard drive. The lower portion of this area is divided by a tabbed interface. Each tab contains the specific setting used to output the file. These settings vary depending on the format you choose, but Audio and Video and other similar settings usually remain constant.

Filters: Use it to add a Gaussian blur to the final exported file. You can use the Gaussian blur to remove graininess that might result from shooting footage in low light conditions.

Multiplexer: Use it to set the way in which the audio and video merge to form the output file. This panel is not available for all output formats.

Video: Use it to specify the settings for the video portion of the output file; these settings range from frame size and frame rate to the type of compression and file bit rate.

Audio: Use it to specify the settings for the audio portion of the output file, for example, the audio channels to output, codec, and audio bit rate.

FTP: Use it to automatically set FTP information to immediately upload the exported file to a server. You can set an FTP server address and input login and password information for your destination server. This option uploads a copy of your exported file, not the original.

Creating a custom export preset

You can use Premiere Pro's built-in presets for different output requirements, but occasionally, you might have to create your own customized settings to output video. In such cases, you will need to determine the video resolutions the target device supports; the best video format and codec to use; and the frame rates the target device prefers. Some useful sources of information are the device manufacturers' websites, white papers, technical sheets, and encyclopedic or knowledge-based sites such as Wikipedia (*wikipedia. com*).

In this part of the lesson, you will create and save a new preset for exporting video to display on a computer screen. You will reduce the output size of the video to compensate for differences between the size of the video frame and monitor display.

1   With **pr1101-working.prproj** still open, if necessary, click the Timeline panel to highlight it and make it active.

2   Choose File > Export > Media to open the Export Settings dialog box.

3   In the Export Settings section of the dialog box, if necessary, set the Format drop-down list to H.264, and the Preset drop-down list to Apple iPad 2, 3, 4, Mini; iPhone 4S, 5; Apple TV 3 – 1080P 23.976 . If you are continuing from the previous part of this lesson, the menus will already be set to the last settings used.

We highly recommend you base your new export preset on an existing preset that matches some of the settings you expect to use, and then modify it as needed.

4   Click the Output Name field, navigate to the pr11lessons project folder, and change the file name to **Reporter at Crime Scene-desktop**. Click the Save button to return to the Export Settings dialog box.

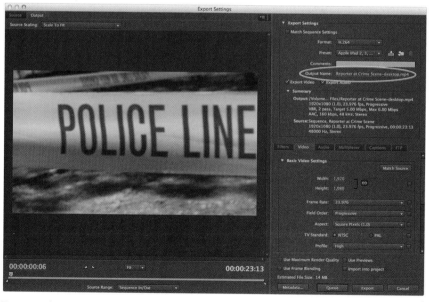

You can use the Output Name field to specify the name and location in which to create the exported file.

5   There is a great deal of variation in the screen size of modern monitors. The video
    frame dimensions of this preset are 1920 × 1080, which can actually fill the entire
    screen for some users. To compensate for this you will reduce the video's export
    dimensions so that they are smaller. In the Video tab, confirm that the link button (⬚)
    to the right of the Frame Width and Frame Height values is enabled. This button
    ensures that changes to either value result in a proportional change that will not distort
    the video. Click the value for the Frame Width property and change it to 1280 pixels.
    The Frame Height property value automatically changes to 720 pixels.

When enabled, the button to the right of the Frame Width and Height fields maintains their proportions.

 You can click any empty area of the Export Settings dialog box to exit text editing mode.

6   Scroll the Video panel to the Bitrate Settings section. The original preset is designed for video displayed on electronic devices and streamed over Apple TV sets, and has a Target Bitrate of 5 Mbps and a Maximum Bitrate of 6 Mbps. The bitrate of a file contributes to that file's size and quality. Raise the Target Bitrate to **8** and the Maximum to **10**.

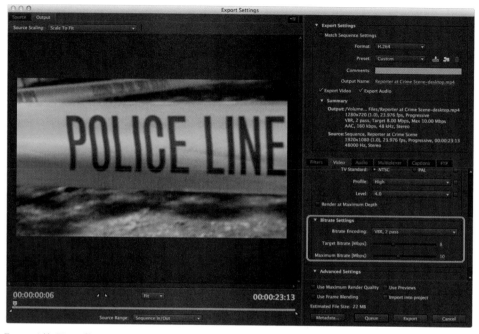

For a variable Bitrate files you can set values for both a target and maximum Bitrate for the encoded file.

The lower the bit rate of a file, the smaller the resulting file will be when stored on your hard drive or device. Notice that the reduction in bit rate produces a smaller estimated file size for the exported file. For future projects, we recommend that you experiment with different devices and footage to find the settings that work for you. For complex graphics, background, text, and transitions higher bit rates to display well when exported to video.

About bit rate

The bit rate, sometimes written bitrate, of a file determines how much data is used to display each second of that video file. When encoding video files, you can use a constant bit rate (CBR) or a variable bit rate (VBR). A constant bit rate file uses a single bit rate for every second of video; a variable bit rate file sets a range of usable bit rates the application can use when encoding the video file.

An important idea to understand when setting the bitrate for your file is that it doesn't help you to exceed the bitrate of your initial video footage. Bitrate is effectively the amount of information you have to describe each second of video. Raising your output bitrate beyond the level of the footage you are working with would result in a larger file but not a higher quality one.

7 Click the Save Preset button (⟐) located to the right of the Preset drop-down list to open the Choose Name dialog box. Change the preset's name to **720P Desktop** and click the OK button to save the preset.

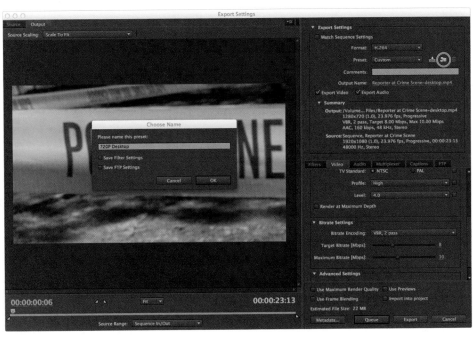

You can access custom presets from the Preset drop-down list just as you would built-in presets.

Don't close the dialog box; you will need it to complete the next portion of this lesson.

Exporting with the Adobe Media Encoder

Earlier in this lesson, you exported footage directly from Premiere Pro. The problem with this approach is that you cannot work with your editing application while the files are rendered. A solution to this problem is to use Adobe Media Encoder for all Premiere Pro's exporting tasks. You can send a file to the Media Encoder's render queue and continue working in Premiere Pro. The Adobe Media Encoder is a separate application that exists not only to function as a render queue for Premiere Pro but also as a stand-alone media transcoder. This allows you to change media from one format into another without having to first import the file into Premiere Pro.

In this part of the lesson, you will send a file from Premiere Pro to the Adobe Media encoder to be rendered.

1 With **pr1101-working.prproj** still open, the Export Settings dialog box still active, and the Reporter at Crime Scene-desktop.mp4 file ready to be exported, you can begin this portion of the lesson.

If you skipped the previous portion of this lesson, you will want to set your format and preset menus now.

2 Confirm that the Preset drop-down list is still set to the 720P Desktop preset you created in the previous part of the lesson.

3 Click the Queue button at the bottom of the dialog box to add the current export job to the Adobe Media Encoder Queue. After a few moments the Adobe Media Encoder application opens.

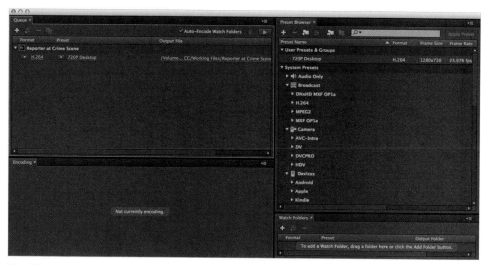

The Adobe Media Encoder is a render queue: you can add multiple export jobs to it and they will be completed in sequence.

4 In the Media Encoder, click the Start Queue button (■) to begin the video rendering process. The video is created using the settings specified in Premiere Pro and saved into the folder you specified in the Export Settings dialog box. The render progress is visible in the Encoding panel in the Media Encoder.

5 To preview the file, minimize the Adobe Media Encoder and Premiere Pro applications and navigate to the pr11lessons folder on your hard drive. Locate the Reporter at Crime Scene-desktop.mp4 and double-click the file to preview it in your default video application.

6 Return to Premiere Pro and choose File > Save or press Ctrl+S (Windows) or Command+S (Mac OS) to save these changes to your project. You can now close this project; you have completed this lesson. Minimize Premiere Pro and return to the Media Encoder and close it as well.

Understanding the Adobe Media Encoder

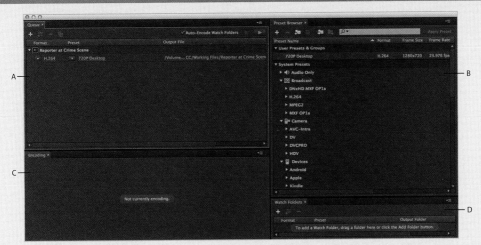

A major advantage and the main reason for using the Adobe Media Encoder is its render queue. You can add multiple files with the same or different output settings to the Media Encoder, and the application will render them in sequence without any other input from you. These export jobs are easy to add, remove, and adjust their settings.

A. Queue. The Render Queue panel displays all your current and pending render jobs. The Add Source button is used to add files to the queue, while the Add Output button is used to add export settings (format, compression & destination) for your source file. This allows you to take a single source file and render out several different versions of it if necessary.

B. Preset Browser. The Preset Browser panel contains all the video, audio, and image output presets that ship with the application as well as all the custom presets that you have created. You can use the Create New Preset button to create additional custom presets directly in the Media Encoder without having to open Premiere Pro.

C.Watch Folder. The Watch Folder panel is used to set a folder on your hard drive for the application to watch and automatically transcode video files that are added to it. You can use the Add Folder button to add a new watch folder, and then use the Preset menu to set the export settings you want to use for all files that the application detects in this folder. This is an excellent feature of the program for users who have to transcode files to multiple output formats for multi-platform distribution.

D. Encoding. The Encoding panel displays the status of the current encoding job. This panel is blank until you actually begin to render the items in the queue.

Self study

Create and save a custom preset to view video on a Smartphone or other mobile device, such as a BlackBerry, Windows Phone 7, or Sony Playstation Vita.

Review

Questions

1. What are the four major players in the web and desktop video deployment market?

2. What are video codecs?

3. What is the advantage of using the Adobe Media Encoder to export your project instead of using Premiere Pro?

Answers

1. The four major players in the deployment of video to the web and desktop are Flash Video, Windows Media Video, QuickTime video, HTML 5 Video (H.264)

2. The word codec is a conjunction of the words *compressor* and *decompressor*. Codecs are mathematical algorithms used to reduce audio and video files to manageable sizes so they can be displayed on the Web, e-mailed, or written to a DVD.

3. Using the Media Encoder lets you continue working on editing projects in Premiere Pro. The Media Encoder also offers additional features for exporting multiple files from a single source.

Appendix A

Premiere Pro Panels

Audio Master Meters Panel

The Audio Master Meters are Volume Unit (VU) meters that displays the volume of the audio on the Timeline when you preview a sequence and also of clips that are being previewed in the Source Monitor. The meters are only monitoring tools and are not used for editing the volume of tracks.

Audio Clip Mixer

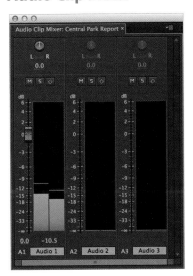

The Audio Clip Mixer lets you monitor and adjust the volume and pan of clips in sequence when the Timeline panel is active. Additionally, when the Source Monitor is active the Audio Clip Mixer lets you monitor audio in the Source Monitor.

Audio Track Mixer Panel

Use the Audio Mixer to adjust the settings of audio tracks while previewing the video and audio in your sequence. Each track in the Mixer corresponds to a track in your active sequence. Unlike the Audio Master Meters, the Mixer contains active controls for adjusting the volume of each track, muting it, or making it play solo. You can also use the Mixer to record audio from a microphone onto an audio track.

Captions Panel

The Captions tab in Premiere Pro lets you make word-level edits of the closed caption clips. You can also make changes to the timing and formatting, like, text alignment, text color, from an intuitive user interface.

Capture Panel

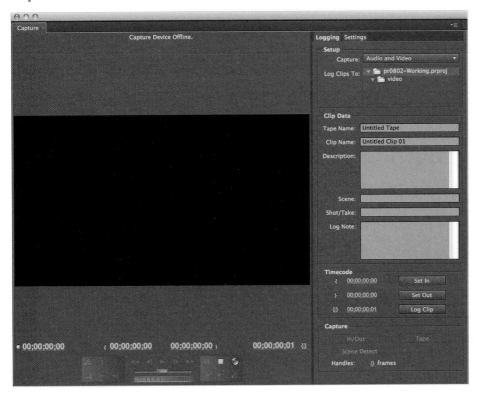

Use the Capture panel to capture footage from a FireWire-based videotape camera or video deck. The panel contains camera controls that let you manage playback on your device. You can capture an entire tape or set In and Out Points to capture only a section of the tape. You can also use this panel to batch capture a group of offline clips.

Effect Controls Panel

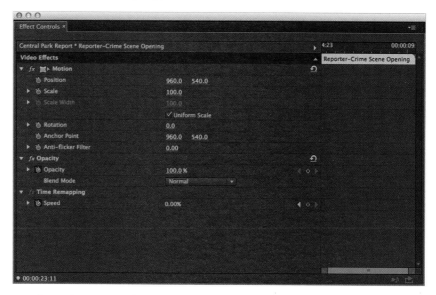

Use the Effect Controls panel to edit video and audio effects of clips in your active sequence. You can view the effects added to a clip by clicking the clip once. Double-click the clip to open it in the Source Monitor and the Effect Controls panel. All clips have built-in editable effects you can edit using the Effect Controls panel. You can also edit effects added from the Effects panel.

Effects Panel

The Effects panel is a storage area and a library of all the video and audio effects and transitions available in Premiere Pro. The Effects and Transitions that appear in this panel are grouped into subcategories; use the search field at the top of the panel to easily find the effect or transition you want.

Events Panel

The Events panel displays warnings, errors, and other information you can use to troubleshoot problems in Premiere Pro. View the Events panel by double-clicking any warning displayed in the status bar or by choosing Window > Events.

History Panel

The History panel displays a list of actions you have performed since opening your project. You can adjust the panel's vertical slider by dragging it upward to undo commands you have performed. The History panel is an alternative to choosing Edit > Undo and Edit > Redo or using the respective keyboard shortcuts.

Info Panel

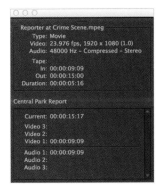

The Info panel contains valuable feedback about any clip or sequence you select from the Project panel. The information that appears in this panel includes clip duration, In and Out points, and track information.

Markers Panel

You can use the Markers panel to see all the markers in an open clip or sequence, along with their color codes, In points and Out points. Clicking on the marker thumbnail in the panel advances the playhead to the starting position of the marker.

Media Browser Panel

The Media Browser is Premiere Pro's built-in file browser. You can browse for files on your hard drive or find the files you want by file type. Unlike the Import dialog box, you can leave the Media Browser open and active while working in the application.

Metadata Panel

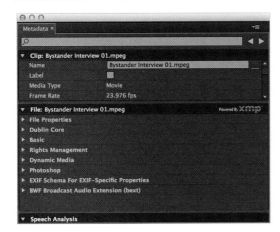

The Metadata panel displays clip-instance metadata and the XMP metadata for any asset you select in the Project Panel or a sequence. Clip-instance metadata is stored in the Premiere Pro project file and used in Premiere Pro only. XMP metadata is accessible in other programs, such as Adobe After Effects and Adobe Bridge.

Multi-Camera Monitor

Use the Multi-Camera Monitor to edit footage from a multiple cameras simultaneously. The multi-camera workflow simulates working with a live video switcher. For best results, we recommend you ensure that all the footage used in a multi-camera edit contains a synchronizing point set with a clapper board or other technique.

Options

The Options panel is the horizontal bar at the top of the application's interface. It was a common feature of the default editing workspace in older versions of Premiere Pro. In the Editing (5.5) interface, the Tools panel is docked to this bar by default. The Options panel also holds the workspace switcher drop down menu.

Program Monitor Panel

Use the Program Monitor to view the content of the Timeline panel at the playhead's current time position. The Program Monitor is the main preview window used when working with sequences.

Project Panel

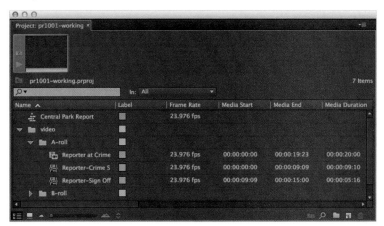

The Project panel is the central hub for all the work you do in Premiere Pro. Links to your media files are stored in this panel when you import them, as well as the content you create with the application, such as titles and sequences. You can organize the panel by creating bins. These are effectively folders that can hold clips, titles, sequences, and even other bins.

Reference Monitor Panel

The Reference Monitor acts as a secondary Program Monitor. You can use the Reference Monitor to compare different frames in a sequence or to view the same frame in different viewing modes; for example, you can use the Composite viewing mode side by side with the Vectorscope.

By default, the Reference Monitor is linked to the Program Monitor such that their respective playheads move in sequence. However, you can unlink these monitors to control one independently from the other.

Source Monitor Panel

The Source Monitor is one of the most important tools you can use to prepare clips for the Timeline. Use the Source Monitor to preview and trim clips before adding them to the Timeline, and to preview all footage you use in Premiere Pro, except for sequence content, which you preview using the Program Monitor. To preview footage in the Source Monitor, double-click a footage item or drag it into the Source Monitor panel.

Timeline Panel

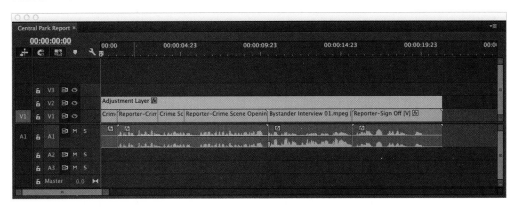

Use the Timeline to edit all your footage. You can add clips to the Timeline directly from the Project panel, Media Browser, or Source monitor. Each sequence you create in Premiere Pro is its own independent Timeline. You can move clips on the Timeline, trim them, or delete them as you craft your project.

Tools Panel

When you select a tool from the Tools panel, the mouse cursor changes appearance based on the tool you have active and the type of content the cursor is hovering over. For example, the Selection tool that you can use to move clips in the Timeline changes to become a Trim tool when you position it at the beginning or end of a clip.

Timecode Panel

The Timecode panel provides you with an enlarged display of the playhead position. The display adjusts depending on whether you have the Program or Source Monitors active.

Trim Monitor Panel

Use the Trim Monitor to refine your edits. When working with adjacent clips on the same track, the Trim Monitor displays the In and Out points of clips at a cut so you can see the frames you are cutting. The left monitor window displays the clip on the left side of the edit line; the right monitor window shows the clip to the right of it.

VST Editor Panel

Premiere Pro supports the Steinberg VST (Virtual Studio Technology) audio plug-in format so you can add VST audio effects from third-party vendors. The VST Editor is available only when you work with VST effects; open the VST Editor by double-clicking a VST effect.

Adobe Premiere Pro Keyboard Shortcuts

Many menu commands have corresponding keyboard shortcuts. Below is a partial list of the keyboard commands available in Premiere Pro. This list is taken from the Adobe Premiere Pro help files, a full and up to date list can be found at: *http://helpx.adobe.com/premiere-pro/using/default-keyboard-shortcuts-cc.html*

Keyboard shortcuts for selecting Tools

RESULTS	WINDOWS	MAC OS
Selection Tool	V	V
Track Select Tool	A	A
Ripple Edit Tool	B	B
Rolling Edit Tool	N	N
Rate Stretch Tool	R	R
Razor Tool	C	C
Slip Tool	Y	Y
Slide Tool	U	U
Pen Tool	P	P
Hand Tool	H	H
Zoom Tool	Z	Z

Keyboard shortcuts for activating Menu Commands

RESULTS	WINDOWS	MAC OS
FILE		
Project/Production...	Ctrl+Alt+N	Opt+Cmd+N
Sequence...	Ctrl+N	Cmd+N
Bin		Cmd+/

RESULTS	WINDOWS	MAC OS
Title...	Ctrl+T	Cmd+T
Open Project/Production...	Ctrl+O	Cmd+O
Browse in Adobe Bridge...	Ctrl+Alt+O	Opt+Cmd+O
Close Project	Ctrl+Shift+W	Shift+Cmd+W
Close	Ctrl+W	Cmd+W
Save	Ctrl+S	Cmd+S
Save As...	Ctrl+Shift+S	Shift+Cmd+S
Save a Copy...	Ctrl+Alt+S	Opt+Cmd+S
Capture...	F5	F5
Batch Capture...	F6	F6
Import from Media Browser	Ctrl+Alt+I	Opt+Cmd+I
Import...	Ctrl+I	Cmd+I
Export		
Media...	Ctrl+M	Cmd+M
Get Properties for		
Selection...	Ctrl+Shift+H	Shift+Cmd+H
Exit	Ctrl+Q	
EDIT		
Undo	Ctrl+Z	Cmd+Z
Redo	Ctrl+Shift+Z	Shift+Cmd+Z
Cut	Ctrl+X	Cmd+X
Copy	Ctrl+C	Cmd+C
Paste	Ctrl+V	Cmd+V
Paste Insert	Ctrl+Shift+V	Shift+Cmd+V
Paste Attributes	Ctrl+Alt+V	Opt+Cmd+V
Clear	Delete	Forward Delete
Ripple Delete	Shift+Delete	Shift+Forward Delete
Duplicate	Ctrl+Shift+/	Shift+Cmd+/
Select All	Ctrl+A	Cmd+A

RESULTS	WINDOWS	MAC OS
Deselect All	Ctrl+Shift+A	Shift+Cmd+A
Find...	Ctrl+F	Cmd+F
Edit Original	Ctrl+E	Cmd+E
CLIP		
Make Subclip...	Ctrl+U	Cmd+U
Audio Channels...	Shift+G	Shift+G
Speed/Duration...	Ctrl+R	Cmd+R
Insert	,	,
Overwrite	.	.
Enable	Shift+E	Shift+Cmd+E
Link	Ctr+l	Cmd+l
Group	Ctrl+G	Cmd+G
Ungroup	Ctrl+Shift+G	Shift+Cmd+G
SEQUENCE		
Render Effects in Work Area/In to Out	Enter	Return
Match Frame	F	F
Add Edit	Ctrl+K	Cmd+K
Add Edit to All Tracks	Ctrl+Shift+K	Shift+Cmd+K
Trim Edit	T	T
Extend Selected Edit to Playhead	E	E
Apply Video Transition	Ctrl+D	Cmd+D
Apply Audio Transition	Ctrl+Shift+D	Shift+Cmd+D
Apply Default Transitions to Selection	Shift+D	Shift+D
Lift	;	;
Extract	'	'
Zoom In	=	=
Zoom Out	-	-
Go to Gap		
Next in Sequence	Shift+;	Shift+;

RESULTS	WINDOWS	MAC OS
Previous in Sequence	Ctrl+Shift+;	Opt+;
Snap	S	S
MARKER		
Mark In	I	I
Mark Out	O	O
Mark Clip	X	X
Mark Selection	/	/
Go to In	Shift+I	Shift+I
Go to Out	Shift+O	Shift+O
Clear In	Ctrl+Shift+I	Opt+I
Clear Out	Ctrl+Shift+O	Opt+O
Clear In and Out	Ctrl+Shift+X	Opt+X
Add Marker	M	M
Go to Next Marker	Shift+M	Shift+M
Go to Previous Marker	Ctrl+Shift+M	Shift+Cmd+M
Clear Current Marker	Ctrl+Alt+M	Opt+M
Clear All Markers	Ctrl+Alt+Shift+M	Opt+Cmd+M
Type Alignment		
Left	Ctrl+Shift+L	Shift+Cmd+L
Center	Ctrl+Shift+C	Shift+Cmd+C
Right	Ctrl+Shift+R	Shift+Cmd+R
Tab Stops...	Ctrl+Shift+T	Shift+Cmd+T
Templates...	Ctrl+J	Cmd+J
Select		
Next Object Above	Ctrl+Alt+]	Opt+Cmd+]
Next Object Below	Ctrl+Alt+[	Opt+Cmd+[
Arrange		
Bring to Front	Ctrl+Shift+]	Shift+Cmd+]
Bring Forward	Ctrl+]	Cmd+]

RESULTS	WINDOWS	MAC OS
Send to Back	Ctrl+Shift+[	Shift+Cmd+[
Send Backward	Ctrl+[	Cmd+[
WINDOW		
Workspace		
Reset Current Workspace...	Alt+Shift +0	Opt+Shift +0
Audio Clip Mixer	Shift+9	Shift+9
Audio Track Mixer	Shift+6	Shift+6
Effect Controls	Shift+5	Shift+5
Effects	Shift+7	Shift+7
Media Browser	Shift+8	Shift+8
Program Monitor	Shift+4	Shift+4
Project	Shift+1	Shift+1
Source Monitor	Shift+2	Shift+2
Timelines	Shift+3	Shift+3
HELP		
Adobe Premiere Pro Help...	F1	F1
Keyboard...		
Add Tracks to Match Source		
Clear Poster Frame	Ctrl+Shift+P	Opt+P
Cut to Camera 1	Ctrl+1	Ctrl+1
Cut to Camera 2	Ctrl+2	Ctrl+2
Cut to Camera 3	Ctrl+3	Ctrl+3
Cut to Camera 4	Ctrl+4	Ctrl+4
Cut to Camera 5	Ctrl+5	Ctrl+5
Cut to Camera 6	Ctrl+6	Ctrl+6
Cut to Camera 7	Ctrl+7	Ctrl+7
Cut to Camera 8	Ctrl+8	Ctrl+8
Cut to Camera 9		Ctrl+9

RESULTS	WINDOWS	MAC OS
Decrease Clip Volume	[	[
Decrease Clip Volume Many	Shift+[	Shift+[
Expand All Tracks	Shift+=	Shift+=
Export Frame	Ctrl+Shift+E	Shift+E
Extend Next Edit To Playhead	Shift+W	Shift+W
Extend Previous Edit To Playhead	Shift+Q	Shift+Q

Keyboard shortcuts for working with the Panels

RESULTS	WINDOWS	MAC OS
AUDIO MIXER PANEL MENU		
Show/Hide Tracks...	Ctrl+Alt+T	Opt+Cmd+T
Loop	Ctrl+L	Cmd+L
Meter Input(s) Only	Ctrl+Shift+I	Ctrl+Shift+I
CAPTURE PANEL		
Record Video	V	V
Record Audio	A	A
Eject	E	E
Fast Forward	F	F
Go to In point	Q	Q
Go to Out point	W	W
Record	G	G
Rewind	R	R
Step Back	Left	Left
Step Forward	Right	Right
Stop	S	S

RESULTS	WINDOWS	MAC OS
EFFECT CONTROLS PANEL		
Remove Selected Effect	Backspace	Delete
EFFECTS PANEL MENU		
New Custom Bin	Ctrl+/	Cmd+/
Delete Custom Item	Backspace	Delete
HISTORY PANEL MENU		
Step Backward	Left	Left
Step Forward	Right	Right
Delete	Backspace	Delete
Open in Source Monitor	Shift+O	Shift+O
Parent Directory	Ctrl+Up	Cmd+Up
Select Directory List	Shift+Left	Shift+Left
Select Media List	Shift+Right	Shift+Right
Loop	Ctrl+L	Cmd+L
Play	Space	Space
Go to Next Edit Point	Down	Down
Go to Previous Edit Point	Up	Up
Play/Stop Toggle	Space	Space
Record On/Off Toggle	0	0
Step Back	Left	Left
Step Forward	Right	Right
Loop	Ctrl+L	Cmd+L

Keyboard shortcuts for working with working with the Multi-Camera panel

RESULTS	WINDOWS	MAC OS
Go to Next Edit Point	Down	Down
Go to Next Edit Point on Any Track	Shift+Down	Shift+Down
Go to Previous Edit Point	Up	Up
Go to Previous Edit Point on Any Track	Shift+Up	Shift+Up
Go to Selected Clip End	Shift+End	Shift+End
Go to Selected Clip Start	Shift+Home	Shift+Home
Go to Sequence-Clip End	End	End
Go to Sequence-Clip Start	Home	Home
Increase Clip Volume	]	]
Increase Clip Volume Many	Shift+]	Shift+]
Maximize or Restore Active Frame	Shift+`	Shift+`
Maximize or Restore Frame Under Cursor	`	`
Minimize All Tracks	Shift+-	Shift+-
Play Around	Shift+K	Shift+K
Play In to Out	Ctrl+Shift+Space	Opt+K
Play In to Out with Preroll/Postroll	Shift+Space	Shift+Space
Play from Playhead to Out Point	Ctrl+Space	Ctrl+Space
Play-Stop Toggle	Space	SpaceRecord Voiceover
Reveal Nested Sequence	Ctrl+Shift+F	Shift+T
Ripple Trim Next Edit To Playhead	W	W
Ripple Trim Previous Edit To Playhead	Q	Q
Select Camera 1	1	1
Select Camera 2	2	2
Select Camera 3	3	3
Select Camera 4	4	4
Select Camera 5	5	5
Select Camera 6	6	6

RESULTS	WINDOWS	MAC OS
Select Camera 7	7	7
Select Camera 8	8	8
Select Camera 9	9	9
Select Find Box	Shift+F	Shift+F
Select Clip at Playhead	D	D
Select Next Clip	Ctrl+Down	Cmd+Down
Select Next Panel	Ctrl+Shift+.	Ctrl+Shift+.
Select Previous Clip	Ctrl+Up	Cmd+Up
Select Previous Panel	Ctrl+Shift+,	Ctrl+Shift+,
Set Poster Frame	Shift+P	Cmd+P
Shuttle Left	J	J
Shuttle Right	L	L
Shuttle Slow Left	Shift+J	Shift+J
Shuttle Slow Right	Shift+L	Shift+L
Shuttle Stop	K	K
Step Back	Left	Left
Step Back Five Frames - Units	Shift+Left	Shift+Left
Step Forward	Right	Right
Step Forward Five Frames - Units	Shift+Right	Shift+Right
Toggle All Audio Targets	Ctrl+9	Cmd+9
Toggle All Source Audio	Ctrl+Alt+9	Opt+Cmd+9
Toggle All Source Video	Ctrl+Alt+0	Opt+Cmd+0
Toggle All Video Targets	Ctrl+0	Cmd+0
Toggle Audio During Scrubbing	Shift+S	Shift+S
Toggle Control Surface Clip Mixer Mode		
Toggle Full Screen	Ctrl+`	Ctrl+`
Toggle Multi-Camera View	Shift+0	Shift+0
Toggle Trim Type	Shift+T	Ctrl+T
Trim Backward	Ctrl+Left	Opt+Left

RESULTS	WINDOWS	MAC OS
Trim Backward Many	Ctrl+Shift+Left	Opt+Shift+Left
Trim Forward	Ctrl+Right	Opt+Right
Trim Forward Many	Ctrl+Shift+Right	Opt+Shift+Right
Trim Next Edit to Playhead	Ctrl+Alt+W	Opt+W
Trim Previous Edit to Playhead	Ctrl+Alt+Q	Opt+Q

Keyboard shortcuts for working with Project Panel

RESULTS	WINDOWS	MAC OS
Workspace 1	Alt+Shift+1	Opt+Shift+1
Workspace 2	Alt+Shift+2	Opt+Shift+2
Workspace 3	Alt+Shift+3	Opt+Shift+3
Workspace 4	Alt+Shift+4	Opt+Shift+4
Workspace 5	Alt+Shift+5	Opt+Shift+5
Workspace 6	Alt+Shift+6	Opt+Shift+6
Workspace 7	Alt+Shift+7	Opt+Shift+7
Workspace 8	Alt+Shift+8	Opt+Shift+8
Workspace 9	Alt+Shift+9	Opt+Shift+9
Zoom to Sequence	\	\
Extend Selection Up	Shift+Up	Shift+Up
Move Selection Down	Down	Down
Move Selection End	End	End
Move Selection Home	Home	Home
Move Selection Left	Left	Left
Move Selection Page Down	Page Down	Page Down
Move Selection Page Up	Page Up	Page Up
Move Selection Right	Right	Right
Move Selection Up	Up	Up
Next Column Field	Tab	Tab
Next Row Field	Enter	Return

RESULTS	WINDOWS	MAC OS
Open in Source Monitor	Shift+O	Shift+O
Previous Column Field	Shift+Tab	Shift+Tab
Previous Row Field	Shift+Enter	Shift+Return
Thumbnail Size Next	Shift+]	Shift+]
Thumbnail Size Previous	Shift+[	Shift+[
Toggle View	Shift+\	Shift+\

Keyboard shortcuts for working with Timeline panel

RESULTS	WINDOWS	MAC OS
Add Clip Marker	Ctrl+1	
Clear Selection	Backspace	Delete
Decrease Audio Tracks Height	Alt+-	Opt+-
Decrease Video Tracks Height	Ctrl+-	Cmd+-
Increase Audio Tracks Height	Alt+=	Opt+=
Increase Video Tracks Height	Ctrl+=	Cmd+=
Nudge Clip Selection Left Five Frames	Alt+Shift+Left	Shift+Cmd+Left
Nudge Clip Selection Left One Frame	Alt+Left	Cmd+Left
Nudge Clip Selection Right Five Frames	Alt+Shift+Right	Shift+Cmd+Right
Nudge Clip Selection Right One Frame	Alt+Right	Cmd+Right
Ripple Delete	Alt+Backspace	Opt+Delete
Set Work Area Bar In Point	Alt+[	Opt+[
Set Work Area Bar Out Point	Alt+]	Opt+]
Show Next Screen	Page Down	Page Down
Show Previous Screen	Page Up	Page Up
Slide Clip Selection Left Five Frames	Alt+Shift+,	Opt+Shift+,
Slide Clip Selection Left One Frame	Alt+,	Opt+,
Slide Clip Selection Right Five Frames	Alt+Shift+.	Opt+Shift+.
Slide Clip Selection Right One Frame	Alt+.	Opt+.
Slip Clip Selection Left Five Frames	Ctrl+Alt+Shift+Left	Opt+Shift+Cmd+Left

RESULTS	WINDOWS	MAC OS
Slip Clip Selection Left One Frame	Ctrl+Alt+Left	Opt+Cmd+Left
Slip Clip Selection Right Five Frames	Ctrl+Alt+Shift+Right	Opt+Shift+Cmd+Right
Slip Clip Selection Right One Frame	Ctrl+Alt+Right	Opt+Cmd+Right

Keyboard shortcuts for working with Titler

RESULTS	WINDOWS	MAC OS
Arc Tool	A	A
Bold	Ctrl+B	Cmd+B
Decrease Kerning by Five Units	Alt+Shift+Left	Opt+Shift+Left
Decrease Kerning by One Unit	Alt+Left	Opt+Left
Decrease Leading by Five Units	Alt+Shift+Down	Opt+Shift+Down
Decrease Leading by One Unit	Alt+Down	Opt+Down
Decrease Text Size by Five Points	Ctrl+Alt+Shift+Left	Opt+Shift+Cmd+Left
Decrease Text Size by One Point	Ctrl+Alt+Left	Opt+Cmd+Left
Ellipse Tool	E	E
Increase Kerning by Five Units	Alt+Shift+Right	Opt+Shift+Right
Increase Kerning by One Unit	Alt+Right	Opt+Right
Increase Leading by Five Units	Alt+Shift+Up	Opt+Shift+Up
Increase Leading by One Unit	Alt+Up	Opt+Up
Increase Text Size by Five Points	Ctrl+Alt+Shift+Right	Opt+Shift+Cmd+Right
Increase Text Size by One Point	Ctrl+Alt+Right	Opt+Cmd+Right
Insert Copyright Symbol	Ctrl+Alt+Shift+C	Opt+Shift+Cmd+C
Insert Registered Symbol	Ctrl+Alt+Shift+R	Opt+Shift+Cmd+R
Italic	Ctrl+I	Cmd+I
Line Tool	L	L
Nudge Selected Object Down by Five Pixels	Shift+Down	Shift+Down
Nudge Selected Object Down by One Pixel	Down	Down
Nudge Selected Object Left by Five Pixels	Shift+Left	Shift+Left
Nudge Selected Object Left by One Pixel	Left	Left

RESULTS	WINDOWS	MAC OS
Nudge Selected Object Right by Five Pixels	Shift+Right	Shift+Right
Nudge Selected Object Right by One Pixel	Right	Right
Nudge Selected Object Up by Five Pixels	Shift+Up	Shift+Up
Nudge Selected Object Up by One Pixel	Up	Up
Path Type Tool		
Pen Tool	P	P
Position Object(s) to Bottom Title Safe Margin	Ctrl+Shift+D	Shift+Cmd+D
Position Object(s) to Left Title Safe Margin	Ctrl+Shift+F	Shift+Cmd+F
Position Object(s) to Top Title Safe Margin	Ctrl+Shift+O	Shift+Cmd+O
Rectangle Tool	R	R
Rotation Tool	O	O
Selection Tool	V	V
Type Tool	T	T
Underline	Ctrl+U	Cmd+U
Vertical Type Tool	C	C
Wedge Tool	W	W

Keyboard shortcuts for working with Trim Monitor panel

RESULTS	WINDOWS	MAC OS
Focus Both Outgoing and Incoming	Alt+1	Opt+1
Focus on Incoming Side	Alt+3	Opt+3
Focus on Outgoing Side	Alt+2	Opt+2
Loop	Ctrl+L	Cmd+L
Trim Backward by Large Trim Offset	Alt+Shift+Left	Opt+Shift+Left
Trim Backward by One Frame	Alt+Left	Opt+Left
Trim Forward by Large Trim Offset	Alt+Shift+Right	Opt+Shift+Right
Trim Forward by One Frame	Alt+Right	Opt+Right

Finding keyboard shortcuts

Finding the keyboard shortcuts for a tool, button, or menu command is as easy as doing any of the following:

- For a tool or button, hold the pointer over the tool or button until its tool tip appears. If available, the keyboard shortcut appears in the tool tip after the tool description.

- For menu commands, look for the keyboard shortcut at the right of the command.

- For the most-used keyboard shortcuts not shown in tool tips or on menus, see the tables in this article. For a complete list of default and current shortcuts, choose Edit > Keyboard Shortcuts (Windows) or Premiere Pro > Keyboard Shortcuts (Mac OS)

- Use the search field in the Keyboard Customization dialog box to find specific commands quickly.

Customize or load keyboard shortcuts

You can set shortcuts to match shortcuts in other software you use. If other sets are available, you can choose them from the Set menu in the Keyboard Customization dialog box.

1 For customizing keyboard shortcuts, choose one of the following:

   In Windows, choose Edit > Keyboard Shortcuts

   In Mac OS, choose Premiere Pro > Keyboard Shortcuts

2 In the Keyboard Customization dialog box, choose an option from the menu:

3 In the Command column, view the command for which you want to create or change a shortcut. If necessary, click the triangle next to the name of a category to reveal the commands it includes.

4 Click in the item's shortcut field to select it.

5 Type the shortcut you want to use for the item. The Keyboard Customization dialog box displays an alert if the shortcut you choose is already in use.

To erase a shortcut and return it to the command that originally had it, click Undo. To jump to the command that previously had the shortcut, click Go To. To simply delete the shortcut you typed, click Clear. To re-enter the shortcut you typed previously, click Redo.

6 Repeat the procedure to enter as many shortcuts as you want. When you're finished, click Save As, type a name for your Key Set, and click Save.

The operating system reserves some commands. You cannot reassign those commands to Premiere Pro. Also, you cannot assign the plus (+) and minus (-) keys on the numeric keypad because they are necessary for entering relative timecode values. You can assign the minus (-) key on the main keyboard, however.

Appendix C

Premiere Pro Input and Output formats

Supported formats for Input and Output

Premiere Pro can import and output a wide variety of different video, still image and audio formats. With the assistance of third party plug-ins, many of which are automatically installed with the application the number of supported file formats is enhanced. Premiere Pro can only import the listed file types when the codec used with the file is installed locally on your computer. So in order to view or edit a file that has been encoded in the DivX codec, that very same DivX codec must be installed on your machine.

This list is taken from the Adobe Premiere Pro help files. A full and up-to-date list can be found at: *http://helpx.adobe.com/premiere-pro/using/transferring-importing-files.html*.

Video File Formats

FILE FORMAT	IMPORT/EXPORT	NOTES
3GPP Movie (.3gp)	Import and Export	QuickTime player required on Windows
Advanced Video Codec (.mts)	Import only	
AVCHD (.m2ts, .mts)	Import only	
DV stream (.dv)	Import and Export	
Flash Video (.flv, .f4v)	Import and Export	
Microsoft AVI (.avi)	Import and Export	Export Windows only
Microsoft NetShow (.asf)	Import only	Windows only
MPEG-1 (.mpg)	Import and Export	Export Windows only
MPEG-2 (.m2v, .mpg)	Import and Export	
MPEG-4 (.m4v)	Import and Export	
Panasonic P2 (.mxf)	Import and Export	
QuickTime Movie (.mov)	Import and Export	QuickTime player required on Windows
Shockwave Flash object (.swf)	Import only	

FILE FORMAT	IMPORT/EXPORT	NOTES
Sony VDU File Format Importer (.dlx)	Import only	Windows only
Windows Media (.wma, .wmv)	Import and Export	Export Windows only
XDCam-EX movie (.mp4)	Import only	
XDCam-HD movie (.mxf)	Import only	

Image file formats

Please note that Adobe Premiere Pro can only import still image files that use the RGB and Grayscale color modes.

FILE FORMAT	IMPORT/EXPORT	NOTES
Adobe Illustrator and Illustrator sequence (.ai, .eps)	Import only	
Adobe Photoshop and Photoshop sequence (.psd)	Import only	Import does not support files that are CMYK, Duotone, LAB, or Multichannel mode. PSDs containing a 32-bit alpha channel are not supported. Convert your image to an 8- or 16-bit PSD before importing.
Adobe Premiere Title (.ptl, .prtl)	Import only	
Animated GIF (.gif)	Import and Export	Windows only
Bitmap and Bitmap sequence (.bmp, .wbm, .dib, .rle)	Import and Export	8-bit per channel (bpc) or better only. Alpha channels in BMP files are not supported.
CompuServe GIF (.gif)	Import and Export	
Encapsulated PostScript (.eps)	Import only	
Icon file (.ico)	Import only	Windows only
JPEG and JPEG sequence (.jpe, .jpg, .jfif)	Import and Export	
PICT and PICT sequence (.pic, .pct, .pict)	Import only	QuickTime player required on Windows
Portable Network Graphics (.png)	Import and Export	Export in Mac OS X only
Targa and Targa sequence (.tga, .icb, .vda, .vst)	Import and Export	
TIFF and TIFF sequence (.tif, .tiff)	Import and Export	8-bit per channel (bpc) files only

Audio file formats

FILE FORMAT	IMPORT/EXPORT	NOTES
Adobe Sound Document (.asnd)	Import only	
Advanced Audio Coding File (.aac)	Import and Export	
Audio Interchange File Format (.aif, .aiff)	Import and Export	
Audio Video Interleaved (.avi)	Import and Export	
Dolby Digital (.ac3)	Import and Export	After 3 free trial uses, purchase SurCode encoder
MPEG Audio (.m4a, .mp3)	Import and Export	
MPEG Audio (.mpeg, .mpg)	Import and Export	
QuickTime (.mov)	Import and Export	QuickTime player required on Windows
Windows Media Audio (.wma)	Import and Export	Windows only

Other file formats

FILE FORMAT	IMPORT/EXPORT	NOTES
Adobe Clip Notes (.pdf)	Import and Export	
Adobe Premiere 6.x Library(.plb)	Import	Windows only
Adobe Premiere 6.x Project (.ppj)	Import	Windows only
Adobe Premiere 6.x Storyboard (.psq)	Import	Windows only
Adobe Premiere Pro Project (.prproj)	Import and Export	
Adobe After Effects Project (.aep)	Import and Export	Production Premium or Master Collection
Advanced Authoring Format (.aaf)	Import and Export	Windows only
Batch list (.csv, .pbl, .txt, .tab)	Import	
Edit Decision List (.edl)	Import and Export	

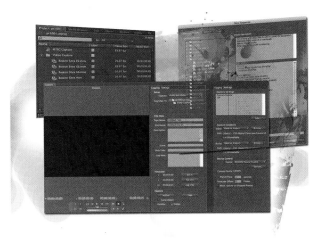

What you'll learn in this lesson:

- Creating a new Premiere Pro project

- Adding bins and set a capture bin

- Capturing footage from a digital video camera

- Adding and editing metadata footage

Capturing and Transferring Footage

In the previous lessons in this book, you worked with footage that was already captured or transferred from a recording source. In this lesson, you will learn to transfer the footage from your camera or storage card.

Starting up

In this lesson, you will work with the project files from the AppDlessons folder. Make sure that you have loaded the prlessons folder onto your hard drive from the supplied DVD. The Starting up section at the beginning of this book provides detailed information about loading lesson files, resetting your workspace, locating missing media, and opening the files in CC. If you have not already done so, please review these instructions before starting this lesson.

When opening the Premiere Pro project files used in this lesson you may experience a missing media message. You must locate any missing media before trying to proceed through the lessons. For more information refer to "Locating missing media" in the Starting up section of this book.

Capturing from a tape-based camera

If you are working with tape-based media, before you can add footage to a Premiere Pro project you must capture it from the digital tape-based medium where you recorded it, to a digital file on your hard drive. To complete the activities in this lesson, you need a digital video camcorder or a video deck connected to your computer via a FireWire cable. FireWire connections are very fast, but capture from a linear device, such as digital video tape, always occurs in real time, so capturing 40 minutes of video takes 40 minutes to accomplish.

Video decks are the digital video equivalent of a VCR (Video Cassette Recorder). Video decks have a FireWire or other connection to attach to a computer, some have a display screen, and they let video editors capture video without connecting a camera.

Before beginning the capture process detailed in this part of the lesson, you should perform the following steps to set up your FireWire equipped digital video camera or video deck and the tape you want to capture:

1   Connect your camcorder or deck to your computer using a FireWire cable, also known as ieee1394 or iLink, and turn it on.

You can connect the FireWire cable when either of the devices you are connecting is on, but we strongly recommend turning the devices off before connecting them to avoid possible damage to the devices.

2   Place the tape you want to capture from into your camcorder or video deck.

3   If you are using a digital camcorder, set it to VCR mode to let Premiere Pro interact and control it.

4   Move your camera's playhead to the location on your tape that you want to capture from.

Understanding the Capture panel interface

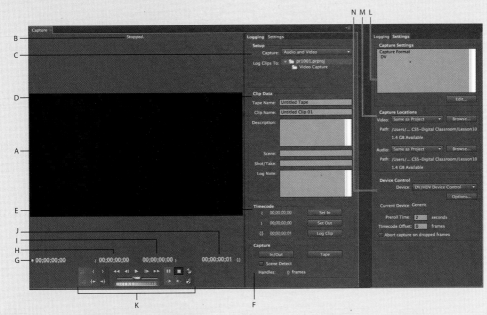

A. Video Preview. B. Camera/Deck status message. C. Capture Setup. D. Clip Data. E. Timecode. F. Capture.
G. Playhead Position. H. In Point. I. Out Point. J. Duration. K. Transport Controls. L. Capture Settings.
M. Capture Location. N. Device Control.

Video Preview: shows the video source from the camcorder or video deck when the video is playing. When paused, the preview shows the video frame at the current position of the playhead.

Camera/Deck status message: displays the status of the capture device.

Capture Setup: use it to specify the capture destination bin, called the Logging Bin, and the source media to capture (video, audio, or both). By default, the capture destination is set to the root of the Project panel.

Clip Data: use it to specify the tape and clip names, add a description, log notes, and any other metadata that can be displayed in the Project panel once the clip is captured. You can use this information as part of the media management task to organize and rate footage for inclusion in a project.

Timecode: displays the current In and Out points set on a tape. Use these points during the logging process to define different clips or the areas on a tape that you can capture from, for example, a specific scene.

Capture: contains the commands to initiate the capture process. You can capture the entire tape or only the area set by the current In and Out points in the Timecode area described above.

Playhead Position: shows the current timecode position of the playhead.

(continues)

Understanding the Capture panel interface (continued)

In Point: shows the currently set In point on the tape. You can set the In point when logging or capturing only a portion of the currently loaded tape.

Out Point: shows the currently set Out point on the tape. You can set the Out point when logging or capturing only a portion of the currently loaded tape.

Duration: shows the duration of the video or the time between the current In and Out points on the tape.

Transport Controls: use them to navigate the tape in the Capture panel much as you would in the Source and Program monitors. You can play and pause the tape, initiate capture using the record button, fast forward or rewind the tape, move forward or back frame-by-frame, and use other navigational controls.

Capture Settings: use them to display and edit the type of capture (DV or HDV) you are performing. Found in the Settings tab.

Capture Location: use it to specify the location for captured footage on the hard drive. You can configure these settings in the Scratch Disks tab of the new project dialog box, and later override them here as necessary. Found in the Settings tab.

Device Control: use them to specify the type of camcorder the capture panel will interact with. For most cameras, the standard, generic settings are enough to let Premiere Pro control device playback. Occasionally, you might need to specify the manufacturer and model of your camera to allow device control. Found in the Settings tab.

Using the Capture panel

You can use the Capture panel to log and capture footage from digital video camcorders or decks. *Logging* is the process of reviewing and annotating every scene and shot recorded on a tape. *Capturing* is the process of transferring the digital video from the tape where it is stored in linear form to a file on your computer, where you can access each clip in a non-linear fashion. The term used is specifically called capturing instead of digitizing because modern video tape camcorders already record footage into a digital format.

When the cost of stable digital storage could not be easily afforded, editors would log everything on a tape and only capture the needed footage. Now, high capacity hard disk drives are affordable and reliable, so many editors capture every piece of footage on a tape and sort it after capturing. Premiere Pro can automatically detect different scenes on your tape based on when recording was started and paused (every time you pressed the Record/Pause toggle button on the camera) through a feature called Scene Detect, which can help you sort and capture all footage on your tape.

In this section of the lesson, we will demonstrate the capture of clips from a tape that contains shots taken in and around the city of Boston, Massachusetts. You can adjust the clip settings used in this exercise when you capture your own tapes; the specific values used in this section are for demonstration purposes only. Later in this lesson, you will discover how to work with non-tape based systems as many devices are now recording directly to removable high capacity memory cards and integrated hard drives.

Due to the nature of the tape-based capture process, this section of the book is intended to be used more for informational purposes so that you have the knowledge to capture your own tapes rather than an actual step by step lesson.

1   With your project open, choose File > Capture to open the Capture panel.

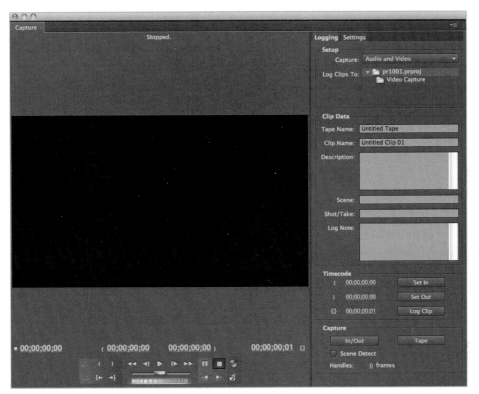

If the capture panel does not detect a device, text at the top to the panel lets you know the capture device is offline.

You can also press the F5 key to open the Capture panel.

2 In the Capture panel, locate the Logging tab on the right and click the Video Capture bin in the Log Clips To menu.

Clips are placed in the root area of the Project panel by default. You can specify a different bin to log clips to.

3 Set your tape and clip names in the Clip Data section of the Logging tab. We recommend matching the name on the physical label on the tape so you can easily find it should you need to recapture your footage due to loss or damage.

For this example, we used the following settings:

Tape Name: Boston Travelogue Tape 1

Clip Name: Boston Sites

Description: Video taken of and around the city of Boston for use in Adobe Premiere Pro Digital Classroom.

The fields Scene, Shot/Take, and Log Note were not used for this footage. These fields are often used when capturing dramatic or narrative works divided into scenes and usually contain multiple takes for each scene.

4   In the Capture section of the panel, select the Scene Detect check box to make this
feature available.

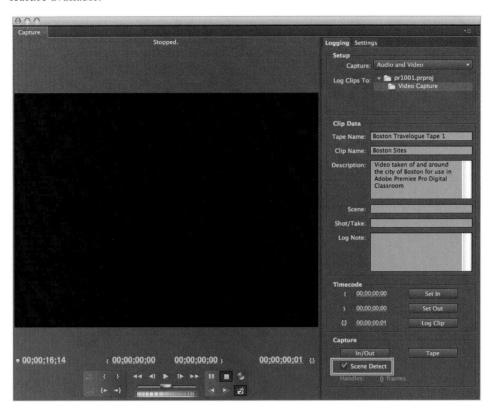

For the purposes of the Capture panel, a scene occurs every time the camera recording is paused.

5   Click the Tape button in the capture section of the dialog box to begin the capture
process. Premiere Pro automatically begins playback on the capture device.

After capturing is complete, the status message displays paused, and the clips appear inside the logging folder you specified.

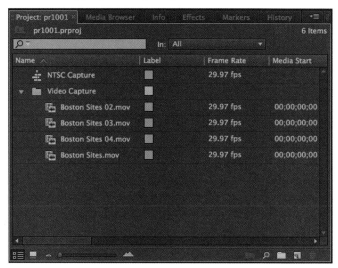

The clip names are automatically enumerated based on the name you indicated in the Capture panel.

6   Close the Capture panel and choose File > Save or press Control+S (Windows) or Command+S (Mac OS) to save the project file. Close this file; you have completed this section of the lesson.

To capture from other tapes, eject the tape from your camera or deck, insert a new tape, and begin the capture process again after changing the tape and clip names.

Capturing from an analog source

The process described in this lesson is only good for capturing footage that is already digital; digital video tape from a FireWire equipped device. If you are working with analog footage from a VHS or Beta tape you can adjust this workflow to accommodate your needs. The process of digitizing footage from an analog video source, such as VCR or non-digital camcorder, is similar to the process of capturing from a digital source. All analog devices have a connection port, such as RCA or coaxial. To digitize from an analog source, you must connect it to a digital converter, such as a dedicated analog-to-digital media converter device, or a FireWire-equipped camcorder or video deck. Many camcorders and video decks have analog inputs you can set to a bypass mode to pass video and audio signals to a computer, thus allowing them to function as digital converters.

To convert an analog source to digital

1   Attach your analog device to your FireWire-equipped camcorder or video deck, or to an analog-to-digital converter.

2   Attach your FireWire-equipped digital device to your computer and turn all devices on. If you are using a camcorder, confirm that it is set to VCR mode.

3   Open the Premiere Pro Capture panel and wait for it to detect your FireWire device.

4   In the Device section of the Settings tab, change the device control from DV/HDV Device Control to None; you cannot rely on the camera control features of Premiere Pro when working with analog devices.

5   Begin the capture process by clicking the Record button in the Transport controls and then pressing the Play button on your analog device. You should see the analog video playing in the video preview area of the Capture panel.

6   When you have captured the part of your analog source that you need, click the Stop button in the transport controls and then stop your analog device.

Transferring from a non-tape based camera

Many of the cameras sold today store footage onto a variety of digital storage media and are not tape-based. These file-based camcorders are produced by different manufacturers with their own specifications; some examples include the Panasonic P2 camcorders, AVCHD camcorders, Sony's XDCAM HD and CDCAM EX camcorders, DSLR cameras and the RED digital cinema cameras. The storage media used by these camcorders varies from hard disk drives to optical media such as a DVD or flash memory cards like CF or SD cards.

As is the case with mini-DV tape-based devices, the tapeless camcorders perform the capture and digitizing process so you do not need to capture or digitize the files before importing them to Premiere Pro. The process of reading the data files from the recording media and then converting it into a format you can use in your projects is called ingesting. Premiere Pro CS5 is designed to ingest and work with the native files of tapeless formats without pre-importing conversions.

Adobe provides specific guidelines and recommendations for working with footage from RED, XDCAM, and other tapeless formats at *www.adobe.com*.

You can import assets directly from the camcorder's tapeless media, but best practice is to transfer the footage to your hard disk drive first and then import it into Premiere Pro. Most tapeless cameras have a built-in USB port you can use for this purpose. For cameras that record onto portable media, such as CF and SD cards, you can use card readers.

Self study

Attach your tape-based camcorder to your computer, and then capture your own footage.

Review

Questions

1   The Premiere Pro project file contains references to the _____ that you import and the other original content, such as _____ and _____, that you create in the application.

2   What are the four types of scratch disks you can set when creating a new project?

3   What do the terms logging and capturing mean?

Answers

1   media (video, audio, images), titles, sequences

2   The four types of scratch disks you can set when creating a new project are: Captured Video, Captured Audio, Video Preview, and Audio Previews.

3   *Logging* is the process of reviewing and annotating every scene recorded on a tape. *Capturing* is the process of transferring the digital video from the tape where it is stored in linear form to a file on your computer, where you can access each clip in a non-linear fashion.

What you'll learn in this lesson:

- Exporting a sequence from Premiere Pro for use in Encore

- Creating menus and building DVD navigation

- Exporting an interactive Flash (.swf) file for display on the web

Using Adobe Encore

Adobe Encore is a powerful application you can use to build projects for DVDs, Blu-ray disks, and interactive Flash (.swf) videos. Encore is included with Premiere Pro.

Starting up

In this lesson you will work with the project files from the AppElessons folder. Make sure that you have loaded the prlessons folder onto your hard drive from the supplied DVD. The Starting up section at the beginning of this book provides detailed information about loading lesson files, resetting your workspace, locating missing media, and opening the files in CC. If you have not already done so, please review these instructions before starting this lesson.

Downloading Adobe Encore

Adobe Encore does not have a Creative Cloud version instead you can download and install Encore CS6 with your subscription. Even though it has not received an update you still have a very powerful and flexible application for Blu-ray disk and DVD authoring available to you. In order to complete this section of the book you must install Encore CS6 from the Adobe Application Manager.

Downloading the Adobe Encore Library Content

In this section of the book you will be working mostly with Adobe Encore. The application has a Library feature that allows you to access menu templates, buttons and other functional content. If you have not already done so you can download this additional functional content by reviewing the Adobe help page on this topic at the following link: *http://helpx.adobe.com/x-productkb/multi/library-functional-content-missing.html*.

Understanding the DVD/Blu-ray/Flash authoring process

The process for authoring projects for use as DVD, Blu-ray disk, or Flash files (.swf) is similar in all cases:

1 Export a Premiere Pro sequence to a format compatible with DVD or Blu-ray disk.

2 Create a DVD or Blu-ray disk Encore project.

3 Import your video and audio files into the Encore project and add them to Timelines.

4 Create menus with buttons, and then link the buttons to Timelines and other menus to generate navigation.

5 Output the completed project to a variety of formats, such as disk image, disk folder, and Flash file (.swf); or burn a DVD or Blu-ray disk directly from the application.

You can author DVD or Blu-ray disk content in the Creative Suite using Adobe Encore, which is included as part of the Creative Suite Production Premium, and the Master Collection when you subscribe to the Creative Cloud and is included with Adobe Premiere Pro when you purchase it individually. However, it is important to keep in mind that Encore is not the only application that can be used to create DVD and Blu-ray disks. Premiere Pro can be used as a stand-alone application and you can always export video files from Premiere Pro and use a third-party application for your disk authoring.

Understanding DVD formatting

DVD is an acronym for Digital Video Disk (also known as Digital Versatile Disk); the technology was created in the mid-1990s by a group of companies that included Phillips and Sony. DVDs are a digital optical storage medium that uses laser to read and write data onto a disk. These disks can store a wide variety of content, including video, audio, and data files. DVDs intended for playback on a console or DVD player follow a specific convention: the video is encoded into the MPEG-2 format; menus and sub-menus can be included to navigate the content; and additional content can be added. The DVD is then written into a standardized file and folder structure and burned to a disk.

The Adobe Suite of products provides you with the end-to-end tools you need to create a DVD project.

Understanding Blu-ray formatting

Officially released in 2006, the Blu-ray disk format was developed by the Blu-ray Disk Association, a group composed of consumer electronics makers, computer hardware makers, and elements of the film industry. Blu-ray disks were created to supersede DVDs and become a distribution medium for high-definition digital content. As with DVDs, Adobe Encore offers a wide range of tools for authoring content to display on Blue-ray disks. High-definition video content is usually encoded using the H.264 codec, but Blu-ray technology supports MPEG-2 to maintain backwards-compatibility with DVDs.

About the project

In this lesson, you will learn to export sequences from Premiere Pro and use them to construct a DVD project in Adobe Encore. You will build a DVD-based demo reel composed of the projects you have worked on in this book. In the two following exercises, you will learn the two most common ways of transferring your sequences from Premiere Pro to Encore. The first is a direct export that converts your sequence into DVD-compatible audio and video files. The second option is called Adobe Dynamic Link and it is a more direct alternative, but requires Adobe Premiere Pro purchased as part of the Production Premium suite or Master Collection. Dynamic Link lets you use an unrendered, Premiere Pro sequence directly inside an Encore project, thus eliminating the need to pre-render your sequence into MPEG-2 format.

Exporting an MPEG-2 DVD file

Any MPEG-2 file works when creating a DVD, but for flexibility, especially to add more than one audio track to your projects, we recommend using the MPEG-2 DVD export preset. This preset produces two separate files: the video portion of the exported sequence is written to an M2V file, and the audio portion of the sequence is written to a separate WAV file. To use a third-party application to author your DVD content, use the MPEG-2 DVD export preset to export your sequences.

In this portion of the lesson, you will open an existing Premiere Pro project and export an MPEG-2 file for use in your Encore project. You can find the media for this section of the lesson in the Media Library folder. Locate the video used for this lesson, **Central Park-NYC-Lake Scene.AVI** and **Central Park-NYC-Fountain Scene.AVI**, in the video sub-folder of the Travelogue-New York folder. You can find the audio used for this project, **Classical Background Music.mp3**, in the Audio folder.

1 From the Premiere Pro Welcome screen, click the Open Project button, or with Premiere Pro already open, chose File > Open Project. Navigate to the AppElessons folder that you copied to your hard drive, and locate the **AppE01.prproj** file. Double-click the file to open it.

This project contains a single sequence called Lake Scene. There are some transitions used in this sequence that you should render before exporting the file, as explained in the next step.

2 Click the Timeline panel to make it active, and then press the Enter (Windows) or Return (Mac OS) key on your keyboard to render all areas of the Timeline that need rendering.

Premiere Pro automatically previews the Timeline when the rendering is done. Press the spacebar on your keyboard or click any area of the Timeline panel to stop the playback.

3 With the Lake Scene sequence still active, choose File > Export > Media to open the Export Settings dialog box.

4 In the Export Settings dialog box, choose MPEG2-DVD from the Format pull-down menu, and from the Preset pull-down menu, choose NTSC 23.976P Wide.

The NTSC high-quality setting lets a DVD store approximately two hours of high-quality content.

Some third-party authoring programs do not import audio and video as separate files. In such cases, use the setting named MPEG2 in the format menu to produce a single file.

5 Click the Output Name field to open the Save As dialog box, and then navigate to the AppElessons folder. Click the Save button on the dialog box to set this folder as the export destination, and then return to the Export Settings dialog.

Only the name of the exported file appears in the Output Name field; nothing else changes.

6 Select the Use Previews check box at the bottom of the dialog box. This option applies only when exporting sequences from Premiere Pro. When selected, you can use any preview files already generated for transitions and effects on the Timeline, thus making the rendering process faster.

If you have already rendered the effects and transitions used on your Timeline, you can save time by selecting the Use Previews check box when exporting.

Click the Export button to export the sequence from Premiere Pro.

7 Choose File > Save As. In the Save Project dialog box that appears, confirm that you are still in the AppElessons folder, rename your file to **AppE-working**, and then click the Save button.

Close the project. You have completed this section of the lesson.

You will use the file you exported after you create a new DVD project in Adobe Encore.

Creating a new Encore project

Encore is available as part of a suite of products and is also included with the individual purchase of Premiere Pro, so you can use Encore to author dynamic DVDs, Blu-ray disks, and Flash files (.swf). After importing media files into an Encore project, you can create menus step by step, or use pre-built templates that are PSD files familiar to Photoshop users. Encore lets you open a menu in Photoshop so you can use it to create new menus or enhance your existing menu content.

In this part of the lesson, you will create a new project and import the files you exported from Premiere Pro in the previous exercise. To continue this part of the lesson, please open Adobe Encore now.

1   From the Adobe Encore Welcome screen, click the New Project button, or with Encore already open, chose File > New > Project to open the New Project dialog box.

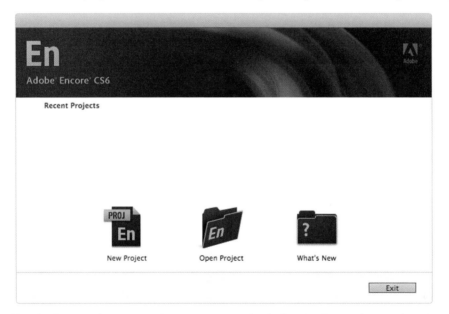

Encore's welcome screen lets you open projects, create new ones, and read information about new features in the version of the software you are using.

2   In the New project dialog box, change the default project name to **Demo Reel**, click the Browse button to navigate to the AppElessons folder that you copied to your hard drive, and choose it as the location to store your project files.

3 In the Project Settings section of the dialog box, click on the radio button next to DVD and from the Television Standard drop-down list choose NTSC.

Click OK to create the project.

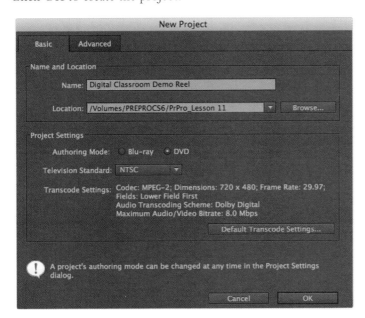

Choosing the Authoring Mode and Television Standard automatically configures the transcode settings used in the project.

The transcode settings control the way in which video brought into the project is converted into a format compatible with DVD or Blu-ray.

When working in Encore, you can choose how to import different types of footage: you can indicate that a specific file be treated as a menu, pop-up menu, Timeline, or Slideshow. Menus are used when creating a DVD or Blu-ray disk project to allow you to navigate to different areas; they are what create the non-linear nature of the disk-based experience. Pop-up menus are a special type of menu used only in Blu-ray disk projects. Timeline is where you place the audio and video resources that you wish a viewer to see, and finally slideshows are used to show a series of still images allowing you to author an image gallery on your disk.

Asset is the default option that you will use when importing audio and video content that you do not want to convert into a Timeline.

4   Choose File > Import As > Asset. Navigate to the AppElessons folder and select the **Lake Scene.M2V** and Lake Scene.wav files that you created earlier in this lesson.

Highlight more than one file on a computer running the Windows OS by pressing and holding the Control key while clicking each file. On a computer running the Mac OS, press and hold the Command key to select multiple files.

5   Click the Open button to complete the Import and return to Encore.

6   Right-click (Windows) or Ctrl+click (Mac OS) any empty area of the Project panel and choose Import As > Asset from the menu that appears.

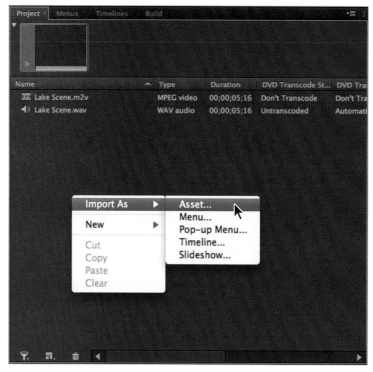

Many of the shortcuts from Premiere Pro work in Encore.

7   Navigate to the Media Library, locate the DVD creation folder, highlight the four files listed in the table below, and then click the Open button to import them.

Jeff Jacobs-I Will.m2v

Jeff Jacobs-I Will.wav

Reporter at Crime Scene.m2v

Reporter at Crime Scene.wav

Name	Type	Duration	DVD Transcode St...	DVD Transcode Settings
Jeff Jacobs-I Will.m2v	MPEG video	00;00;29;10	Don't Transcode	Don't Transcode
Jeff Jacobs-I Will.wav	WAV audio	00;00;29;10	Untranscoded	Automatic
Lake Scene.m2v	MPEG video	00;00;05;16	Don't Transcode	Don't Transcode
Lake Scene.wav	WAV audio	00;00;05;16	Untranscoded	Automatic
NYC-Central Park.m2v	MPEG video	00;00;32;15	Don't Transcode	Don't Transcode
NYC-Central Park.wav	WAV audio	00;00;32;15	Untranscoded	Automatic
Reporter at Crime Scene.m2v	MPEG video	00;00;24;15	Don't Transcode	Don't Transcode
Reporter at Crime Scene.wav	WAV audio	00;00;24;15	Untranscoded	Automatic

The Project panel displays files in alphabetical order, thus letting you see how your audio and video files relate to each other.

8   Choose File > Save or press Ctrl+S (Windows) or Command+S (Mac OS) to save these changes to your project. Do not close this file; you will need it in the next part of the lesson.

Next, you will use Adobe Dynamic Link to import the final piece of footage you will need for this project.

The Adobe Encore Tools

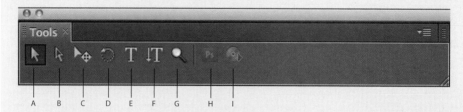

*A. Selection Tool. **B.** Direct Selection Tool. **C.** Move Tool. **D.** Rotate Tool. **E.** Text Tool. **F.** Vertical Text Tool. **G.** Zoom Tool. **H.** Edit Menu in Photoshop. **I.** Preview.*

A. Selection Tool: Use it to select and move button layers when working with menus. You can also use it to scale or rotate the selected content using the content's bounding box.

B. Direct Selection Tool: Use it to select and move text and image layers when working with menus. You can also use it to scale or rotate the selected content using the content's bounding box.

C. Move Tool: Use it to move any currently selected item in a menu. You can also use it to scale and rotate the selected content using the content's bounding box.

D. Rotate Tool: Use it to rotate any item you selected with the Selection or Direct Selection tools.

E. Text Tool: Use it to select and edit any existing text layer or create new ones. Create new text layers by clicking and dragging to create an area with defined boundaries, or by clicking and releasing the mouse to create a boundless text area.

F. Vertical Text Tool: This tool works like the Text tool, but the text is oriented vertically instead of horizontally.

G. Zoom Tool: Use it to zoom in or out in the menu panel. Click to zoom in incrementally; click and drag an area to zoom in on a region of the screen. Press and hold the ALT (Windows) or Option (Mac OS) key to zoom out. Double-click the Zoom tools icon in the tools panel to set the menu panel's zoom level to 100%.

H. Edit Menu in Photoshop: Active only when working with a menu. Use it to edit the original menu file in Photoshop.

I. Preview: Use it to test your DVD or Blu-ray project.

Creating a Timeline

Encore has Timelines that work somewhat differently from the Timelines in Premiere Pro. In Encore, Timelines hold video and audio files, but unlike Premiere Pro, you can only have a single video track per Timeline. However, Encore Timelines can have multiple audio tracks, so you can have several language tracks. This is how DVD players can switch between multiple dubbed language tracks on a single disk. Encore Timelines can also contain tracks for sub-titles.

In this portion of the lesson, you will create a Timeline for the four sets of video and audio clips you imported. For this DVD, you will have a single Timeline, and then use chapter markers to create the ability to navigate to different points along the Timeline.

1   With the **Demo Reel.ncor** project open, choose File > New > Timeline to create a new Timeline for your media files.

A new item called Untitled Timeline appears in the Project panel and a Timeline appears at the bottom of the application interface.

2   Click the Untitled Timeline in the Project panel to highlight it; its properties appear in the Properties panel at the right of the interface.

In the Properties panel, change the Timeline name to **Demo Reel**, and then add the following description: **This is a demo reel of the projects created using the Premiere Pro Digital Classroom**. You may need to expand the panel to read the entire description.

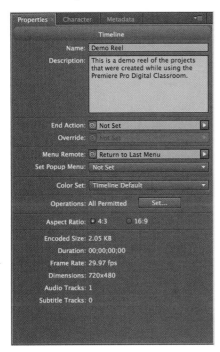

Names and Descriptions help you keep a project organized.

3 In the Project panel, select the video (**Jeff Jacobs–I WIll.m2v**) and audio (**Jeff Jacobs–I WIll.wav**) files for the Jeff Jacobs–I Will music video and drag them to the Demo Reel Timeline at the bottom of the interface.

The beginning of the Video and Audio 1 tracks automatically become highlighted; place your files at the highlighted points.

The Audio 1 track is automatically set as the English track. Add more tracks by right-clicking (Windows) or Ctrl+click (Mac OS) the track head and selecting Add Audio Track from the menu that appears. Make sure you assign the proper language to each track using the drop-down menu to the right of the track name.

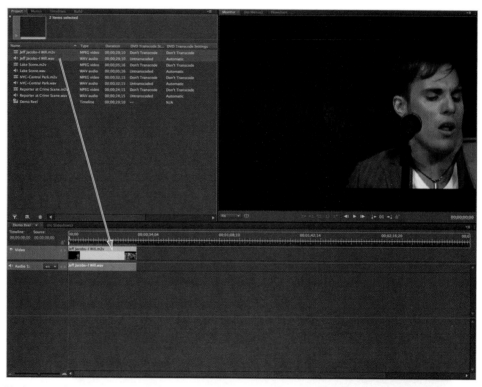

The beginning of the music video clip appears in the monitor.

4   Click the Reporter at Crime Scene audio and video files and drag it onto the Timeline; notice that they will automatically snaps into place next to the first few clips.

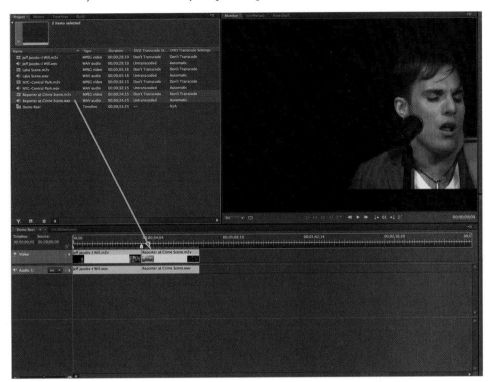

In Encore, clips you add to the Timeline automatically snap to the end of the clips already on the Timeline.

5   Select the audio and video file for the NYC–Central Park clips and add them to the Timeline after the Reporter at Crime Scene clips.

     Repeat this procedure for the Lake Scene clips and add them to the end of the Timeline.

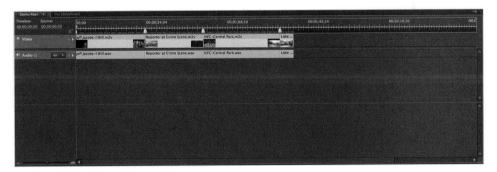

Be careful when adding clips to the Timeline: if you drag your clips below the Audio 1 track, you will create another audio track.

6 Choose File > Save, press Ctrl+S (Windows), or press Command+S (Mac OS) to save changes to your project. Do not close this file; you will need it in the next part of the lesson.

In the next part of the lesson, you will work with the chapter markers that were automatically added at the beginning of each pair of clips.

Renaming chapter markers

In the previous exercise, a chapter marker was automatically added to the Timeline as you added a pair of clips. Chapter markers help you create menu navigation because each marker creates a unique point along the Timeline that can be navigated to independently.

1 With the **Demo Reel.ncor** project still open, click the first chapter marker to see its properties in the Properties panel.

2 In the Properties panel, change the name of this first marker to **Jeff Jacobs**.

Click on the other chapter markers one at a time and assign the following names to each of them respectively.

MARKER NUMBER	NEW NAME
2	Reporter
3	Central Park
4	Lake Scene

You will use these names when you build the navigational menus for this DVD.

3 Choose File > Save, press Ctrl+S (Windows), or press Command+S (Mac OS) to save changes to your project. Do not close this file; you will need it in the next part of the lesson.

In the next portion of the lesson, you will organize the project panel so it is not cluttered.

Organizing the Project panel

Media management is an important aspect of working with Encore, as it is with Premiere Pro. A disorganized Project panel can complicate a project, because media becomes more difficult to locate.

1   With the **Demo Reel.ncor** project still open, click on the project panel to highlight it, then choose File > New > Folder to open the New Folder Name dialog box. Change the default folder name to Assets and click the OK button to create the folder in the Project panel.

Similar to Premiere Pro, Encore uses folders to organize the Project panel content.

2   Select all the video and audio files in the Project panel, then drag and drop them into the new Assets folder you just created.

The folder becomes highlighted to indicate you will add the selected content.

3   Choose File > Save, press Ctrl+S (Windows), or press Command+S (Mac OS) to save changes to your project. Do not close this file; you will need it in the next part of the lesson.

In the next portion of the lesson, you will build the menus that will link the content of this project.

Creating Menus

Menus are the basis for all navigation in a DVD or Blu-ray project:

- They contain navigational buttons so viewers can access the project's content.

- They can be used to play a timeline, navigate to individual chapter points, navigate to other menus, or set the active audio and sub-title tracks.

With Adobe Encore, you can create custom menus using assets from the Encore Library, or edit those assets in Adobe Photoshop to create new and unique content. You can also use pre-built menus downloaded from Adobe Resource Central, modify those pre-built menus in Photoshop, or create original menus directly from Photoshop PSD files.

All the menus installed with Encore or downloaded as templates from the Internet are native Photoshop documents (.psd), thus letting you customize existing content or create unique, new content from the beginning. Because the files are native Photoshop files, you can also use animation programs like Adobe After Effects to create motion graphics using the same assets available for your menus.

In this portion of the lesson, you will import and customize two Photoshop files already prepared for use as the main menu and sub-menu of this project.

1   With the Demo Reel.ncor project still open, choose File > New > Folder, and in the New Folder Name dialog box, change the default folder name to **Menus**. Click the OK button to create the new folder.

2   In the Project panel, click the Menus folder to highlight it, and then choose File > Import As > Menu to open the Import as Menu dialog box. Navigate to the DVD Creation folder in the Media Library and highlight the **Digital Classroom Menu SD NTSC.psd** and **Digital Classroom Submenu SD NTSC.psd** files. Click the Open button to import them directly into the Menus folder. Click the reveal triangle to the left of the folder name to show its content.

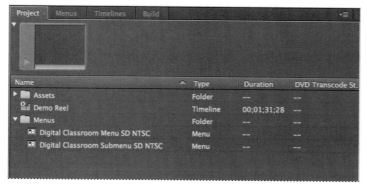

In Encore, the folder reveal triangle is always available, even if the folder is empty.

3 If necessary, click the dividing line between the name and type in the Project panel and drag it to the right to reveal the full file name of both menus.

Double-click the Digital Classroom Menu SD NTSC to select it and make it active.

Double-clicking the menu opens it in the Menu panel and brings that panel in front of the monitor.

4 Click the Layers panel in the lower-right side of the interface to make it active and bring it to the front of the display. Notice that the menu is divided into several layers and layer folders; this is the content created in Photoshop that you can add to, delete, or customize in Encore.

Notice also that each button is contained within its own layer folder. Click the reveal triangle to the left of the layer folder called (+) Special Features and notice that it is composed of a text layer and another layer called (=1) highlight. All the other button layer folders are created in the same way.

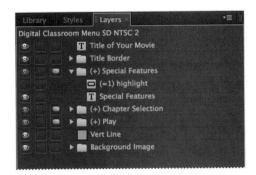

The (=1) highlight layer is only available when the button is activated during the DVD playback.

The special symbols at the beginning of the layer folders let Encore recognize these layers as buttons.

5 Double-click the Zoom tool in the Tools bar to set the menu panel zoom level to 100%, and then click the Selection tool to activate it.

Click the Special features button in the menu panel to select it.

With the button selected, press the Backspace (Windows) or Delete (Mac OS) key on your keyboard to delete it. This menu only needs two buttons: one to play the Demo Reel Timeline, and the other to take you to the sub-menu to navigate to each individual clip.

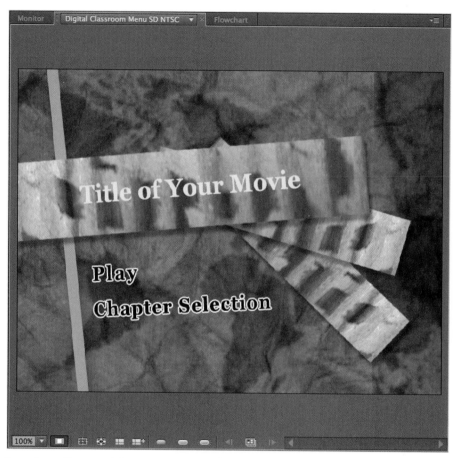

You need to modify most pre-built menus to suit your specific project.

6   Click the Show Safe Area button (⊞) at the bottom of the Menu panel to show the Action and Title Safe Margins.

Click the Chapter Selection button with the Selection tool and drag it toward the bottom of the menu; make sure to keep it within the safe margins.

The safe margins used in Encore are similar to the ones in Premiere Pro.

7 Click the Text Tool in the Tools panel to activate it, and then click the text for the Chapter Selection button three times. This selects all the text for this button so you can edit it without affecting the rest of the button.

With the text selected, change it to **View Individual Clips**.

Clicking three times with the text tool selects all the text in the button; double-clicking selects a single word.

When text is selected, editing it is similar to using the Titler in Premiere Pro. You can edit text properties using the Character panel located at the upper-right of the application interface. From the Character panel, you can edit the font, font style, size, tracking, leading color, and other properties of the selected text.

8   With the Text tool still active, click the Title of Your Movie text three times to select it.

Change this text to **DEMO REEL 2012**.

You can also select text by clicking and dragging with the Text tool, just as you would in a word processing application.

9   With the *DEMO REEL 2012* text still selected, click on the Character panel to activate it and make it visible.

Click on the color swatch and in the Color Picker that appears, set the R, G, and B values to zero by clicking the current values and changing them.

Click OK to close the Color Picker and change the text color to black.

You can enter colors into the color picker using HSB, RGB, or Hexadecimal values. You can also click the color field to the left to visually set the active color.

RGB (Red, Green, and Blue) are the primary colors of the RGB color mode used for all on-screen design for computer monitors, projectors, and television sets.

10 Click in any empty part of the Menu panel to deselect the text.

You can also select text by clicking and dragging with the Text tool, just as you would in a word processing application.

In the next part of this lesson, you will edit the sub-menu to link its buttons to the chapter markers in the Timeline.

To deselect items in your menu, you can also use the Edit > Deselect All command or the keyboard shortcut Ctrl+Shift+A (Windows) or Command+Shift+A (Mac OS).

11 Choose File > Save, press Ctrl+S (Windows), or press Command+S (Mac OS) to save changes to your project. Do not close this file; you will need it in the next part of the lesson.

Linking buttons to chapter markers

In this part of the lesson, you will use the menu items you created in the last section to build your project's navigation.

1   With the **Demo Reel.ncor** project still open, double-click the Digital Classroom Submenu SD NTSC in the Project panel to open it in the Menu panel.

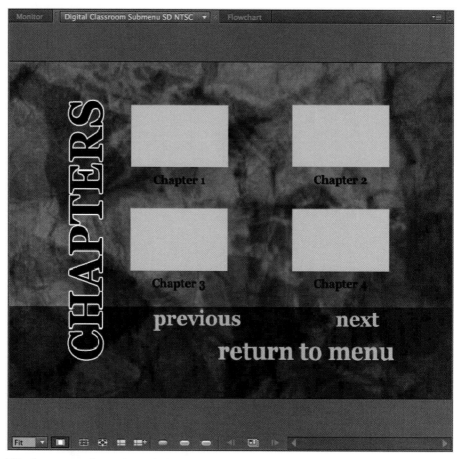

This submenu contains buttons that can display a video preview of the chapters they link to.

2 Activate the Selection tool and click the button labeled Chapter 1. Note the button includes the gray rectangle along with the text "Chapter 1."

The button properties appear in the Properties panel on the right. The property used for navigation is called Link.

Use the Properties panel to add navigation and set item properties in Encore.

3 In the Properties panel, enable the Set Name from Link check box, and then from the Link pull-down menu, choose Demo Reel > Jeff Jacobs.

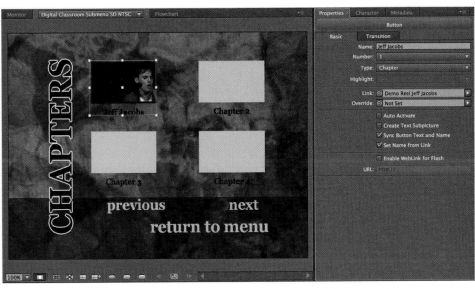

The name of the button and the on-screen text of the button change to match the name of the chapter marker.

4 The Timeline panel remained fixed on the Demo Reel Timeline when you edited the menus in this and the preceding exercise. You will now use the Timeline to set a link for the remaining buttons on the menu.

Again with the Selection tool active, click the Chapter 2 button to highlight it. In the Properties panel, enable the button's Set Name from Link check box switch.

Click the Pick Whip (☜) to the left of the Link property in the Properties Panel and drag it to the second chapter marker on the Timeline.

As do most Adobe applications, Encore lets you perform the same task in several ways.

5   Set the links for the final two chapter buttons using the method outlined in the previous two steps.

Link the Chapter 3 button to the third chapter marker called Central Park.

Link the Chapter 4 button to the fourth chapter marker called Lake Scene.

Make sure you click each button's Set Name from Link check box. You can do this before or after setting the Link property.

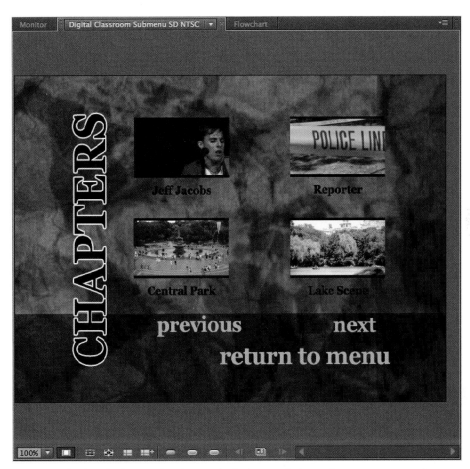

The image displayed in video buttons such as these is set by the chapter marker's poster frame property; you can select a marker to change it.

6   With the Menu panel active, deselect all the items on your menu by choosing Edit > Deselect All, or use the keyboard shortcut Ctrl+Shift+A (Windows) or Command+Shift+A (Mac OS). When none of the items on the menu are selected, the menu properties appear in the Properties panel.

Click the Motion property tab to view the menu's Motion options. These options let you set the background audio and video to display when the menu is on the screen; you can also use the options to set other properties to create animated, engaging menus.

Enable the check box next to the Animate Buttons property to convert the still video frames into looping video buttons. You will see the effects of enabling motion once you preview the menu.

7   Click the Selection tool to activate it, click the previous button on the menu, and press the Backspace (Windows) or Delete (Mac OS) key on your keyboard to delete it.

Next, select the next button on the menu and delete it as well.

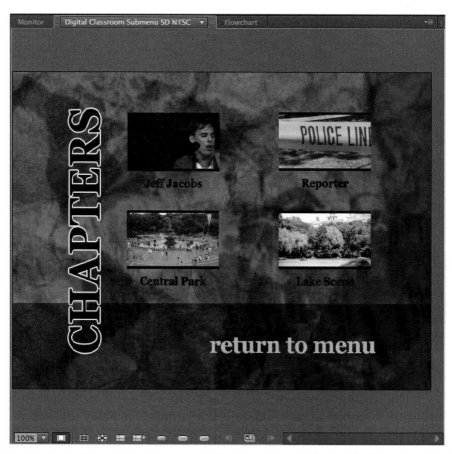

For this project, the Next and Previous buttons are redundant when combined with the Main Menu button because there are only two menus.

8   Choose File > Save, press Ctrl+S (Windows), or press Command+S (Mac OS) to save changes to your project. Do not close this file; you will need it in the next part of the lesson when you add the links to allow the menus to connect to each other.

When editing menus in Adobe Photoshop, do NOT remove the special symbols at the beginning of the button names. You can easily add and copy button layer groups, but the special symbols in the button names help Adobe Encore recognize the button type. Your buttons will not work without the symbols.

Linking menus to each other

To build navigation, you must link the two menus created for this lesson to each other.

1   With the **Demo Reel.ncor** project still open, confirm that the Digital Classroom Submenu is active in the Menu panel. If necessary, double-click the Digital Classroom Submenu in the Project panel to make it active.

2   With the Selection tool, click the Return to Menu button to activate it.

In the Properties panel, change the button name to **Main Menu** to match screen shot below; the button text in the menu panel itself changes after clicking another text field in the panel or after pressing Enter (Windows) or Return (Mac OS).

Click the Link property Pick Whip and drag it to the **Digital Classroom Menu SD NTSC** located in the Project panel.

Use the Pick Whip to link to any item visible in the Project panel and to chapter markers on the Timeline.

3   Double-click the Digital Classroom Menu in the Project panel to make it active, and then click the Play button with the Selection tool to highlight it.

In the Properties panel, change the Play button name property to **PLAY DEMO**; the button text in the menu changes after clicking another text field in the panel or after pressing Enter (Windows) or Return (Mac OS).

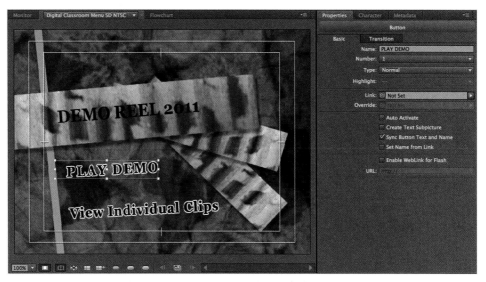

The Sync Button Text and Name check box links the button name property with the button text that appears in the menu.

4   Click the button's Link property drop-down menu and choose Demo Reel > Jeff Jacobs as the target for this button. This links the button to the beginning of the Demo Reel Timeline.

5   With the Selection tool, click the View Individual Clips button to make it active; set its Link property drop-down menu to Digital Classroom Submenu SD NTSC > Default to set the submenu as the button's target.

6   Choose File > Save, press Ctrl+S (Windows), or press Command+S (Mac OS) to save changes to your project. Do not close this file; you will need it in the next part of the lesson to complete the DVD project.

Setting a first play item

The first play item is the menu or Timeline that automatically appears when a DVD first starts. You need to set your main menu as the first play item so it appears on the screen and your DVD navigation works.

1   With the **Demo Reel.ncor** project still open, right-click (Windows) or Ctrl+click (Mac OS) the Digital Classroom Menu SD NTSC menu in the Project panel to open a contextual menu.

2   From the contextual menu, choose Set as First Play; a small play icon appears on the menu icon in the panel.

A small play icon above the menu's icon in the Project panel marks the menu as the first play item.

3   Choose File > Save, press Ctrl+S (Windows), or press Command+S (Mac OS) to save changes to your project. Do not close this file; you need to test it to ensure everything works properly.

Previewing a DVD

You can test your project at any point in the authoring process after setting your first play item. A good best practice to follow is to test throughout the authoring process to avoid costly, time-consuming mistakes, and then again before releasing the project.

1   With the **Demo Reel.ncor** project still open, click the Preview button in the Tools panel to open the Project Preview window.

2   The main menu appears; you can now test your project's navigation.

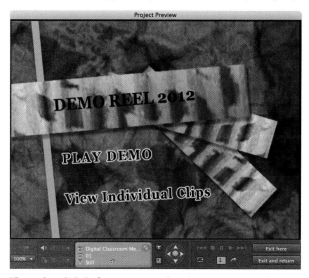

The speed at which the first preview starts depends on your system configuration.

Click the PLAY DEMO button to play the Demo Reel Timeline.

3   After ensuring the button works, return to the menu by clicking the Remote Control
Title Button at the base of the Preview window.

Use the controls at the bottom of the Preview window to simulate the buttons on a remote control.

4   From the main menu, click the View Individual Clips button to navigate to the sub-menu.

From the project sub-menu, click the Reporter clip to navigate to the second chapter
marker on the Timeline.

*There might be a lag when the project is previewing. This is normal and depends on your system
configuration.*

Let the entire clip play to the end; notice that the next clip begins immediately. This is
not the correct behavior for this type of button; the clip should return to the sub-menu
after it finishes playing to allow the user to select a different clip, not automatically start
a new clip. You can correct this behavior by setting End and Override actions.

5   Close the Preview window by clicking the Exit Here button on the lower-right side of the window.

Choose File > Save, press Ctrl+S (Windows), or press Command+S (Mac OS) to save changes to your project. Do not close this file; you will need it open in the next part of the lesson.

Setting End and Override actions

You can use the End and Override actions to control the way in which the user navigates from one section of a Timeline to another. You can apply End actions to Menus, Timelines, and Chapter Markers to set the event that should follow when a specified item finishes playing. You can add Override actions to buttons to override the default end actions of items such as Chapter Markers.

For the exercise in this lesson, the PLAY DEMO button from the main menu should play the entire Demo Reel Timeline; the buttons on the sub-menu should navigate back to the originating menu after the individual clips finish playing.

1   With the **Demo Reel.ncor** project still open, click the first Chapter Marker in the Demo Reel Timeline to select it.

2   In the Properties panel, set the first marker's End Action to go to the next clip on the Timeline by choosing Demo Reel > Reporter from the End Action drop-down menu.

3   Click the second Chapter Marker and set its End Action to Demo Reel > Central Park.

4   Click the third Chapter Marker and set its End Action to Demo Reel > Lake Scene.

5   Click the fourth and final Chapter Marker and set its End Action to Return to Last Menu.

This pattern sets the end action of each Chapter Marker to advance to the next clip on the Timeline. The final Chapter Marker's End Action is set to return to the menu the user was previously on.

The next step of this process is to assign actions to the buttons on the sub-menu to override these end actions and return to the sub-menu when the specified clip has finished playing.

6 Double-click the Digital Classroom Submenu SD NTSC 2 in the Project panel to open it in the Menu panel.

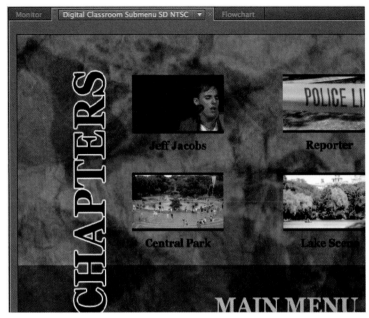

Setting Override Actions is optional; if you choose to use the Override actions, you must set each button.

7 With the Selection tool, click the Jeff Jacobs button to activate it, and in Basic tab of the Properties panel, set its Override property to Link Back to Here.

The actual menu name appears in the drop-down menu when you select Link Back to Here as the Override.

8 Select each of the remaining three buttons and set each Override action to Link Back to Here.

9 Click the Preview button in the Tools panel to open the Project Preview window.

Click the View Individual Clips button to navigate immediately to the sub-menu. Click any of the buttons to view the corresponding clip.

10 Close the Preview window by clicking the Exit Here button on the lower-right side of the window.

Choose File > Save, press Ctrl+S (Windows), or press Command+S (Mac OS) to save changes to your project. Do not close this file; you will need it open in the next part of the lesson to output your project.

Outputting the project

Encore can create projects for distribution to DVD, Blu-ray, or the web. There are several options for distributing to optical disks; for example, you can burn a DVD or Blu-ray disk directly from Encore; or create a disk image, master, or folder for use in a third-party authoring program. Regardless of the output format, you can use the Build panel to output your project.

1 With the **Demo Reel.ncor** project still open, click the Build panel to make it active and visible.

2 From the Build Panel Format drop-down menu, choose DVD; from the Output drop-down menu, choose DVD Folder.

Confirm that the Source area drop-down menu is set to Create Using the Current Project.

Your specific output format varies depending on your needs.

To burn a DVD directly from Encore, choose DVD Disk from the Output drop-down menu. The DVD output method you choose depends on the specific uses for the DVD disk: if you have a burner and want to make a test copy, choose DVD Disk. If you want your DVDs created at a replication facility, the facility should tell you the output they prefer.

3 If necessary, use the scroll bar on the right side of the Build panel to reveal the disk's Destination options.

In the Destination area of the panel, click the Browse button and choose a location to which to write your DVD folder. For this project, use the AppElessons folder as the destination.

Name the Project in the Disk Info section and set the size of the disk you are going to to burn. For example, the figure below shows the Disk name set to Demo Reel and standard single layer DVD as the output media.

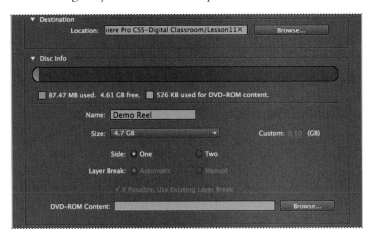

A single layer DVD can hold 4.7 GB of data; a dual layer DVD can hold 8.5.

4   Again if necessary, use the scroll bar on the right side of the Build panel to reveal the disk's Region Coding options.

In the Region Codes section of the panel, set the Region Coding you want to use. For example, to create a DVD without any regional restrictions, choose the All Regions option button. Any other choice will prevent the disk from playing back in DVD players that are set for any unchecked region.

Specify the type of Copy protection to use when creating your disk: you can set the option to make zero, one, or an unlimited number of copies of a disk. For this exercise, disable copy protection to allow an unlimited number of copies to be made.

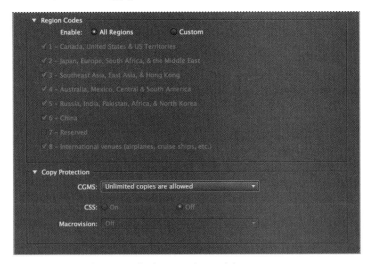

Region coding is a tool to prevent illegal pirating of DVD disks.

5   Click the Check Project button in the top-right corner of the Build panel to open the Check Project panel. Using this panel to check the project before building it is an optional step, but it is very helpful to double-check errors or omissions.

In the Check Project panel, click the Start button to begin checking.

Checking your project is an optional step you can perform at any point in the authoring process.

6   For this exercise, the Project Check indicates that the Demo Reel Timeline does not have an End Action set.

Click the error in the Check Project panel to see the Demo Reel Timeline properties in the Properties panel.

Set the Timeline's End Action to Return to Last Menu, and then close the Check Project panel.

7   Click the Build button on the Build panel to complete the DVD authoring process. A status bar appears on the screen to indicate the progress made. The time it takes to build the DVD depends on the media used and the configuration of your computer.

You can stop the Build process anytime by clicking the Cancel button on the status bar.

8   Choose File > Save, press Ctrl+S (Windows), or press Command+S (Mac OS) to save changes to your project. Close the file; you have completed this lesson.

A note about authoring Blu-ray disks and Flash files

Blu-ray disks were created to replace DVDs. With a capacity approximately five times greater than dual-layer DVD disks, the Blu-ray disk offers content creators the ability to author disks that can hold high-definition video content and allow for much greater depth to create interactive branching experiences. The menu navigation for Blu-ray disks is built in the same way as DVDs, but the content fits one of the high-definition standards. Additionally, the high-definition video you use in the project is encoded using the H.264 codec.

Adobe Encore is not only a tool for creating DVD and Blu-ray disks; you can also output your projects to Adobe Flash. These interactive projects offer an alternative to the traditional optical disk distribution. You can upload Flash projects to a web server and view them online as any other Flash-based content. You can author projects you want to output to Flash as you would other projects; Flash is just an additional output channel for your work.

Self study

Use your own content to create your disks. If you are not familiar with Photoshop, use the pre-built menus from the Library or download menus from Adobe Resource Central.

Review

Questions

1   What is the result of using the MPEG-2 DVD export format in Premiere Pro?

2   The templates, buttons and other elements used in Adobe Encore are all
_____ files, so if you are already a _____ user, you can easily modify or create new menu items.

3   What is the point of setting End and Override actions?

Answers

1   The MPEG-2 DVD export format creates two separate files: the video portion of the exported sequence is written to an M2V file, and the audio portion of the sequence is written to a separate WAV file.

2   PSD, Photoshop

3   You can use the End and Override actions to control the way in which the user navigates from one section of a Timeline to another.

Index

volume keyframes, 233–235
VST Editor Panel, 292

W

Warp Stabilizer, 194–196
Watch Folder panel, Adobe
    Media Encoder, 279
waveform, 89
Web Link markers, 64
welcome screen (Adobe Encore),
    326
widescreen format, 12
windowboxing, 268
Windows, 2

Windows Media Video, 264
wipes, 100
workspace
    customizing, 24–29
    deleting, 28
    description of, 20
    Editing, 20
    panels, 20–22
    setting, 297
    tools, 22–23

X

XDCAM, 14–15
XDCAM EX, 14–15

XDCAM HD, 14–15, 319
XDCAM HD422, 15
XMP metadata, 287

Y

YUV, 140

Z

Zoom In button, 108
Zoom Tool, 23, 330

John Wiley & Sons, Inc.
End-User License Agreement

5. Limited Warranty.

(a) WILEY warrants that the Software and Software Media are free from defects in materials and workmanship under normal use for a period of sixty (60) days from the date of purchase of this Book. If WILEY receives notification within the warranty period of defects in materials or workmanship, WILEY will replace the defective Software Media.

(b) WILEY AND THE AUTHOR(S) OF THE BOOK DISCLAIM ALL OTHER WARRANTIES, EXPRESS OR IMPLIED, INCLUDING WITHOUT LIMITATION IMPLIED WARRANTIES OF MERCHANTABILITY AND FITNESS FOR A PARTICULAR PURPOSE, WITH RESPECT TO THE SOFTWARE, THE PROGRAMS, THE SOURCE CODE CONTAINED THEREIN, AND/OR THE TECHNIQUES DESCRIBED IN THIS BOOK. WILEY DOES NOT WARRANT THAT THE FUNCTIONS CONTAINED IN THE SOFTWARE WILL MEET YOUR REQUIREMENTS OR THAT THE OPERATION OF THE SOFTWARE WILL BE ERROR FREE.

(c) This limited warranty gives you specific legal rights, and you may have other rights that vary from jurisdiction to jurisdiction.

6. Remedies.

(a) WILEY's entire liability and your exclusive remedy for defects in materials and workmanship shall be limited to replacement of the Software Media, which may be returned to WILEY with a copy of your receipt at the following address: Software Media Fulfillment Department, Attn.: *Adobe Premiere Pro CC Digital Classroom*, John Wiley & Sons, Inc., 10475 Crosspoint Blvd., Indianapolis, IN 46256, or call 1-800-762-2974. Please allow four to six weeks for delivery. This Limited Warranty is void if failure of the Software Media has resulted from accident, abuse, or misapplication. Any replacement Software Media will be warranted for the remainder of the original warranty period or thirty (30) days, whichever is longer.

(b) In no event shall WILEY or the author be liable for any damages whatsoever (including without limitation damages for loss of business profits, business interruption, loss of business information, or any other pecuniary loss) arising from the use of or inability to use the Book or the Software, even if WILEY has been advised of the possibility of such damages.

(c) Because some jurisdictions do not allow the exclusion or limitation of liability for consequential or incidental damages, the above limitation or exclusion may not apply to you.

7. U.S. Government Restricted Rights.
Use, duplication, or disclosure of the Software for or on behalf of the United States of America, its agencies and/or instrumentalities "U.S. Government" is subject to restrictions as stated in paragraph (c)(1)(ii) of the Rights in Technical Data and Computer Software clause of DFARS 252.227-7013, or subparagraphs (c) (1) and (2) of the Commercial Computer Software - Restricted Rights clause at FAR 52.227-19, and in similar clauses in the NASA FAR supplement, as applicable.

8. General.
This Agreement constitutes the entire understanding of the parties and revokes and supersedes all prior agreements, oral or written, between them and may not be modified or amended except in a writing signed by both parties hereto that specifically refers to this Agreement. This Agreement shall take precedence over any other documents that may be in conflict herewith. If any one or more provisions contained in this Agreement are held by any court or tribunal to be invalid, illegal, or otherwise unenforceable, each and every other provision shall remain in full force and effect.